Designing Information:
New Roles for Librarians

Papers presented at the 1992 Clinic on Library Applications
of Data Processing, April 5-7, 1992
Sponsored by
Graduate School of Library and Information Science
University of Illinois at Urbana-Champaign

Clinic on Library Applications
of Data Processing: 1992

Designing Information:
New Roles for Librarians

Edited by
LINDA C. SMITH
and
PRUDENCE W. DALRYMPLE

Graduate School of Library and Information Science
University of Illinois at Urbana-Champaign

© 1993 by The Board of Trustees of the University of Illinois
ISBN 0-87845-088-2   ISSN 0069-4789

Printed in the United States of America
on acid-free paper

CONTENTS

Contents *(Cont.)*

Introduction

The twenty-ninth annual Clinic on Library Applications of Data Processing was held April 5-7, 1992, at the University of Illinois at Urbana-Champaign. The clinic theme, "Designing Information: New Roles for Librarians," reflects the availability of increasingly sophisticated hardware and software that provide librarians with new tools for designing information. Tools include software for electronic publishing, database development, and interface design, as well as hardware and software for hypermedia/multimedia. These developments present an opportunity for librarians in all types of libraries to assume new roles and to collaborate with others to produce new products and services.

INFORMATION DESIGN

Simon (1981, p. 129) has observed that "design . . . is the core of all professional training; it is the principal mark that distinguishes the professions from the sciences." Increasingly there is recognition that librarians in the future will have opportunities to serve not only as "information navigators," but also as architects or designers of information products (Borah, 1992). Orna (1992, p. 305) suggests that to be successful as designers, librarians need to

> Know about users and what they do
> Understand the nature of the information they need
> Have understanding and skills in
> 1. Conceptually organizing information
> 2. Visually organizing it

1

The work of Edward R. Tufte (1983, 1990), keynote speaker for the clinic, provides a rich source of ideas and principles for information design. His *The Visual Display of Quantitative Information* and *Envisioning Information* offer numerous illustrations of effective means of communicating complex information. Attention to visual design "with care given to color, typography, layout, icons, graphics and coherency" can contribute to the quality and usability of information delivered through computer screens as well as on paper (Tufte, 1992, p. 15). Ronnie Peters's paper on "Designing for the Computer Screen," included in this volume, offers additional guidance for the task of organizing a large amount of information in the small area offered by current computer screens.

NEW ROLES FOR LIBRARIANS

As M. E. L. Jacob observes in her paper summarizing the clinic, the authors represented in this volume are among the leaders, pioneers, and early adapters of new technology. Their descriptions of projects in which they have been involved provide insights into roles that librarians can fill.

Richard E. Lucier and Carolyn M. Gray explore roles for librarians in knowledge management. Lucier proposes a new role for librarians in collaboration with scholars as creators and maintainers of scholarly and research databases and presents the Genome Data Base at Johns Hopkins University as a working prototype. Gray describes the Gesher Project, a joint effort of Digital Equipment Corporation's Cambridge Research Laboratory and the Brandeis University Libraries to understand the changing nature of scholarly research and to develop computer-based tools to assist in these activities.

Two specific design projects to enhance library users' access to information are described by Virginia Tiefel of Ohio State University and by a group of librarians from the University of Illinois at Urbana-Champaign (Timothy W. Cole, Leslie Troutman, William H. Mischo, and Winnie Chan). Ohio State University's Gateway to Information provides guidance and instruction for students on how to proceed through an information search that integrates the use of print and computerized information. The Illinois Library Information Workstation project gives integrated and largely transparent access from a single terminal to a wide range of library resources. Its user-friendly interface facilitates patron searching of bibliographic databases, with flexibility to allow terminal-specific customization of the interface to accommodate localized patron needs and library resources. Both projects seek to provide "one-stop shopping" for the user and to address problems that users have in selecting information resources and formulating questions.

In the area of instructional design, Ruth V. Small reviews principles and strategies for designing effective computer-mediated instruction, recognizing that librarians are increasingly asked to design or adapt instructional programs. Joe C. Rader describes the development of computer-based materials for staff training at the University of Tennessee Libraries. Rader's case study explains each step in the development process, including choice of librarians to serve on the development team, topic selection, selection of hardware and software (HyperCard), development of instructional materials, evaluation, implementation, and replication at another site.

Jean Armour Polly and David V. Loertscher address applications in diverse environments. Polly demonstrates that the Internet has a number of resources of potential value to public library patrons. While eventually users may be able to access such material from home, Polly sees a place for librarians as long as the Internet remains difficult to use. To encourage librarians to get connected to the Internet, she identifies resources for getting onto the Internet and learning more about it through user guides. Loertscher describes the various ways in which school librarians have applied technology, identifying certain trends such as the use of microcomputers in managing school libraries and the possibilities for involving students in online searching, creating local databases, data gathering and analysis, and creation of multimedia productions. Those students who gain experience with storage, retrieval, and production of text, sound, and pictures will come to expect access to such technology in public and academic libraries as well.

Librarians have an important role to play in making information available via networks. Peter Scott explains the use of hypertext tools in the development of HYTELNET, a tool providing instructions for and access to information resources available on the Internet. The challenge is to organize the information necessary to access these diverse sites in as simple and straightforward a fashion as possible, and Scott demonstrates that hypertext is well suited for this purpose. Katharina Klemperer describes the different categories of information resources that libraries handle (indexes, structured full text, full text, numeric, and multimedia) and the different needs of each with regard to access and delivery. The challenge is to develop the tools that will accomplish this. Arlene Moore Sievers provides an overview of the Free-Net concept and its operation in Cleveland through Case Western Reserve University. Sievers notes that major libraries in Cleveland have been actively involved in Free-Net from the beginning and that public libraries have been active in Free-Nets in other cities. Librarians can both contribute to the development of information resources made available through

Free-Nets and use such databases as community resource files to enhance their services to library users.

OTHER COMPONENTS OF THE CLINIC

In addition to the papers assembled in this volume, the clinic included a keynote speech by Edward R. Tufte on "Envisioning Information" and an illustrated talk by Richard Greenfield entitled "Tying It All Together: Designing Graphical User Interfaces to Integrate and Evaluate Information Resources." The clinic began with three preconference workshops covering desktop publishing (presented by Nan Goggin and Kathleen Chmelewski), database design (presented by Carol Tenopir and Gerald W. Lundeen), and expert systems (presented by Lloyd A. Davidson, Judy E. Myers, and Craig A. Robertson), made possible with support provided by the Council on Library Resources. A poster session gave several clinic participants an opportunity to make presentations on topics related to the clinic theme. Presenters included James E. Agenbroad on "Browsing Classification Data: Feasible? Useful?," Mark Crook and Craig Henderson on "OCLC's Batch Services," James S. Foster, Javed Mostafa, and Beatriz Calixto on "CAI Packages for Microcomputer Competency," Gregory B. Newby on "WAIS: A New Model for Information Retrieval," and Eric Rumsey on "Use of HyperCard to Teach Medline CD-ROM." The editors gratefully acknowledge the contributions of all these individuals to the success of the clinic.

LINDA C. SMITH
PRUDENCE W. DALRYMPLE
Editors

REFERENCES

Borah, E. G. (1992). Beyond navigation: Librarians as architects of information tools. *Research Strategies, 10*(3), 138-142.

Orna, L. (1992). Information design and information services: What information professionals should know about design, in order to deliver value-added information products. *Aslib Proceedings, 44*(9), 305-308.

Simon, H. A. (1981). *The sciences of the artificial* (2nd ed.). Cambridge, MA: MIT Press.

Tufte, E. R. (1983). *The visual display of quantitative information*. Cheshire, CT: Graphics Press.

Tufte, E. R. (1990). *Envisioning information*. Cheshire, CT: Graphics Press.

Tufte, E. R. (1992). The user interface: The point of competition. *Bulletin of the American Society for Information Science, 18*(5), 15-17.

RICHARD E. LUCIER

University Librarian and Assistant Vice Chancellor
for Academic Information Management
University of California, San Francisco

Embedding the Library into Scientific and Scholarly Communication through Knowledge Management

ABSTRACT

Knowledge management is a new role for academic research libraries that has the potential to integrate the library into scholarly and scientific communication in a significant way. Work in knowledge management is advancing in both the sciences and humanities. The Genome Data Base at the Johns Hopkins University is currently the most advanced knowledge management prototype. As part of its new Center for Knowledge Management, the University of California, San Francisco is undertaking several initiatives to create a campuswide knowledge management environment.

INTRODUCTION

The University of California, San Francisco (UCSF) is one of the nine campuses of the University of California (UC) system. With schools in medicine, pharmacy, nursing, and dentistry, and graduate programs in the behavioral and social sciences, UCSF is unique within UC in that it is the only campus devoted to research, education, and service in the health sciences.

In September 1990, as the result of a decade of planning, UCSF opened a new library building of great beauty and utility that is a visual representation of the importance of the library to the UCSF faculty and student community (Cooper, 1991). The critical challenge in the current decade is to articulate and realize a programmatic vision that will (a) embed the library into the scientific and clinical research, educational curricula, and professional practice programs of this diverse and distributed campus; (b) position the library as a campus focal point for knowledge-based applications of information technology; and (c) establish the library's leadership in the development of knowledge bases and online tools for the health sciences.

OUR VISION:
A KNOWLEDGE MANAGEMENT ENVIRONMENT

Historically, the function of the research library has been storage and retrieval. This will remain at the core of the library's responsibilities. More recently, the library has extended its role to include information transfer, or the delivery of information over high-speed communications networks. Responsibilities and activities in this area are increasing rapidly, driven by users' needs and the growing availability and reliability of the Internet or the National Research and Education Network (NREN). A new, more experimental and challenging role for the library is that of knowledge management, the insinuation of the library at the beginning of the scientific and scholarly communication process for the purpose of building and maintaining specialized knowledge bases in unique collaborations with scientists and scholars.

Our vision for the UCSF Library, and its innovative new Center for Knowledge Management, embraces all three functions: storage and retrieval, information transfer, and knowledge management. Figure 1 graphically represents this vision, which we call a Knowledge Management Environment.

This Knowledge Management Environment is an integration of knowledge sources, access and delivery systems, education and training programs, and personalized services with the following components:

- online bibliographic databases of the library's physical collection;
- the "full text" of the published literature online, including images;
- high-quality, interactive knowledge bases *critical* to the daily work of scholars and scientists;
- online tools for the peer review of data and collaborative knowledge base management;
- high-speed communications for the conduct of scientific and scholarly work from the local to international levels; and

- an integrated access tool, or wide area information server, to retrieve information from local and remote bibliographic databases, "full-text" information sources, and specialized knowledge bases.

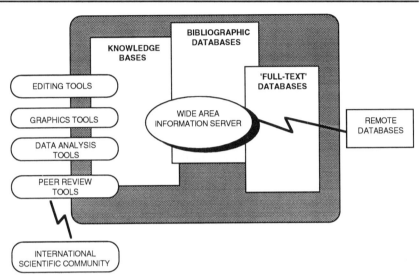

Figure 1. The Knowledge Management Environment

SCIENTIFIC AND SCHOLARLY COMMUNICATION

The need for a Knowledge Management Environment emerges from problems inherent in the current scientific and scholarly communication process. Figure 2 depicts the information transfer cycle as we know it today. Scientists and scholars discover new knowledge and communicate it through both writing and teaching. Publishers disseminate that information through a variety of primary and secondary information products. In their traditional storage and retrieval role, research libraries build collections and make available to users the world's published literature. Since the 1970s, network access (information transfer) to this stored knowledge through online catalogs and indexes, along with a new emphasis on service and education, has assumed major importance. However, the roles and functions of scholars, publishers, and librarians have remained fundamentally the same.

By the late 1980s, the limitations of this prevailing model for scientific communication were becoming apparent. The length of the hard-copy publishing process makes it increasingly difficult for scholars

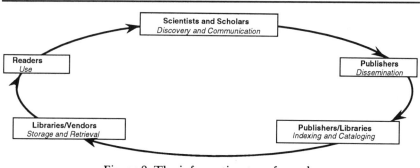

Figure 2. The information transfer cycle

and scientists to communicate their findings in a timely fashion. With the rising cost of publishing and a limited resource base, libraries and universities can no longer afford to support comprehensive collections. The financial crisis facing libraries is not short-term; rather, it is structural in the current environment. Most importantly, it is clear that the presentation of knowledge in static form, whether in print or as part of the emerging electronic library, is grossly inadequate. Scientists and scholars, often on their own and with inadequate support, are augmenting this passive presentation of knowledge with a growing number of interactive, discipline-based knowledge bases that are developed, maintained, and shared across networks. Knowledge management has emerged from this situation as a creative response to managing the world's knowledge base.

THE LIBRARY AS KNOWLEDGE MANAGER

Knowledge management represents a new model for scientific and scholarly communication in which faculty and research librarians share the responsibility for the collection, structuring, representation, dissemination, and use of knowledge using electronic information technologies. Encompassing the entire information life cycle, from creation of new knowledge to its dissemination and use, knowledge management is a collaborative enterprise, where scholars, scientists, and research librarians work together to develop and maintain knowledge bases and derivative information products. Knowledge bases are developed and maintained through knowledge management processes, which ensure content integrity and usefulness. A variety of products and services can be derived from the knowledge base. The collaborative nature of knowledge management, embodied in techniques of shared development of functional specifications, rapid prototyping, and user acceptance testing, fosters an interdependency among all involved. The ongoing management of the knowledge base also requires funding and administration strategies that crosscut traditional departmental, disciplinary, and institutional boundaries.

Knowledge management consists of four primary components:

1. Collaboration: the shared responsibility for the development and management of knowledge bases, products, and services. Effective collaboration requires a balanced relationship among peers, recognizing the unique value of each person's contributions to the success of shared work. A multidisciplinary team of collaborators includes discipline-based scholars and scientists, librarians, computer scientists, and software engineers.

2. Knowledge base: a collection of scholarly knowledge structured for computational storage and representation. A knowledge base may contain all or some part of the intellectual core of a scholarly discipline. The contents of the knowledge base are chosen and validated by consensus at some level within the scholarly community that develops, uses, and maintains it.

3. Knowledge management processes: those activities of collaborators related to the creation, structuring, representation, dissemination, and use of scholarly knowledge. They result in knowledge bases, patterns of collaboration and communication that ensure the integrity and continuing usefulness of those knowledge bases, and knowledge products.

4. Knowledge products and services are the output derived from the knowledge base: books, articles, computer-based educational materials, database subsets, and typesetting tapes are examples of knowledge products. Knowledge products are market driven, developed in response to the immediate information needs of scholars, scientists, educators, students, and other information seekers. Product services are the customer support activities associated with each knowledge product. Examples include production of typesetting tapes or camera-ready copy for hard-copy publication or education and training programs to provide skills and abilities needed for full and appropriate use of knowledge products derived from the knowledge base.

What is remarkably different about the knowledge management role is that it insinuates the library at the beginning of the information transfer cycle rather than at the end and focuses on information capture rather than access and use (Figure 3).

The long-term implications for building and maintaining a portion of the library's collection in this manner are enormous. Knowledge management transforms the various roles in the scientific communication process and potentially places ownership and control back in the hands of the scholarly community. It also has enormous potential for closing the gap between research faculty and their students and integrating the library into research and education programs in a significant way.

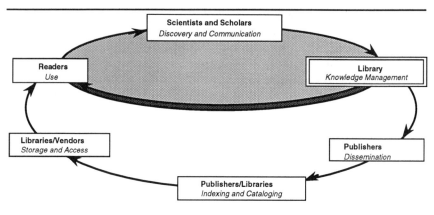

Figure 3. New roles in a Knowledge Management Environment

THE GENOME DATA BASE:
A KNOWLEDGE MANAGEMENT PROTOTYPE

To date, the most advanced knowledge management prototype is the Genome Data Base (GDB), developed at the Laboratory for Applied Research in Academic Information, William H. Welch Medical Library, the Johns Hopkins University. (The following section is an adaptation of sections from Lucier [1990].) GDB is a working prototype, which serves the international scientific community on a daily basis. The most technologically advanced systems possible are not our primary goal in knowledge management; instead we are more concerned with designing systems that work and that people use in their everyday environments.

GDB is a gene-mapping database that serves as a repository for data collected by scientists engaged in the international human genome effort. GDB integrates several types of data including descriptions and map locations of human genes and other markers, descriptions of DNA probes used to characterize the markers and polymorphisms, contacts for obtaining probes, and more than 25,000 linked bibliographic citations.

To see GDB as an example of knowledge management, it is essential to have an understanding of the sociology of the human genetics community, namely the Human Gene Mapping (HGM) Workshops. The First International Human Gene Mapping Workshop, held in 1973, was instituted to develop and maintain a consensus human gene map. Since that time, similar workshops have been held either annually or biennially. These workshops are one of the community's primary data filters. The HGM workshops are organized by committee, one for each chromosome as well as several specialized committees, e.g., nomenclature, DNA, mitochondrial, and comparative (mouse). These committees collect, review, analyze, and synthesize all the mapping data from the published literature to produce the consensus human gene map.

Two aspects of HGM work have specially driven the need and design for GDB: (a) the growing volume and complexity of data and (b) the interactive character of the peer review work of HGM committees. The amount of information that committees must process has increased proportionately with the greatly heightened scientific activity in this area. It is estimated that the information doubles every two years. In 1973, 75 people attended HGM 1, and 25 genes were mapped. At HGM 10 in 1989, 700 scientists were in attendance, and 1,630 genes were mapped. Until now, during the four- or five-day workshop, members would collect and input information concerning their particular chromosome. With the larger volume of data, this has become a nearly impossible task, even with the introduction of computers to the workshops beginning in 1983. Making use of the Internet and public data networks, GDB provides the committees with an online, continuous, interactive system into which information can be added and verified at the committee members' convenience throughout the year. The committees will continue to meet annually, but the workshops can now focus on science and the analysis and significance of data rather than on data entry.

Although the various chromosome committees do their work mostly independent of each other, there is considerable interaction among the chromosome, nomenclature, and DNA committees. Certain data elements are shared; these elements, e.g., gene symbol, cannot become part of the database until they have been validated by the appropriate members of various committees, in consultation with each other. An "online peer review process" has been integrated into GDB editorial interfaces, again making significant use of national and international networks and a completely modularized design.

At present, GDB draws primarily on the HGM workshops and the literature for the major portion of its data. Already, it is beginning to include unpublished and unvalidated data submitted directly by users for consideration and subjected to quality control by both GDB staff and a special group of scientific editors. Figure 4 illustrates this data flow and highly dynamic form of scientific communication possible in a networked environment. It also represents a true electronic journal in a knowledge management environment.

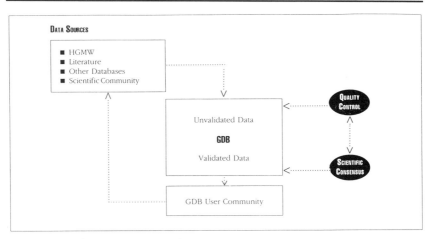

Figure 4. GDB data flow in a networked environment

GDB is designed so that it is possible to develop other information products that the user community demands in order to accomplish its work. In addition to the various interfaces provided for HGM committees and GDB Editors, a more generalized online searchable version of GDB is available to the scientific community. The HGM Reports, published by Karger in a special issue of the journal *Cell Genetics and Cytogenetics,* are produced from GDB data structures.

IMPLEMENTATION OF A KNOWLEDGE MANAGEMENT ENVIRONMENT AT UCSF

Although the library will continue to build a high-quality paper-based collection in the health sciences, excellent service in a distributed environment as well as educational programs will assume a far higher priority than in the past. We anticipate a rapidly increasing emphasis on information transfer and knowledge management over the next 10 years, and we will focus our technology-based efforts on these roles.

Figure 5 depicts the primary areas in which we plan to develop or adopt technological innovations over the next three to five years, as we implement the first phase of our Knowledge Management Environment.

Driven by the needs of our customers, the continuously changing external environment, and new advances in technology, we are fashioning a dynamic, multidisciplinary organization with three programmatic divisions.

	CONTENT	ACCESS	EDUCATION	SERVICE
STORAGE & RETRIEVAL	Bibliographic db's Online Indices 'Full Text'			
INFORMATION TRANSFER	Delivery of 'Full Text' information on-demand	Wide Area Information Server (GALEN) for integrated access to local/remote db's	Training programs which facilitate access and use	Information services to distributed faculty and student workplaces
KNOWLEDGE MANAGEMENT	Discipline-specific knowledge bases of high currency, value, and integrity Interactive tools for collaborative data maintenance in a networked environment	Information Retrieval Software for 'Full Text' Electronic Library Online tools for information access and analysis	Practice-based health sciences Informatics Curriculum Information products to support curriculum	Direct collaboration between faculty and librarians in the development/ maintenance of knowledge bases and products

Figure 5. Development areas for the first phase of the Knowledge Management Environment

1. *Information Resources and Services* is responsible for storage and retrieval and information transfer functions including the following:
   - collection management and processing;
   - public information services to our distributed customer base;
   - document and information delivery;
   - special collections including the History of the Health Sciences, the Oriental Collection, and University Archives; and
   - bibliographic instruction component of a broad educational program.
2. The *Center for Knowledge Management,* created by the Division of Academic Affairs and the library, is responsible for information transfer and knowledge management functions. In collaboration with faculty, the center's staff performs the following functions:
   - develops new information products and services, e.g., knowledge bases and online tools for the health sciences;
   - pursues applied research projects related to UCSF informatics problems;
   - advises graduate students in computer science and the health sciences who are using the center as their laboratory;
   - consults with faculty, staff, and students in the development of private databases, etc.; and

- supports the state-of-the-art systems and infrastructure that underpin the development, maintenance, and use of knowledge resources and information services.
3. The *Interactive Learning Laboratory* has primary responsibility for our educational and instructional programs including the following:
   - development of a health sciences informatics curriculum;
   - integration of educational technology resources into the curriculum of the various schools and professional training programs;
   - instructional computing and the development of multimedia software for education; and
   - educational and external publications.

A fourth division, *Finance, Planning, and Administration,* supports our storage and retrieval, information transfer, and knowledge management functions through the efficient and effective management of our financial and human resources and facilities. This division is also responsible for development. In order to implement the UCSF Knowledge Management Environment, it is critical for the library to implement long-term financial planning for the effective use of state funds as well as broaden its financial resource base beyond state-appropriated funds. Important sources of support include grants, contracts, business-university agreements, gifts, and information consulting and brokering activities. An endowment for the Center for Knowledge Management has been established as an important priority in an upcoming campus capital campaign.

As we move towards realizing our Knowledge Management Environment vision, it has also been necessary for us to examine and refashion the library's organizational culture as well. Several principles guide us in this challenging and long-term task that has been greatly aided by the opportunity to recruit several new professional staff from the library, computing, and biomedical science professions:

- high value placed on technological innovations that solve practical and recognized problems;
- continuous involvement of faculty, staff, and students in the University of California tradition of shared governance;
- an informed, knowledgeable, and service-oriented staff a critical factor;
- technology a tool, not an end;
- strong management essential for program development and the effective use of human and financial resources;
- processes and tasks organized around outcomes;
- pragmatism and principle as a dual basis for decision making;
- outcomes as the principal evaluation measure; and

- entrepreneurial responsiveness to environmental changes, opportunities, and emerging information technologies a key to success.

Several new projects have already begun. In collaboration with our Human Gene Mapping Center, we have successfully sought funding to build and maintain a chromosome 4 database, which will be our first efforts at collecting and making available source data. Discussions are continuing with (a) Springer-Verlag for an experiment with several important online journals, (b) clinical researchers for an AIDS knowledge base, and (c) medical educators for the creation of a comprehensive database that would support undergraduate medical education.

CLR STUDY OF KNOWLEDGE MANAGEMENT

In 1987, the Council on Library Resources (CLR) awarded a grant to Richard E. Lucier and Nina W. Matheson to address the changing roles of research libraries, the scholarly community, and university publishers in scientific and scholarly communication through examination of the knowledge management model as implemented in Lucier's work at the Laboratory for Applied Research in Academic Information, the William H. Welch Medical Library, the Johns Hopkins University. (This following section is an adaptation of sections from Lucier & Matheson [1992].) The CLR grant had three major objectives:

1. *Documentation of the knowledge management model.* The collection, examination, and synthesis of statements, definitions, and descriptions of the knowledge management model and its components have been major documentation activities of the project. Briefing materials for the Symposium on Knowledge Management drew heavily upon these files. A monograph on the knowledge management model, coauthored by the principal investigators, will be published by the Johns Hopkins University Press in late 1992.
2. *Diffusion of the knowledge management model to academic settings outside medicine.* Initial diffusion of the concept of the model occurred through presentations made by the principal investigators to high-level staff at numerous academic institutions that seemed to possess the requisite human, technical, and financial resources to implement the model. Follow-up calls, interviews, and site visits monitored the possibility of actual implementation in these settings. Presentations were also made at several national meetings over the life of the grant.
3. *Sponsorship of a national meeting on knowledge management.* Early on, the principal investigators formed a special executive committee

to oversee this component of the project. This group decided on the strategy of a special invitational symposium as most appropriate to a full discussion of the key issues raised by the knowledge management model.

From October 27-29, 1991, 63 invited guests gathered at the Coolfont Conference Center in Berkeley Springs, West Virginia, for the Invitational Symposium on Knowledge Management, a policy-level forum for examination of knowledge management. Included among these experts were scholars, university administrators, academic librarians from major public and private universities, association directors, independent consultants, and others whose work and interests have led to innovations in scholarly and scientific information management. Major private and public funding agencies such as the National Science Foundation, the National Endowment for the Humanities, and the Andrew W. Mellon Foundation were also represented. During the three-day gathering, participants' time was divided between working group meetings and plenary sessions.

Symposium registrants directed their attention and activities toward four desired outcomes:

1. *Shared understanding* of the knowledge management model, including the economic and political advantages and disadvantages of different approaches and social and other noneconomic barriers to wider implementation of knowledge management.
2. *Clarification of implications* for scientific/scholarly communication, comparing the current situation to communication in knowledge management environments, and suggesting solutions for problem areas.
3. *Scenario development* outside human genetics, applying knowledge management to other scholarly information problems; examining existing knowledge management projects, especially in the humanities; and identifying the advantages, disadvantages, opportunities, and barriers to knowledge management within particular disciplines.
4. *Recommending implementation strategies* for knowledge management, providing a rationale, time frame, level of intensity, projected resource requirements, technological initiatives, and, where possible, priority audiences.

At the symposium's concluding session, the leaders of these groups presented recommendations for future actions in each of the five areas. *Strong consensus emerged in support of wider implementation of knowledge management.* In the words of Donald N. Langenberg, registrants should take action to colonize carefully selected distant locations in intellectual space with the practice of knowledge management. Groups also pinpointed a set of complementary actions to develop the conceptual and curricular infrastructure for knowledge management environments.

Knowledge management is a transformational activity. Working examples of knowledge management serve as proof of concept for the approach. They also help to highlight the areas where immediate work is needed if an infrastructure to nurture new implementations is to emerge in the next three to five years. Next steps involve actions with national and international impact; individual initiatives must be supplanted by broader based, mainstream action targeted to reduce barriers and leverage opportunities.

Themes running through the plenary and working group discussions and recommendations highlight three action items that require immediate attention:

1. *Financial strategies.* The future diffusion and success of knowledge management rests in large part on the development of reasonable and creative financial strategies and on an economic model that considers the needs of all important players. In particular, the model must consider that the current state of research institutions and information producers, in an era of limited resources and constrained public agencies, requires the ability to mesh pricing, costing, and allocation strategies among various organizations and groups both internal and external to the research enterprise.

2. *Intellectual property.* As a next logical step in moving towards a knowledge management environment, it is increasingly important to convert existing published works to electronic form for online access and management. The symposium's work group on intellectual property proposed pulling a group together to describe the climate needed for knowledge management, particularly the elements of collaborative ownership. Such a group would identify current copyright status for each class of information (e.g., source data, consensus data, the published literature, and bibliographic records), project what is needed, and recommend actions to be taken over the next five years.

3. *Technology strategy.* A functional architecture that will serve as a reference model is needed for knowledge management. This structural definition can serve as a rationale for institutional infrastructure planning and technological development. The architecture should take into account the available technologies but must also offer a plan for incorporating future developments. Though there will ultimately be several architectures for knowledge management, a general one is needed to begin with that defines how to deal with communications, content organization, standards, and other related issues.

CONCLUSION

It is clear that the knowledge management concept is a vital, effective approach to scientific communication in networked environments. Working implementations of knowledge management exist, and numerous projects in the sciences and humanities can be identified where the knowledge management approach will provide identifiable benefits to disciplines and institutions. Wider implementation of knowledge management approaches requires that the focus of action and attention be redirected to issues beyond those that arise from individual university- or discipline-specific projects. Enthusiasm exists for initiating new knowledge management experiments in a number of disciplines, but it is not likely that any coordinated effort can emerge until additional work is done to reduce technological, legal, and financial barriers. The involvement of new participants, including people who bring legal and economic expertise and who share an interest in and commitment to shaping new roles and processes in scholarly and scientific communication, is critical.

REFERENCES

Cooper, R. S. (1991). A library for the fifteenth through the twenty-first centuries. *Bulletin of the Medical Library Association, 79*(2), 147-158.

Lucier, R. E. (1990). Knowledge management: Refining roles in scientific communication. *EDUCOM Review, 25*(3), 21-27.

Lucier, R. E., & Matheson, N. W. (1992). *Invitational symposium on knowledge management: Overview and recommendations.* Baltimore, MD: Welch Medical Library.

CAROLYN M. GRAY

Associate Director
Brandeis University Libraries
Waltham, Massachusetts

Building Electronic Bridges between Scholars and Information: New Roles for Librarians

ABSTRACT

Through a description of information science, communications, and knowledge utilization information models, this paper provides an introduction to the conceptual framework for the use of information in knowledge work activities and outlines one approach to studying knowledge work. The Gesher Project—a design effort undertaken by Brandeis librarians and Digital Equipment Corporation software engineers—is presented, with details of a group study of the Brandeis Radio Astronomy Group (BRAG). A prototype information management system developed by Digital Equipment Corporation researchers is also described.

INTRODUCTION

The traditional response of librarians to the study of information needs has been to study what users are doing in the library—studying how they are using information that is available. Maurice Line has suggested that we should instead hypothesize about need based on the nature of the activities in which individuals are involved (Line, Brittain, & Cranmer, 1971). Whether one is involved in designing a new bibliographic tool, designing a new approach to library instruction, or designing a new library system, it is important to understand what the needs of end-users are in relation to a specific information activity.

19

Libraries have been developing in an evolutionary process in relation to information products and information services. Each new product has been built upon the models of the past. Edward Tufte (1990) has suggested that we must envision information and information activities in a different manner in order to develop products and services that are truly revolutionary. If one assumes that a major library constituency is the scholars and researchers in the user community, then one can begin to think about their "needs." Instead of building better tools based upon historical precedent, librarians can begin to think beyond the confines of the past by beginning to examine the knowledge work of scholars.

This paper provides an introduction to the conceptual framework for the use of information in knowledge work activities, outlines one approach to studying knowledge work, and presents an overview of a design effort undertaken by Brandeis librarians and Digital Equipment Corporation software engineers.

INFORMATION AND KNOWLEDGE WORK

Consider three potential outcomes that are desirable and possible by examining "knowledge work":

- Through the process of examining scholarly activity, librarians may be able to assist in the development of scholarly support software that is not just an electronic analogue of existing electronic- or print-based library reference works but a medium for a kind of scholarly support activity that is genuinely new and three-dimensional.
- By examining how scholars use information, librarians can develop simulations of complex information activities. It is possible to simulate for the undergraduate the complex situation of a scholar analyzing a literary text. Librarians can develop truly innovative, interesting, and educational library instruction programs.
- By examining how scholars use information, we can begin to develop collections and connections to collections that truly reflect scholars' needs and support their scholarly work in an enabling fashion.

Elsewhere, the author (Gray, 1992) has suggested that information is a dynamic process with distinct phases forming a life cycle that can be defined, isolated, and examined. In this criterion, information is said to be a dynamic process, to be diverse and cumulative in effect, and to lead to informed action (Kochen, 1970; Taylor, 1980, 1986). Following are three types of models that contribute to understanding the dynamic nature of information. It may be helpful to view information as having a distinct life cycle that begins with creation, involves dissemination, collection by a potential user, analysis, subsequent use, and storage. Various iterations of these phases in the information life cycle are present in the models described. To study the "information life cycle," one must combine elements of each of the models into an iterative model that includes data collection, analysis, action, and feedback loops.

To understand the concept of "information" as a dynamic process, various linear models that depict information on a continuum are reviewed. The Kochen (1970) model depicted in Figure 1 shows a progression from information to wisdom with two intermediate transformations along the way.

Information--> transformation into knowledge--> assimilation of knowledge into understanding--> fusion of understanding into wisdom

Figure 1. Kochen information model

Another version of the Kochen model can be seen in Taylor (1980) as he outlines four steps for refining data and transforming it into information for decision making. The first step is the *organization* of data, in which he includes collection, sorting, grouping, classifying, formatting, presenting, and displaying. The second step is *synthesizing,* which is a systematic approach to selecting, analyzing, interpreting, adopting, and compressing. The third step is *judgment,* which is a more critical act of selecting and evaluating against established parameters. The final step in the model is the *decision process.* In the decision process, useful knowledge is assessed and decisions are made based upon the goals of the organization or decision maker. Choosing among alternatives, compromising, bargaining, and consultation with experts are all elements of this final process.

The Taylor model is often depicted as a pyramid rather than as a linear model, with the raw data forming the base of the pyramid and the decision process forming the apex. In a later work, Taylor (1986) retains the steps but depicts the model as an hierarchical spectrum from data to action.

The Taylor model shown in Figure 2 illustrates the unrefined "data" at the base of the hierarchy, followed by "information," the first level of refinement or organization of data. "Informing knowledge" is organized and synthesized to create in the recipient some greater understanding. "Productive knowledge" has attached to it some form of critical or evaluative element. The apex represents the action of the decision maker.

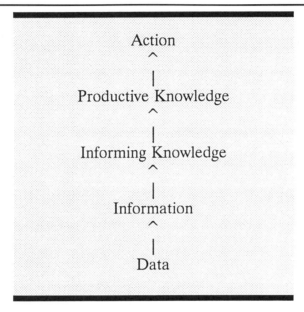

Figure 2. Taylor information model

Variations on these models can be found in the management information systems (MIS) literature. Boulton and Saladin (1983) and Hodge, Fleck, and Honess (1984) depict a flow from raw data to a decision point in their information system continuum illustrated in Figure 3. The "data processing" step is roughly analogous to the "informing knowledge," and "data output" corresponds to "productive knowledge" in the Taylor model. In the MIS school of research, "information utilization" has as an underlying assumption that some refining process has been undertaken to turn raw data into useful information.

One may contrast these models to a model used in communications theory as depicted in Davis and Olson's (1985) general model of a communication system. The above models place more emphasis upon the use, and Davis and Olson study the process. The communications school approach is depicted in Figure 4. The communications model begins with a message or information source, a transmission device, a channel or conduit through which the message travels, and a receiver

Raw data or Input -->
Data Processing-->
Data Output-->
Information--> Decision

Figure 3. MIS information model

source--> transmitter-->
channel--> receiver/decoder-->
destination

Figure 4. Communications model

that relays the message to its destination. In this model, there is concern that the message remain intact from source to destination. The ideal is for the "destination" to understand the message as it was intended by the "source." Noise and distortion often arise in the channel. Thus, the communication approach is concerned with maintaining the integrity of the message, and the information-processing approach focuses upon transformation.

These variations reflect the difference in approaches between the information scientist and the communications theorists. There is yet a third approach that arises out of the knowledge utilization literature. Havelock (1972, 1976) develops what he calls a knowledge flow system. The unique nature of this system is that it is not a strict linear model but has a series of "feedback loops."

Figure 5 depicts a strict linear model, but in fact there are a series of feedback loops with information from applied research feeding back to basic research, e.g., engineers feeding information back to basic research scientists, information from consumers being fed back to practitioners or retailers, or practitioners feeding information to the applied researcher to create understanding of what is or is not working. The field of knowledge utilization is primarily concerned with studying the flow of research to practitioners. Some of the earliest studies in knowledge utilization were done in the agricultural field, which studies the utilization of advances in applied agricultural techniques literally at the "grass roots" level. More recently, we see the use of knowledge utilization studies in the human services field to assess the use of innovations (both techniques and technology).

Basic research-->
Applied Research -->
Practitioners/Producers/
Manufacturers/Retailers-->
Consumers/Clients/Citizens

Figure 5. Havelock knowledge system

The information science, communications, and knowledge utilization information models contribute to understanding the dynamic nature of information. This conceptual framework is a part of the foundation needed for the study of knowledge work activity. Knowledge work may entail using the scientific method of research, or it may involve activities such as literary analysis that cannot be framed by the scientific method. Knowledge work assumes reliance upon information-intensive sources for "work" to be accomplished. It may be helpful to examine one attempt to frame the concept of knowledge work by analyzing the activities that may be involved when one engages in knowledge work. Davis and Olson (1985) identified seven major categories of knowledge work activity:

- Diagnosis and problem finding
- Planning and decision making
- Monitoring and control
- Organizing and scheduling
- Authoring and presentation
- Communication
- System development

Davis and Olson's divisions of knowledge work are complemented by Mackenzie Owen and van Halm's (1989) description of the information cycle that includes the following:

- Production
    processing of data

      text processing

      communication

- Distribution

      editing (link between production and distribution)

      quality control, e.g., peer review

      marketing

      physical production

- Acquisition (booksellers and libraries)

      selection, physical acquisition, and storage of materials

      cataloging and indexing

      provision of documents by selling or lending

      instruction and advice to the end-user

- Use

      orientation

      problem formulation

      searching and selecting relevant information

      acquisition of selected information

      processing of information

      establishing relationships between various items of acquired information

      production of new information

The Gesher Project team began their research with this broad conceptual understanding of knowledge work. The project is designed to build a bridge between the information cycle and scholars to support their knowledge work.

GESHER PROJECT

What follows is a description of a joint project between Brandeis University Libraries and Digital Equipment Corporation's Cambridge Research Laboratory (CRL) that seeks to understand the changing nature of scholarly research and to develop computer-based tools to assist scholars in their research activities. This joint project is entitled the "Gesher Project." Gesher is a Hebrew word meaning bridge, which is intended to symbolize a link between the scholar and the scholarly information most traditionally found in libraries.

The Gesher Project had its birth when computer scientists at Digital's CRL and librarians at Brandeis began to discuss the possibility of building a personal information management system for scholars that would use bibliographic data from our online catalog. As discussions evolved, we tried to imagine what scholars might want to do and how a system might be designed to meet their scholarly information needs. A project was designed with the following broad goals:

1. to study the information-seeking process within a research university setting as a paradigm of how people locate and utilize information in the course of their work, and
2. to assist DEC/CRL staff in evaluating a personal information management system to be developed by CRL project members with participation by Brandeis faculty, doctoral candidates, and senior research librarians.

As the project team began work, a set of assumptions were developed that have helped to guide the research. These assumptions include the following:

1. Scholarly research is changing.
2. Understanding the scholarly research process can help librarians design services to address the changing needs of researchers. (See Belkin et al., 1990.)
3. Scholars must participate in the design of any new and improved system that aims to help manage their scholarly information.
4. Ethnographic field research techniques are useful in understanding the scholarly process.
5. The role of academic librarians in relation to scholarly research support is changing or needs to change.
6. Skills for librarianship are changing.

Grounded in the conceptual foundations of knowledge work, with the broad project goals in mind, and these diverse assumptions, the project team began its research.

Participative Design

Librarians in the project have concentrated on the goal of understanding the scholarly information management process. The research team from CRL and Brandeis decided to use a participative design technique in the system development. To understand our initial work, it is helpful to have a general knowledge of the tenets of participative design. Participative design is a technique pioneered by Mumford and MacDonald in the 1980s in their expert system design efforts. Participative systems design means giving responsibility for all, or part, of the design of a new system to the group who will use it.

Participative design is a concept that is best applied in a single organization where workers are engaged in a common pursuit. Scholarly research, of course, varies by discipline. But as Mumford and MacDonald (1989) point out, "Participation is a means to an end and not an end in itself. It is there to assist the creation of good systems that work efficiently, increase human effectiveness and contribute to a stimulating and satisfying work environment" (p. 27).

The participative design technique developed by Mumford and MacDonald is called "The ETHICS Method." (ETHICS stands for *E*ffective *T*echnical and *H*uman *I*mplementation of *C*omputer-based *S*ystems.) Initial examination made it apparent that the ETHICS method was not appropriate to adopt wholesale for the Gesher Project, but rather it was decided to use the elements of the method that seemed to match project needs. The five steps in participative design follow:

Step 1. Diagnosis of Need
Step 2. Discrepancy Analysis
Step 3. Agreeing on Objectives
Step 4. Designing the System
Step 5. Implementing the System

The initial research efforts concentrated on step 1, which involves the following:

- *Describing* the existing scholarly research systems being used by scholars at Brandeis. In this descriptive process, it is important to look at day-to-day tasks in the scholarly process of collecting information, storage, and retrieval.
- It is important to assess the *efficiency needs* of the scholar by asking such questions as the following: What are the problems impeding progress in the scholarly process? Slowing it down? Causing errors?
- It is important to assess the *effectiveness needs* by describing the key tasks and establishing which contribute to scholarly goals. One can do this by asking two questions: Are the tasks being performed effectively? Are there tasks that are not being performed that should be introduced? In scholarly work, effectiveness may be related to the coordination of activities of other scholars in the same discipline locally or at other institutions.
- It is important to understand *future change:* How is scholarship changing in general, and how will this impact the individual scholar or institution?
- It is important to understand the needs of the scholar on several different levels:
    Knowledge needs. How, ideally, would each scholar or group like their existing skills and knowledge to be used? What opportunities for developing them further would be advantageous? How well are needs being met?
    Psychological needs. What are scholars' needs for responsibility, status, esteem, security, and advancement, and how do they define these needs?
    Support and control needs. What kind of support services would enable them to carry out their work responsibilities more efficiently?

Task needs. What kinds of task structures and role responsibilities do different kinds of scholars find motivating, interesting, and challenging? What opportunities exist for self management, for developing new methods and services? This area is very relevant to the teaching role of faculty and an area where new working relationships can be developed among teaching faculty, computer professionals, and librarians.

Ethical needs. How do scholars wish to be treated by the library? Do policies on communication, consultation, and participation meet their expectations?

An examination of the ETHICS method helped to clarify project staff understanding of what kinds of questions to ask about the scholar's work, but this method did not help in knowing "how to ask" to ensure that the eventual design solves the right problem or set of problems. After an examination of alternative methods of surveying or interviewing faculty, it was decided to use ethnographic field research techniques as a way to interview scholars.

To carry out the research, a two-stage process of interviews was designed. The first stage of interviews involves an in-depth small group study in a specific discipline. The second stage involves using the findings from initial interviews to design a broader survey in other disciplines.

Ethnographic field research techniques were adopted for this study for four primary reasons. First, the method helps the researcher to understand behaviors according to how they are embedded in social and historical fabric of everyday life. The focus is on the relationships between the parts. The design of any component has implications for the rest of the system. Scholarly research is thus placed in the context of the discipline and the day-to-day work life of the scholar.

Second, because the method is descriptive, the researcher withholds judgment about the behavior described or observed. The researcher can look for how seemingly inefficient behavior is embedded in the social system. By describing first, the researcher does not jump to offer technical solutions.

Third, ethnographic research helps researchers understand other people's behavior from their point of view. The researcher must focus on how they categorize their activities and functions and not on artifacts of the environment. The interviewer must not impose her view of the world on the situation being observed.

And fourth, researchers learn about others by encountering their situation firsthand. Researchers look at everyday, naturally occurring talk and action. An important part of a work group's interaction may occur around the coffeepot or watercooler. By making naturalistic observations, researchers can record and understand the use of technology within the environment of its use.

In studying the ethnographic approach, the project team learned that it is not a method to generate good questions in a mechanical way; that is, researchers cannot go into every interview with a script to be followed for three reasons. First, good questions emerge from an understanding of the group. Second, good questions emerge in the course of the interview. And third, results emerge from the interaction between interviewer and interviewee.

The Small Group Study

The following case study was prepared by Sue Woodson-Marks who has training and experience in ethnographic research. The assignment to the research team was to describe the research habits of a single research group in terms of their use of information.

The group studied was the Brandeis Radio Astronomy Group (BRAG) that includes the following:

- two faculty members;
- one advanced graduate student;
- two post-docs, one who is still working at Brandeis and one who has already moved to another area university but returns to Brandeis to attend "Astrolunch";
- several lower-level graduate students who are in the process of deciding whether they want to join the group; and
- one honors undergraduate student.

For Gesher Project purposes, the faculty and advanced graduate students are considered the core members of the group—the ones concentrated on in the interviews. They are all working on various aspects of a single issue: measuring the linear polarization of astronomical objects. In his dissertation work, the senior scientist devised a means of measuring this aspect of astronomical objects that has not been previously recorded. Their work now involves developing the technology for taking these measurements and using the data they gather to better understand the structure and function of these radio sources.

The approach used was to conduct in-depth interviews of the core group with an eye towards understanding how BRAG works as a group, what work they do, and how they do it. Project team members also observed at two "Astrolunches," the lunchtime forum for reviewing current literature in the field and presenting work done for the group. This report is based upon five interviews in all, lasting from one to three hours, which have been conducted by a team including the ethnographer and a librarian with the software engineer participating in one interview.

Although the **BRAG** members are each individually involved in a number of different activities (e.g., teaching, taking classes, serving on university committees, etc.), this project has concerned itself primarily with the work they do as researchers in astrophysics. The information-related tasks involved in this research include designing research projects, gathering and organizing data, producing and refining tools for analyzing the data, analyzing the data, and disseminating the results of their work.

Designing New Observations and Writing Proposals for Grant Money and for Time on the Radio Telescopes

Like most other astronomers, **BRAG** members collect their data using groups of radio telescopes owned by other institutions. They must not only petition for funds to support their research, they must compete with other radio astronomers around the world for time on these telescopes. Although one particular grant may cover more than one year, proposals for research funds and time on the telescopes are generally written each year. These proposals are generally written by the faculty, although graduate students may be writing their own grant proposals as well. In either case, the writer must not only have a clear notion of the work being proposed, he must also know what has been done in the field recently and how the proposed work fits into ongoing, already funded, research.

A weekly lunch seminar, Astrolunch, serves, in part, the function of keeping **BRAG** members up to date on current literature. Members of the group are assigned individual responsibility for reporting on particular journals in this seminar. When new issues of a journal arrive, the responsible member reviews the abstracts and table of contents of the new issues and reports on any articles that would be of interest to members of the group. Faculty members also use this venue to report to students on current funding issues. Although this may seem a rather labor-intensive means of reviewing the literature, project staff cannot recommend a streamlining of this process through computerization because it seems clear that the Astrolunch serves an important teaching function. The field of issues covered in this seminar is much greater than "the most recent developments in astrophysics." Here students learn about the values that guide research, the appropriate ways of evaluating other researchers' work, the nature of collegiality, and the history of the field including important personal information about the researchers that would not easily be available otherwise.

Collecting and Organizing Data on Radio Sources

Though this is central to the activities of BRAG, it does not serve the purposes of this paper to describe this process in detail. Suffice it to say that there are two types of data that are collected and organized—the group's own data and data from other radio astronomy groups. The control over the BRAG members' data is managed in-house and seems to work quite well.

More problematic is the retrieval, recording, and organization of information gathered from other researchers. It is the understanding of the needs in this area where the Gesher Project may be able to provide some assistance. The need for information generated by others is a relatively common bibliographic problem—finding a work in which the desired data is reported. Access to NASA's intergalactic database may prove to be the best bibliographic solution.

The other half of the problem is capturing the needed information in a useful form. The data may be in the form of a spreadsheet with many different observations of a number of different objects, and no one is interested in keying pages and pages of this data into their own computers. Project staff have recommended that rather than investing time and money in solving this technical problem, BRAG would be better off using a service that scans documents for a fee.

Writing Software for the Analysis of Data Collected by the Group

Although BRAG members use a number of programs from other institutions to manage their software, a substantial portion of the group's work seems to involve writing and updating computer programs developed by the group for reducing their data and representing it graphically. This constant "tinkering" can cause significant difficulties; a proliferation of versions develops, and one loses track of which version is the appropriate one to use. The software engineer on the Gesher Project has proposed a software management program solution to this problem.

Disseminating the Results of the Group's Work through Published Writings, Attendance at Meetings, Correspondence with Other Radio Astronomers, and Public Lectures

Though the Gesher Project may have design components that aid in the development of formal papers, such as creating bibliographies, this was not explored very extensively in the initial interviews.

Conclusions from the Small Group Study

The approach of asking how the whole process of doing research in astrophysics works allowed project staff to place information needs in context. Without spending time at the Astrolunch seminar—just relying on interviews—there would only have been evidence like one scientist's complaint that even having the journals delivered to his mailbox is inconvenient—he wants someone to read the journals and tell him which articles to read. Project staff would not have been able to see the broader role that Astrolunch plays in the process of keeping abreast of the literature.

Spending the time up front, trying to learn the basics of their research project, and doing multiple interviews within a single research group are strategies that paid off in the end. The issues of loading masses of data into spreadsheets and managing software updates both came out of the last interview with the senior researcher. Both had been mentioned in passing in earlier interviews, but their importance was only evident in the last interview because one could see the research in a larger context.

This was not an in-depth ethnographic study. Project staff were only able to conduct a few interviews and attend a couple of seminars. If there were more time, it would be good to attend more seminars besides Astrolunch and some graduate level classes. Even with this minimal work, the Gesher Project team was able to come up with several interesting ideas about how the BRAG team members do their research and what some of their information needs are.

SYSTEMS DESIGN IMPLICATIONS

Digital Equipment Corporation researchers are developing a prototype information management system. The prototype has been developed using a medical model and was first previewed publicly at DEC World in Boston in April-May 1992. The medical model includes menuing capability, live links to in-room patient monitors, graphic images such as radiology reports, patient records, physician records, databases resident at various locations, security levels, and links out to external sources such as MEDLINE. The system is running on a DecStation 5000 as a server with DecStation 2000s as primary workstations. Primary requirements of the system design include high-resolution graphics terminals with windowing capabilities.

The library system, yet to be programmed, includes the following design elements:

- a menu of possible activities that can be customized for a scholar or group of scholars;
- network links to bibliographic databases, catalogs, indexing and abstracting services;
- links to local custom programs and files such as BRAG's own data analysis system;
- personal databases created with pointers to external files;
- bibliography-formatting software;

- PC/fax to receive scanned images; and
- high-resolution graphics capability and links to image files.

CONCLUSION

The work presented here is preliminary and reflects research-in-progress at Brandeis University. The work offers one model of how librarians can be involved in the design of new computer products for library users. The primary contribution at this time is methodological. Using qualitative research techniques, involving users in the design of systems, and librarian participation in research and design reflect new roles for librarians.

REFERENCES

Belkin, N. J.; Chang, S.-J.; Downs, T.; Saracevic, T.; & Zhao, S. (1990). Taking account of user tasks, goals and behavior for the design of online public access catalogs. In D. Henderson (Ed.), *Information in the year 2000: From research to applications* (Proceedings of the 53rd ASIS Annual Meeting) (Vol. 27, pp. 69-79). Medford, NJ: Learned Information.

Boulton, W. R., & Saladin, B. A. (1983). Let's make production/operations management top priority for strategic planning in the 1980s. *Managerial Planning, 32*(1), 15.

Davis, G. B., & Olson, M. H. (1985). *Management information systems: Conceptual foundations, structure, and development* (2nd ed.). New York: McGraw-Hill.

Gray, C. M. (1992). *Information for management planning and decision making: Toward a comprehensive model.* Unpublished doctoral dissertation, Brandeis University, Waltham, MA.

Havelock, R. G. (1972). *Bibliography on knowledge utilization and dissemination.* Ann Arbor, MI: Center for Research on Utilization of Scientific Knowledge, Institute for Social Research, University of Michigan.

Havelock, R. G. (1976). *Planning for Innovation through dissemination and utilization of knowledge.* Ann Arbor, MI: Center for Research on Utilization of Scientific Knowledge, Institute for Social Research, University of Michigan.

Hodge, B.; Fleck, R. A., Jr.; & Honess, C. B. (1984). *Management information systems.* Reston, VA: Reston Publishing.

Kochen, M. (1970). Stability in the growth of knowledge. In T. Saracevic (Ed.), *Introduction to information science* (pp. 44-55). New York: R. R. Bowker.

Line, M. B.; Brittain, J. M.; & Cranmer, F. A. (1971). *Information requirements of researchers in the social sciences.* (Investigation into information requirements of the social sciences: Research report no. 1). Bath, England: Bath University of Technology, University Library.

Mackenzie Owen, J. S., & van Halm, J. (1989). *Innovation in the information chain: The effects of technological development on the provision of scientific and technical information.* London: Routledge.

Mumford, E., & MacDonald, W. B. (1989). *XSEL's progress: The continuing journey of an expert system.* New York: Wiley.

Taylor, R. S. (1980). Value added aspects of the information process [Summary]. In A. R. Benenfeld & E. J. Kazlauskas (Eds.), *Communicating information* (Proceedings of the 43rd ASIS Annual Meeting) (Vol. 17, p. 344). White Plains, NY: Knowledge Industry Publications.

Taylor, R. S. (1986). *Value-added processes in information systems.* Norwood, NJ: Ablex.

Tufte, E. R. (1990). *Envisioning information.* Cheshire, CT: Graphics Press.

VIRGINIA TIEFEL

Director, Library User Education
Ohio State University Library
Columbus, Ohio

The Gateway to Information:
Development, Implementation, and Evaluation

ABSTRACT

The Ohio State University Library has developed The Gateway to
Information, which is a computer-assisted program for undergraduate
students. The program guides students in identifying, locating,
evaluating, and selecting information independently. The Gateway has
been in development for six years, funded by four grants, and has
undergone continuous evaluation. No help screens or handouts are
needed to use the system.

INTRODUCTION

The Gateway to Information was designed to help undergraduate
and eventually graduate students identify, locate, evaluate, and select
the most useful information for their needs. Running on Apple
Macintosh workstations, The Gateway provides guidance and
instruction for students on how to proceed through an information
search that integrates the use of print and computerized information.
The microcomputer program serves as an online "bridge" to other
computer-based systems, enabling the user to apply major elements of
a search strategy process by gaining ready access to the text of relevant
CD-ROM-based encyclopedia articles and journal indexes as well as
print sources. Each time users begin to search the catalog, the

34

microcomputer program offers a comprehensive search strategy option to lead the user through information sources beyond the catalog. Goals of the project are to teach students the following skills:

- find, evaluate, and select materials that meet their needs regardless of format;
- access and integrate the content of online catalogs and CD-ROM databases easily (even as novice researchers); and
- apply information-seeking and critical-thinking skills with a high degree of independence.

The Gateway has been continuously evaluated by users, and revisions have been made based on the results of the evaluations. Available on nine workstations since spring 1991, access to The Gateway will steadily increase as the library replaces 50 to 100 public catalog terminals with workstations that provide Gateway access. The Gateway's technology is basic and adaptable so the project is transferable to other libraries both conceptually and technically.

THE NEED

Effective problem solving in a complex society requires educated citizens who possess the ability to identify, acquire, and evaluate available information on a particular topic, question, or set of problems. With vast increases in the quantity of information available, most people are simply not capable of coping with this phenomenon, especially because of the increasing necessity for them to use computerized databases to gain access to much of this information.

College students, in particular, need instruction not only in the use of individual databases but, much more importantly, in a comprehensive approach to finding and integrating information—whether in print sources or in online sources. Most instruction that has taken place at the postsecondary level, however, has focused on teaching use of individual sources, including databases, with little if any guidance provided in how to integrate and weigh the usefulness of information obtained from a variety of online and print sources. Moreover, the proliferation of information has intensified the need for students to be able to evaluate information: the challenge often lies not in students' being able to find enough information but in their being able to evaluate and select the most useful for meeting their specific needs. Thus, two instructional needs in "information-seeking" skills must be satisfied: to teach students how to find needed information, using whatever formats are most efficient, then to evaluate that information to select what is most appropriate to the task at hand.

Many studies have shown that most undergraduate students never learn how to use libraries or other information sources effectively. Without instruction specific to information seeking, it has been found that most students will scan the library catalog to identify a few books on a topic, check out the titles that may be available, and attempt to complete the assignment. This is obviously a wholly inadequate approach to information seeking in today's society.

The Gateway to Information was conceived six years ago in the Office of Library User Education at the Ohio State University (OSU) Library in response to the burgeoning demands of the library user education program. The user education program has been in place since 1978, and as OSU Library Director Bill Studer observed, the program had become the victim of its own success. Meeting the staffing demands of the program was becoming increasingly difficult, and given the library's budget, there would be no additions to the staff. The program was reaching annually over 30,000 students with some form of course-related instruction, and another 5,000 students were taught in clinics and workshops. Although that is a large number, it was an inadequate one considering the 53,000 students on campus. Furthermore, it was recognized that to become information literate, students need multiple sessions of instruction. An additional point of concern was the realization that students were beginning to use remote access to the online catalog; this practice resulted in students' reversion to total dependence on the catalog—a dependence librarians had been trying to break by instructing students about the variety of library resources beyond the catalog.

DEVELOPMENT OF THE GATEWAY

Most of the library instruction at OSU has focused on the search strategy concept that is a step-by-step process moving from general to specific information through evaluation and selecting the best information for the need (see Figure 1). In pursuing how to continue the expansion of the instruction program without more staff, it was decided to try putting the search strategy on a computer that would be connected to the online catalog and to CD-ROMs. A grant was sought from the Fund for the Improvement of Postsecondary Education (FIPSE), a granting agency that funds innovative but largely embryonic projects. The proposal came close to acceptance in 1986, and the following year a revised proposal received funding. The project has subsequently received two grants from the Higher Education Act II-D, College Library Technology and Cooperation Grants Program, and a grant from the William Randolph Hearst Foundation for a total of half a million dollars. These four grants were critical to The Gateway's development.

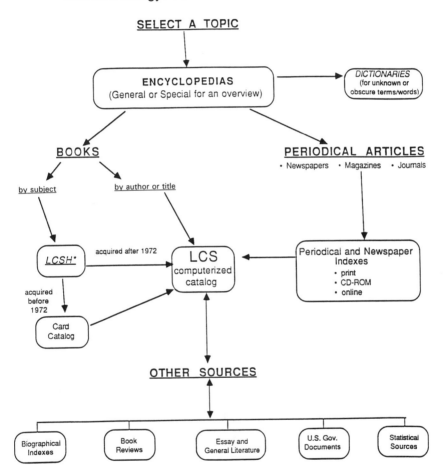

Figure 1. Search strategy concept taught at Ohio State University

The University Library provided a full-time equivalent (FTE) position for directing the project, two FTE professional positions, and considerable staff time. The library assigned a professional librarian to the project full time for four months and provided some equipment. The university's Instructional Development and Evaluation unit provided a 10% equivalent FTE evaluation and computer technology expertise for the first two years, with the assistance of a graduate teaching associate. University Systems, the support and provider for the library's online catalog, loaned $30,000 worth of equipment and provided one-third of a programming position. The Academic Computing Center also provided staffing and equipment support.

The library has provided student programming time, fees for lines to the library's online catalog, software and equipment, and valuable space in the library for The Gateway team. When the project was begun, the programmer/analyst-senior and the systems programmer participated in the evaluation of needed computer equipment. Based on their findings, equipment and software were selected and purchased using funds provided by the University Library and the related university computer center. This equipment included microcomputer workstations, a local area network (LAN), and a connection to the university's Amdahl mainframe computer, which runs the online catalog system.

Macintosh HyperCard 2.0 was used for prototyping The Gateway narrative because it offered the easiest method for creating the narrative and making the necessary revisions. In the beginning, programming activities centered on developing the microcomputer "front-end" for the University Library's mainframe catalog system. This was complicated by the need for the microcomputer to process special characters (e.g., diacritical marks) that are needed for the several foreign languages supported by the online catalog system. The development of this capability, however, had other benefits. It permitted a more flexible user interface that could place all or part of the catalog information anywhere on a microcomputer screen and make possible the combining of catalog data with that from other information sources. Like most online catalog systems, the OSU online catalog was developed for mainframe display terminals that have a fixed display format and access to only one information source. Therefore, this new capability offered a major improvement over existing library information systems and could be adapted by many institutions that had the same limitations in their catalogs.

Programming was started with these underlying structures because they were necessary for implementing the overall project design—to bring together information from different sources utilizing various learning and access strategies. Work began on a single user workstation connected to the library's mainframe-based catalog system and conversion to the LAN environment where users on several workstations could share a single link to the library's online catalog system.

Incorporated into the project's design was the ability to update both information sources and the narrative/instruction. These features were needed to keep pace with the always changing environment within information systems and information itself. It also enhanced the project's transferability by permitting other institutions to tailor the system to their particular needs. The data communications connection to information sources was intended to be transportable to other institutions with little or no modification: there are only a limited number of ways to connect microcomputers for data transfer, and most of them will have been included in the design of The Gateway.

The Gateway software runs on Apple Macintosh IIcx computers that are connected to the campus computer network through which the library user may access available information services. Currently, The Gateway workstation user may access the University Library's online catalog and 12 CD-ROM databases that are housed in CD-ROM towers and mounted on a LAN. The Gateway software, which includes HyperCard 2.0, MAC/TCP, and MitemView, is installed on each Gateway workstation. The Gateway workstation was designed to function as the catalog workstation with the intent that every public terminal for the OSU Library's online catalog would, in time, be a Gateway workstation. The OSU Library also intends to make The Gateway available for remote users of the online catalog. The content of the narrative, instruction in The Gateway software, and the system design have been developed to migrate easily to other library environments.

The design group decided to begin writing the narrative with the journal section, and when that became operable, attention was turned to the development of the first step of the search strategy—encyclopedias. The intent was to design a common interface to the databases so users would see the same screen design regardless of the database they were using. The *Academic American Encyclopedia* was added to The Gateway, which also now offered the journal section.

The first step in the search strategy is finding background information on the topic, for which an encyclopedia is usually the best source. Using a dictionary for definitions of unknown words and terms is the next step, with searches of journals usually a third step, depending on the topic. The additional steps of the search strategy were added until all were operable.

When the technology to link the CD-ROM versions of the encyclopedia, dictionary, and indexes was perfected, The Gateway incorporated that format into its instruction. The Gateway continued to add indexes in electronic format as they became available. The decision, however, on what to instruct the students to use was not decided by what was available in electronic format but by what was deemed the best choice to meet the students' needs. The Gateway is designed to make the best use of technology but not to be driven by it. Links from the microcomputers to the catalog and CD-ROMs were completed near the end of the second year.

IMPLEMENTATION OF THE GATEWAY

As of May 11, 1989, a Macintosh workstation with The Gateway prototype was set up in the main library for library personnel to use and evaluate. For security reasons, the workstation was located in the administrative wing, and librarians and staff were encouraged to schedule a time or simply to stop by to use it. Evaluation forms were available at the terminal.

Based on the evaluation data, the journal section was revised, and a number of subjects and indexes were added to this section. This development was supervised by Nancy O'Hanlon, head of the Reference Department at the Undergraduate Library, who was on temporary assignment to the project. She brought to the project considerable knowledge of how undergraduates seek information and what is needed. Her appointment ran from March through June 1989, and she did an excellent job of pulling the narrative and the staff ideas together, adding consistency to the screen design, and expanding the journal search and other sections of the narrative. Testing and evaluation involving 10 randomly selected students were conducted by the Center for Teaching Excellence evaluation personnel in May. Based on the evaluations, The Gateway was revised and the narrative was expanded. Considerable time was spent on how to determine and analyze user needs. As a help in accomplishing that goal, as well as to provide baseline data, a user study was conducted in the 1988 fall quarter.

The highest priority of the project's programmers was to program and implement the instructional design ideas of the library staff and others. Thus far, programming had been done using a high-level language. Programming using an authoring system that allowed easier and faster development was preferable, but a graphics-based authoring system with the required communications features had not been found. The search for tools that would allow easier implementation and modification of design ideas continued.

At the end of two and one-half years, the narrative had been developed from the original journal search into five major areas of information: Facilities, Explain, Strategies, Sources, and LCS (online catalog). The Gateway provided a subject approach to encyclopedias and journal indexes, recommending which materials students should use depending on their information needs. The Gateway also answered simple questions about the library system, e.g., library locations, floor plans, and services.

By early 1990, connectivity between The Gateway, CD-ROM materials, and LCS had been achieved. This meant that from a single Gateway workstation, the user could access the *Academic American Encyclopedia* on CD-ROM, the catalog, periodical indexes, and the needed guidance to make decisions about what to use and where the information was. A prototype LAN was set up with five workstations sharing a line to the library's online catalog system and databases on CD-ROM. Project goals were seamless access to the CD-ROM database from within The Gateway program. This was a real breakthrough for the project in both instruction and technology.

The Gateway has met the needs of many students and programs. One specific program can be cited as an example of improved library instruction with The Gateway. The Young Scholars Program was implemented by the university in 1988 and is designed to prepare minority students for college. Beginning with a class of pre-seventh graders the first year, the program brings to campus for two weeks 400 students at each grade level. They are taught subject matter and certain skills including information-seeking skills. The first year of the library's involvement with the program was 1990, and the library instruction was ineffective. In 1991, a special limited edition of The Gateway was prepared for the class of tenth graders to use in completing an assignment on Martin Luther King. Students did their work in a computer lab, and evaluations showed that use of The Gateway was very successful. Students liked it and appeared to learn from it. Without The Gateway, the library would have had a difficult time creating and implementing a meaningful library assignment that was also popular with students.

EVALUATION OF THE GATEWAY

Evaluation results provide evidence of how The Gateway has benefited students and improved library services. In 1988-1989, copies of proposed narrative sections were periodically distributed to library and faculty and staff who had expressed an interest in critiquing them. About 30 copies were distributed, and a wide variety of responses were received. These provided some of the material Nancy O'Hanlon used in the development of the search strategy narrative.

The project has been continuously evaluated, primarily through written evaluation forms left at the workstations. The first evaluation study, which is a summative evaluation, was done in fall 1988 when baseline data were collected on how students found information in the library using traditional methods. This will be compared with how students use The Gateway, and the results of both methods will be examined. This comparative analysis has not yet been done. The other evaluations have been formative ones, and the results have been used to revise and expand the narrative. In mid-1989, the first public workstation was set up, and library staff evaluated The Gateway using forms that asked about screen design, logic of the narrative, and the content. In addition, 11 students were intensively interviewed using The Gateway in fall 1989.

When the first public workstation became available in the main library in January 1990, evaluation forms were placed next to the terminal. These forms were similar to the staff evaluation forms. In mid-1990, two freshman classes of 41 students were required to use The Gateway for an assignment. Evaluations were very positive. The evaluation form was changed considerably in mid-July of 1990 and has remained much the same since. After the CD-ROM access became available on The Gateway in mid-February 1991, satisfaction and usage both increased.

The Gateway was also evaluated by special classes—a graduate class and two industrial design classes. Their comments were not summative but formative, i.e., how to improve The Gateway. The Center for Teaching Excellence provided an industrial design expert to evaluate The Gateway in January 1990. In spring 1990, a library science class evaluated The Gateway.

The Gateway was designed for use by lower level undergraduates with the intention of increasing its complexity and sophistication in materials to meet the needs of advanced undergraduate and graduate students and ultimately faculty. Evaluations showed that upper level students, faculty, and staff used The Gateway and were successful in their searches. Of 1,190 evaluation forms turned in voluntarily at the workstations from July 16, 1990, to July 31, 1991, the breakdown by academic level of user was as follows: freshman, 106 (9%); sophomore, 127 (11%); junior, 170 (14%); senior, 226 (19%); graduate students, 306 (26%); faculty and staff, 77 (6%); other, 102 (9%); no answer, 72 (6%). In summary, 629 or 53% of the users were undergraduates, 306 (26%) were graduate students, and a total of 935 students made up 79% of The Gateway usage during that period.

Nine Gateway to Information workstations help students to identify their information needs and locate, evaluate, and select the information. The Gateway's success rate in accomplishing this is documented in the results of the project's evaluations. Results of 1,656 evaluation forms dated from July 16, 1990, to January 31, 1992, indicated that 78% were "completely" or "mostly" successful in their searches: 89% rated the screens "very" or "mostly" clear. Ease of use of The Gateway was rated "very" or "mostly" easy by 84%. From 964 of those evaluations, 83% said they would use The Gateway again.

Sample topics searched included reflexology, women in politics, waste water pollution, medieval period dress and costumes, gum chewing/bubble gum, reunification of Germany, and social welfare. Comments were varied but mostly very positive. Some examples included the following: "Easy as pie." "This thing takes your hand and leads you right down the path." "This was incredible! What a time saver." "I could see exactly what I was doing, and I knew my status all the time." "Everything you could want is at your fingertips!" "I'm addicted: great visual format." "Really easy to use—please get more of these."

Design issues were settled by evaluation results when possible, and the impact of evaluation can be seen in Figure 2. The improvement in the evaluation results can be directly attributed to the revisions that were made based on the evaluations. Figure 3 shows two screens in the Gateway's early development. These were opening screens on The Gateway before it was made available to the public when it was still being evaluated by library staff only. The first screen showed type of material—books or journals—and was too limiting in its options. The second screen attempted to anticipate the user's needs and was also too limiting: users were unable to identify with the options. Neither approach worked well. Opening screens of The Gateway now offer a research strategy diagram that works well (Figure 4): the screen provides the users with several options and allows them to better control their searching.

The evaluation studies revealed some basic tenets. One was that most students will not read more than two lines: they prefer to skim text. Another was that students usually select the first or second choice, especially when using the system for the first time. As they become accustomed to using the system, this tendency diminishes. Most users did not understand the meaning of icons or how to use them. This lack of knowledge extends to arrows, but they do understand boxes.

THE FUTURE OF THE GATEWAY

The Gateway will continue to undergo expansion in its narrative and number of available databases and workstations. Immediate plans include continued revision of the narrative based on evaluations and the addition of special subject sections. The first one of these sections is on communication and is being tested by students. A business section

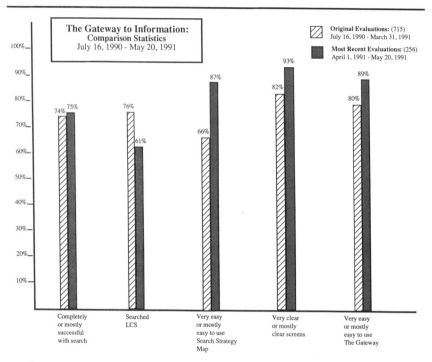

Figure 2. Evaluation results of revisions made on The Gateway

will soon be ready, and by fall 1992, a section of women's studies will be available. These additions will be tested by users and revised until they are as user friendly as the existing Gateway narrative. Commercial databases will be added to The Gateway as money becomes available.

Replacement of public online catalog terminals began in spring 1992, and 20 new workstations with Gateway capability will be available by the end of May. The library will continue this replacement activity until all 106 public workstations have Gateway capability. All of these activities—narrative revision and expansion and addition of databases—will be ongoing. The project will never be finished: it is a forever project. It was envisioned that way, and its development has substantiated that vision.

Plans are already underway to expand the subject list of 100 topics to one based on the Library of Congress Subject Headings classification. The Gateway now recommends specific materials for each subject, and the enhanced list of subjects with recommended sources will expand The Gateway's ability to guide users to the best information. Some have suggested that The Gateway ultimately be programmed to respond

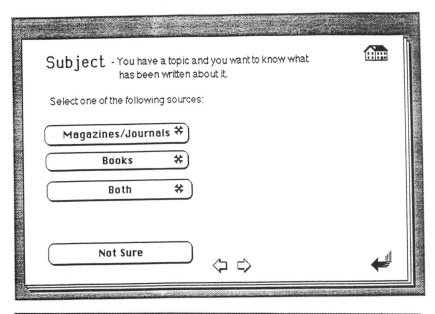

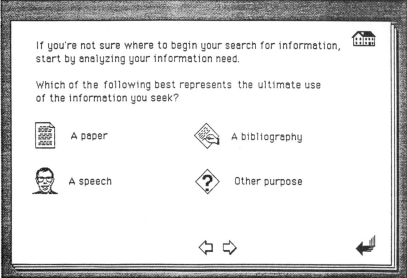

Figure 3. Two screens used in early versions of The Gateway

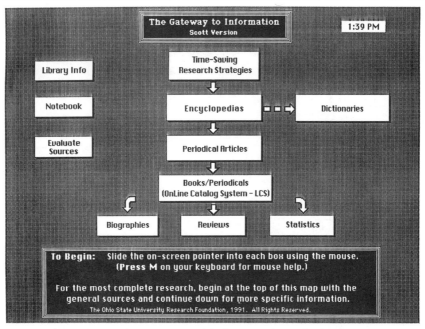

Figure 4. Opening screen used in later versions of The Gateway

to the user's selected subject with not only which materials to use but pages, subject headings used, etc. Some say the cost of doing this would be prohibitive, and from a librarian's viewpoint, it doesn't teach information skills: it's the vending machine approach. However, it is a concept worth exploring.

In The Gateway's immediate future is the development of a UNIX-based system. This would provide remote access and make The Gateway compatible with any type of computer. The narrative would probably not be as appealing as the Macintosh version, but the use of windows would permit the use of some graphics. It is hoped to have this version ready next year, but obtaining money to buy the equipment and do the programming will determine the timetable.

Formative evaluation will continue to provide the basis on which The Gateway narrative is revised and expanded. It would be valuable to do a summative evaluation to determine what impact The Gateway has on students' information seeking. Do they find more or less material using The Gateway than with traditional searching? Is the information found more or less appropriate for their needs? How does The Gateway affect students' attitudes?

In terms of physical expansion, The Gateway will be available on 59 terminals in the library system by summer 1992. This is more than half of the number of public terminals in the library system. The remaining 47 terminals will be replaced within the next year making The Gateway available in all OSU libraries. When the UNIX version is finished, The Gateway will be available across campus in dormitories and offices and off-campus for OSU users who have access to computers. This will be a very popular move; it is one our students have consistently asked for from The Gateway's inception.

The OSU Library plans to share The Gateway with other academic institutions and school and public libraries. The complication is the Library's inability to support such sharing, having neither the necessary staff nor the resources. There have been ongoing talks with several companies about marketing The Gateway. And although there is some interest in a collaborative effort, there is nothing definite to date. Many other academic libraries have expressed an interest in acquiring The Gateway for their institutions. The leaders of a statewide project to link all Ohio primary and secondary schools electronically are interested in incorporating The Gateway into their project. Public libraries have expressed a desire to collaborate on a Gateway version for public libraries. Envisioned is an information system that teaches and guides students from primary through secondary and postsecondary institutions to the public libraries on how to find, evaluate, and select information. The system based on the search strategy concept will make students information literate. In fact, students will learn the search strategy so well that they will be able, ultimately, to apply the concept in libraries without Gateway terminals.

The Gateway to Information is already a success with users, and its potential for development and expansion is virtually limitless. User satisfaction and usage are very encouraging, and The Gateway has demonstrated that it can change how libraries are used. Although no other institution has the right to use The Gateway, there is promise of and an interest in transporting it to other institutions. OSU is committed to sharing The Gateway and to encouraging its adoption by as many other institutions as possible.

Evan Farber, the preeminent expert on bibliographic instruction in the world and one of The Gateway consultants, summarized the project this way:

> I was so pleased with the progress you all have made with Gateway. As I told you I said to the LOEX group, I felt proud to be associated with the project. It's very impressive, and I think academic librarians are going to feel indebted to you for many, many years. To be sure, others will build on it, improve it, but the credit for developing the first really effective computer-assisted bibliographic instruction program will belong to you. Congratulations—and thanks so much for permitting me to take part in it. (E. Farber, personal communication, May 28, 1991)

TIMOTHY W. COLE

Assistant Engineering Librarian
University of Illinois at Urbana-Champaign

LESLIE TROUTMAN

Music Library User Services Coordinator
University of Illinois at Urbana-Champaign

WILLIAM H. MISCHO

Engineering Librarian
University of Illinois at Urbana-Champaign

WINNIE CHAN

Automated Records Maintenance Coordinator
University of Illinois at Urbana-Champaign

Design and Development of a Library Information Workstation

ABSTRACT

This paper describes the design and continuing development of the University of Illinois at Urbana-Champaign Library Information Workstation, which provides the primary, in-library patron access to ILLINET Online Plus, the Library's extended online public access catalog system. The automated library information resources and information processing environment are briefly described as they have influenced the design and development of the Library Information Workstation. The Library Information Workstation philosophy and approach are discussed in the context of relevant information access issues and patron needs and requirements. Features of the current Library Information Workstation implementation are then described using illustrations focused particularly on integrated access to local (resident on individual workstations) information files and an integrated end-user interface for bibliographic database searching. Ongoing development plans also are discussed briefly.

48

INTRODUCTION

This paper discusses general principles and precedents relating to library information workstation design and development, focusing specifically on interface and workstation development at the University of Illinois at Urbana-Champaign (UIUC) Library. The paper is divided into five sections: (a) a brief description of the ILLINET Online Plus (IO+) extended online catalog, (b) an overview of the UIUC Library Information Workstation (LIW) philosophy and approach, (c) a discussion of user searching behaviors and needs and the interface design considerations that have driven the UIUC LIW design and development, (d) an examination of the local file access capability integrated into the UIUC LIW, and (e) a detailed look at the integrated UIUC LIW interface developed to facilitate end-user searching of bibliographic databases accessed via the local BRS/SEARCH implementation.

Concurrent with the Library Information Workstation developments described in this paper, and to an extent the driving force behind it, has been the emergence of the Extended Online Public Access Catalog (E-OPAC). These developments in turn have been possible because of improvements in telecommunications technologies, computer hardware and software, and advances in the accessibility and breadth of bibliographic databases. Together these developments are allowing libraries to provide enhanced access to local and remote bibliographic resources. This is being done principally through the model of the E-OPAC (Hildreth, 1989, 1991; Potter, 1989).

E-OPACs typically provide value-added access to resources beyond the conventional OPAC such as campus or community information resources, locally created bibliographic files, locally mounted and remote periodical index databases, online bibliographic database vendors and utilities, and the OPACs of other major Association of Research Libraries (ARL) or regional libraries. One of the primary roles of the E-OPAC is to serve as a node in a campuswide information system (CWIS).

Supporting the E-OPAC have been a number of important emerging information technologies such as powerful yet affordable microcomputer workstations; optical disk and enhanced magnetic storage media; graphical and imaging technologies and standards; local, campus, regional, and national telecommunication networks; and sophisticated information retrieval search engines (e.g., BRS/SEARCH). These technologies supply system designers and developers with the tools needed to provide enhanced access within the E-OPAC environment.

The UIUC Library has incorporated certain of these technologies into the IO+ E-OPAC (Mischo, Sandore, Clark, & Gorman, 1990). The development and implementation of IO+ has been integrally connected to the evolving UIUC LIW, a multifeatured microcomputer workstation developed in the Library to serve as a public terminal for IO+ (Mischo & Cole, 1992). The UIUC LIW is the primary means of accessing the IO+ information resources and plays a key role in integrating the multiple technologies that comprise IO+.

Specifically, the LIW provides interface, gateway, and database management software to facilitate direct patron access to IO+ resources and services. The major objectives of the UIUC LIW are (a) the integrated and largely transparent access from a single terminal to a wide range of library and information access resources, (b) the inclusion of user-friendly, expert-system interfaces that facilitate patron searching of bibliographic databases and lessen end-user searching difficulties, (c) the built-in flexibility to allow terminal-specific customization of LIW menus and interfaces to accommodate localized patron needs and library resources, and (d) the utilization of emerging multimedia and image transmission technologies to enhance end-user interfaces and to provide more rapid and more complete patron access to information.

The later sections of this paper illustrate some of this functionality with specific examples, focusing on two of the information resources available in the current UIUC LIW implementation: the capability of storing, searching, and integrating local, customized databases stored on the workstation hard disk and a microcomputer-based interface for the locally mounted BRS/SEARCH implementation IBIS (Illinois Bibliographic Information Services). These two particular LIW features serve as illustrations of the enhanced information access provided jointly by the LIW and the E-OPAC.

Finally, the paper concludes with a brief discussion of current planning and development work in progress to further extend the scope and functionality of the UIUC LIW.

ILLINET ONLINE PLUS

The IO+ extended OPAC provides access to a variety of local and remote information resources via two different campus networks. These resources include the following:

1. The statewide online catalog ILLINET Online (IO) with holdings data from over 800 libraries in the state of Illinois, totalling over 9 million records. Access to IO is through both microcomputer and mainframe interfaces.

2. A locally mounted mainframe-based BRS/SEARCH retrieval system (IBIS) and attendant periodical index databases, presently comprised of Current Contents (seven sections, updated weekly), eight Wilson databases (Readers' Guide Abstracts, Social Sciences Index, Humanities Index, Business Periodicals Index, Applied Science and Technology Index, Biological and Agricultural Index, General Science Index, and a combined file), and the ERIC databases. The IBIS system is presently comprised of 5.1 million periodical citations.

3. Locally generated and maintained data files stored on the microcomputer workstation hard disk and searched using a locally developed sequential search database management system. These files can be customized by departmental library site and include databases such as hot topic bibliographies, faculty interest profiles, staff directories, new book lists, and reserve lists.

4. A gateway to the CARL (Colorado Alliance of Research Libraries) UnCover periodical database system.

Additional information resources are currently being tested and integrated into the LIW at selected UIUC campus library sites. These resources include the following:

1. Gateway access to database and telecommunications resources on the campus fiber-optic network (UIUCNet), which include the Oxford English Dictionary (OED), weather information, current news, class listings, and campus telephone directory.

2. Gateway access to Internet resources, including the OPACs of selected Committee on Institutional Cooperation (CIC) and ARL research libraries and consortia, such as Northwestern University, Indiana University, and the MELVYL California statewide union catalog, and access via a local Gopher client to many other Internet resources.

3. Access to databases stored on CD-ROM networks (including full-text files such as the UMI periodical article data) using the CD vendor search engines, run from the interface using shell software.

4. Multimedia and graphical files (in .PCX format) such as building maps, floor plans, and mixed graphics, sound, and text (including hypermedia files). Software has been developed to retrieve and display scanned images with voice-over being provided by a programmable speech synthesizer.

5. The capability of invoking specific commercial microcomputer software application packages such as expert system and database management packages from the interface and returning to the interface menu level using shell software.

In addition, several important access and linking mechanisms are in place within the Information Workstation and IO+ for providing maximum access to available information resources. These mechanisms include the following:

1. UIUCNet file transfer capabilities used to transmit **BRS/SEARCH** search results (bibliographic citations and abstracts) to users' electronic mailboxes.
2. The on-the-fly linking and display of call number and limited holdings information from a displayed **BRS/SEARCH** search citation.
3. Software-controlled gateway paths within the workstation including automatic logon to local and remote resources and hidden password entry for applications requiring passwords.

The above information resources and linking technologies are made available to library users and staff through the LIW software, presently deployed in 39 UIUC departmental libraries on some 110 public terminals. The software is also being tested at selected institutions in the 40-member ILCSO (Illinois Library Computer System Organization) network consortium. The workstation software is also being tested in networking environments utilizing TCP/IP telecommunications protocols.

LIBRARY INFORMATION WORKSTATION

The UIUC LIW is presently implemented on a range of IBM PS/2 platforms from Model 30 286 machines to PS/2 Model 70s. The LIW employs interface, gateway, and database management software to enhance user access to local and remote information resources available in IO+. The LIW is the center of a client-server user access model for IO+ that features a distributed retrieval network with databases on local and remote file servers and the interface and gateway functions residing on the microcomputer workstation. Our implementation of this model is illustrated in Figure 1.

The information resources accessed by the LIW may reside on local or remote mainframes, on CD-ROM files in stand-alone or networked environments, or as files stored on the microcomputer hard disk and accessed via a microcomputer database management application. One of the advantages of the microcomputer workstation approach is that the main search menu presented to the user can be customized to suit the needs of specific departmental libraries. A sample main menu from the UIUC Music Library is shown in Figure 2.

The LIW project has focused on the development and testing of microcomputer software and hardware technologies to (a) enhance the user-computer interface, (b) provide expert-system searching techniques

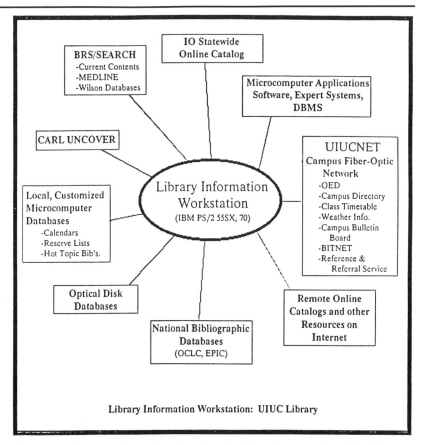

Figure 1. Library Information Workstation: Implementation of a client-server user access model for IO+

and guided assistance in user searching, (c) utilize multimedia technologies in providing assistance with user instruction and point-of-contact help, and (d) provide extended access to information resources on the IO+ statewide network, the campus network, and the Internet.

This approach facilitates a "one-stop-shopping" approach to a broad array of information resources. The LIW is designed to use multimedia techniques in providing access to bibliographic, numerical, graphical, and full-text resources. The long-range goal of the LIW is to merge the three types of workstation technology: bibliographic database and gateway services, multimedia and imaging technologies, and scholarly user needs such as data analysis, scientific computing, and word processing.

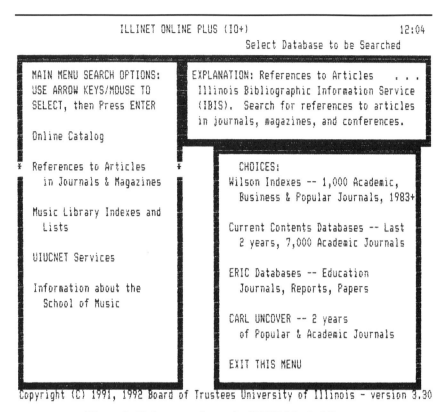

Figure 2. Main menu from the UIUC Music Library

Several academic and special libraries have pursued the development of microcomputer scholar's workstations or similar multifunctional microcomputer-based desktop systems (Arms, 1990). These institutions include Brown University, the University of Southern California, Ohio State University (Tiefel, 1991), and Carnegie-Mellon University.

USER SEARCHING BEHAVIORS AND NEEDS

In May 1990, the UIUC Library Online Catalog Advisory Committee formed an Interface Design Subcommittee with the charge to design and implement LIW interfaces, beginning with the interface to the local BRS/SEARCH implementation IBIS (Norlin et al., 1992a, 1992b). To provide context for planning the design of interface features for the LIW, the literature on user needs and searching behaviors was examined.

Numerous studies of both online catalog and end-user bibliographic searching services have been reported and reviewed (Mischo & Lee, 1987; Drabenstott, 1991; Hildreth, 1989). As Borgman (1986) has noted, the users of all online bibliographic retrieval systems exhibit similar behavior patterns and have the same types of mechanical and conceptual difficulties. Studies of direct end-user search services and online catalog use show the following:

1. Users are enthusiastic about performing searches on easy to use, quickly learned, inexpensive search systems.
2. Search strategy formulation and the use of Boolean operators pose difficulties for users.
3. Users have difficulty with the simpler interfaces provided in the after-hours services and CD-ROM systems.
4. Several recent online catalog and CD-ROM transaction log analyses and repeat search studies show high user failure rates for both subject searches and known-item searches (Peters, 1989; Hunter, 1991; Charles & Clark, 1990; Puttapithakporn, 1990; Schultz & Salomon, 1990).
5. High levels of reported user satisfaction with search results may not reflect true success rates (Ankeny, 1991; Nielsen, 1986).
6. End-user search services can demand a significant investment of library staff time in training and assistance.
7. End-users resist formal training sessions and the use of printed instructions, preferring computer-assisted instruction (CAI) and direct one-to-one instruction from library staff or peers.
8. The typical user searches relatively infrequently; even the frequent users search infrequently enough so as to require retraining or refamiliarization with the system.

In addition, the online catalog use studies have revealed several facts important to designers of E-OPACs containing periodical index databases:

1. Most catalog users want materials on a topic.
2. Subject searching is the predominant mode of searching; it accounts for more than one-half of all searches.
3. Catalog users report the most problems with subject searching.
4. One-third to one-half of searches result in no items retrieved.
5. Conversely, a large percentage of subject searches provide a partial match with controlled vocabulary terms and produce a large number of retrieved citations.
6. User-entered subject search terms match the Library of Congress Subject Headings controlled vocabulary only 20% to 40% of the time.

7. Systems with keyword searching appear to receive more subject searching.
8. Catalog users place the highest priority for improvements on various subject search enhancements.
9. Users approach online catalogs expecting to find access to a broader field of materials, including periodicals, than are covered by the traditional card catalog.

The results of the end-user and online catalog use studies have important ramifications for the design of all bibliographic retrieval systems, including OPACs, online periodical index databases, and optical disk search systems.

On the one hand, the overwhelming acceptance of E-OPACs by users and the high degree of user satisfaction with such systems can be interpreted as a mandate for enhanced subject access (Hildreth, 1987; Mathews, 1991). Historically, the card catalogs of the late 19th century provided access to periodical articles via 3 × 5 cards supplied by vendors or prepared in-house, so the renewed interest in shaping the modern online catalog into an "analytic" catalog capable of providing the same function is not surprising. Locally mounted periodical index databases provide users with access to the periodical literature from the same terminals used to search the online catalog. They serve to complement periodical index databases made available in stand-alone and networked CD-ROM workstations. Local access to the periodical literature has become a common feature of the E-OPAC (Seiden, 1991; Locally loaded databases, 1989).

On the other hand, the use studies also show that the objective quality and success of end-user searches often are not high. The interface plays a particularly critical role in the searching of bibliographic retrieval systems that employ sophisticated information retrieval techniques and contain records with subject-rich fields.

Yet, while it has become clear to library system designers that better interfaces and "front-end" technologies can greatly enhance end-user searching of today's large bibliographic databases, examination of the information science and computer science literature reveals that there are no prescriptive models that can be followed to arrive at an optimum interface design (Grudin, 1989; Sutcliffe & McDermott, 1991; Yee, 1991). There are no complete human-computer interaction theories (Fischer, 1989), and stable and complete guidelines for interface design are felt to be several decades away (Shneiderman, 1987, p. 417), although a few key interface design principles have been identified and accepted (Gould & Lewis, 1985; Wilson & Rosenberg, 1988, p. 865). The LIW end-user searching interface described below, therefore, was developed from first principles and in response to the specific considerations described above rather than according to any existing prescription. It continues to be refined and developed based on experience and observation.

A CUSTOMIZED IMPLEMENTATION EXAMPLE

As an illustrative example of the UIUC LIW as currently implemented, Figure 2 shows the opening LIW menu as defined for the UIUC Music Library installation of the system. Menu pick number 1, "Online Catalog," provides access to the statewide online catalog (IO). At the Music Library, as at most sites on the UIUC campus, access to IO is provided via user-friendly microcomputer interface software developed by UIUC Prof. C.-C. Cheng (1985). Elsewhere in the state, most patron access to IO is via the more recently developed mainframe interface.

Menu pick number 2, "References to Articles in Journals & Magazines," provides access to the statewide BRS/SEARCH implementation for searching bibliographic databases (IBIS). Note that the database availability indicated in Figure 2 is specific to UIUC. Exact database availability varies slightly on other campuses in the statewide ILSCO consortium. The LIW interface to IBIS is discussed in detail in a later section.

Menu pick number 4, "UIUCNet Services," provides access to database and telecommunications resources on the UIUC campus fiber-optic network. In this particular installation, one may access the electronic version of the OED, the campus phone and e-mail address directory, and preselected OPACs from other institutions. Figure 3 shows a selection of UIUCNet resources specific to the Music Library implementation of the LIW.

Data files generated and maintained by each library (menu picks number 3 and 5) are stored on the microcomputer hard disk and searched using a locally developed, sequential search database management system integrated into the LIW. The search software, written in the Microsoft BASIC Professional Development System language, was authored by UIUC faculty members William Mischo, Timothy Cole, and David Stern. A primary goal of developing the search software in-house was to facilitate the interchange between IO+ applications.

This sequential search application is intended for ASCII files up to a few megabytes. Since data files are unindexed and standard ASCII in format, they can be created in a variety of ways. Data files can be created by downloading from sources such as IO or IBIS; files may also be created with standard word processors and saved as ASCII text. The

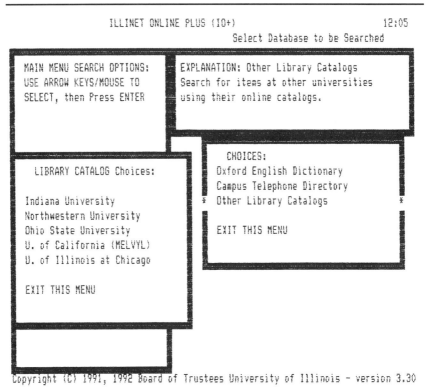

Figure 3. UIUCNet resources specific to the Music Library

files can be customized for a very specific user population. Files created for the Music Library include the Journal List, Current Acquisitions List, Cumulative Acquisitions List, Compact Disc List, Video List, Dissertation List, and Resource Guide (see Figure 4). A help screen supplements the description given for each of these files in the IO+ menu "Explanation Box" (see upper right-hand corner of Figure 4).

In some cases, files are created to complement access to materials in the online catalog. For example, in IO it is not possible to limit one's search to only CDs, yet many of the Music Library's clientele request CDs specifically. For several years, a separate dBase III database was maintained. When that was no longer feasible, the sound recording portion of the electronically prepared monthly acquisition list was appended to a printout of the dBase III file. These files have now been combined and may be searched using this application. Because files are unindexed, they are updated easily; new material is simply appended.

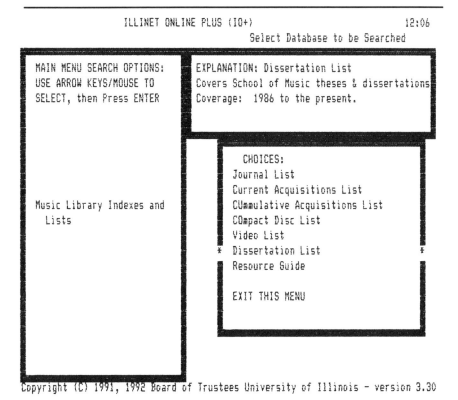

Figure 4. Files and help screen created for the Music Library

Files are searched sequentially from beginning to end, byte by byte. The inherent power and speed of the IBM PS/2 machine—the IBM PS/2 Model 30 286 is the recommended minimum platform for LIW implementation—combined with recent improvements in Microsoft BASIC permits a file to be searched very quickly, even in this sequential search manner; file indexing is unnecessary. Since the files are not indexed, the user need not worry about searching specific fields or using controlled vocabulary. The string search algorithm used permits both right- and left-hand truncation.

For flexibility, the integrated LIW sequential search software does accommodate record delineation. By creating discrete records within the file, the use of Boolean logic becomes possible. A set of reversed brackets is used to delineate the end of a record. End-of-record markers may be introduced into a file by means of a word processing macro.

```
           UNIVERSITY OF ILLINOIS MUSIC LIBRARY VIDEORECORDING LIST

                                 OPERAS

Beethoven, Ludwig van, 1770-1827.
     Fidelio [videorecording] / Beethoven ; libretto, Josef Sonneleithner. New
York : Video Arts International, c1985. Cast: Elisabeth Soderstrom, Anton de
Ridder, Robert Allman, The London Philharmonic Orchestra and Glyndebourne
Chorus.
VIDRECM1500B33F521985


VIDRECM1500B33F521985   BEETHOVEN, LUDWIG VAN, 1770-1827.   FIDELIO$ NEW YORK
     NOLC      3320793   1985      1   ADDED:  870927    NENG
01    001 4W    MUG RCALL 921030/930104 UC
02    001          SAVE  921212       UC
Press ENTER to resume search, or type an LCS command.
```

Figure 5. Local file search results and their circulation status

In addition, files created by downloading from IO using another locally created library staff application, Illinois Search Aid, can be automatically supplied with reverse brackets between bibliographic records.

Available options include searching a single term, searching for two or more terms within one record (the logical operator "and"), and searching for any of two or more terms in a record (the logical "or").

Mentioned above was the goal of facilitating the interchange of information between applications. One example is a local data file that contains catalog call number information. The LIW software permits a dynamic link between local file search results and current IO circulation status and holding information (see Figure 5).

SEARCHING FOR JOURNAL ARTICLES ON THE LIW

Selection of the "References to Articles in Journals & Magazines" LIW main menu pick starts a microcomputer-mediated session on IBIS, the local implementation of the BRS/SEARCH information retrieval system. Figure 6 shows the opening IBIS interface menu screen for an ERIC database search. The three-windowed approach of the LIW main menu screens is preserved providing a sense of integration and continuity. In addition to this basic three-windowed menu approach, the IBIS interface also uses pop-up dialog boxes and pop-up and bar menus. Wherever possible, the interface uses menus to solicit user inputs. Where dialog boxes are required, illustrations and detailed prompt texts are provided.

The extensive use of menus minimizes the need for IBIS users to know explicit command syntax or specific database features or nomenclature. Instead, menus tailored to each IBIS database are provided. Using the menu shown in Figure 6, even users unfamiliar with ERIC are immediately made aware of powerful ERIC search features such as educational level terms and age descriptor codes. The menu approach allows patrons to use these features without having to learn and memorize specific field or search codes. Similar special feature search menus are provided for other IBIS databases. Consistent across these search menus, selections are listed from broad (e.g., keyword searches;

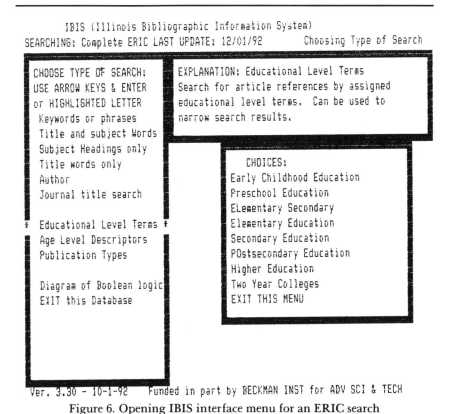

Figure 6. Opening IBIS interface menu for an ERIC search

title and descriptor searches) to narrow (e.g., corporate author searches; publication type searches).

The IBIS microcomputer interface uses an "expert systems approach," incorporating a great deal of experienced searcher expertise behind the scenes. All entered search terms and phrases are parsed and checked by the microcomputer interface software before being formulated into the proper syntax and sent off to the mainframe BRS/ SEARCH implementation for processing. Appropriate operator and search field codes are added. Search phrases are checked for database-specific stopwords, system-reserved words (e.g., Boolean operators; adjacency operators) that might lead to ambiguous results and obvious redundancy or incompatibilities with previously entered terms. The end-user is warned or asked to reenter the search argument according to the nature of the specific problem.

To further facilitate end-user searching, the microcomputer IBIS interface uses a search strategy formulation technique centered around the software creation and combination of user-entered search terms and concept groups. This approach is patterned after the "concept building block" approach to online searching, one of three classical techniques for performing effective searching (Pfaffenberger, 1990, pp. 106-107). The concept group approach was demonstrated by Marcus (1981) in an experimental system and has been adapted in several commercial systems, including the DIALOG CONNECTION systems (Large, 1990, pp. 30-32) and BRS/AFTER DARK (Guidelines, 1989), and several academic end-user systems (Pollitt, 1990; SearchMate, 1990). In addition to being a logical method for building and modifying search strategy, the concept building block approach also facilitates bibliographic instruction, both in group settings and one-to-one, and eliminates the need for user mastery of the various Boolean search operators.

Figure 7 shows the help screen that describes and illustrates this building block search approach as implemented in the LIW IBIS interface. This screen comes up automatically when the user begins his or her search. A more elaborate, extensive description of this search process can be requested by the patron from this summary help screen. Experience with this approach in various forms at UIUC has shown that it indeed helps address and reduce many of the end-user searching difficulties described above (Mischo & Moore, 1989).

Of course, not all cases can be covered in manageable menus, and there may be unanticipated occasions where parsing of a search string may not be desirable. To accommodate this case and to allow for a librarian to help a patron without having to exit the IO+ interface code, two forms of BRS native mode command "pass-thru" are allowed

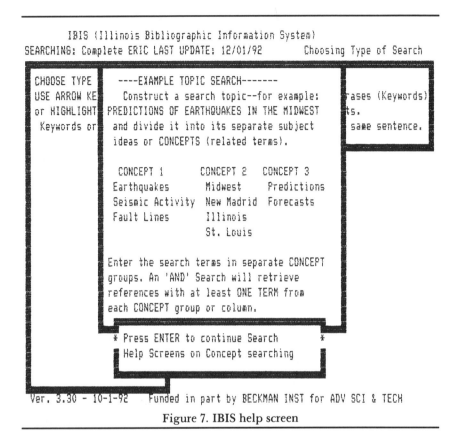

IBIS (Illinois Bibliographic Information System)
SEARCHING: Complete ERIC LAST UPDATE: 12/01/92   Choosing Type of Search

CHOOSE TYPE   ----EXAMPLE TOPIC SEARCH-------
USE ARROW KE   Construct a search topic--for example: rases (Keywords)
or HIGHLIGHT   PREDICTIONS OF EARTHQUAKES IN THE MIDWEST   ts.
  Keywords or and divide it into its separate subject   same sentence.
               ideas or CONCEPTS (related terms).

               CONCEPT 1   CONCEPT 2   CONCEPT 3
               Earthquakes   Midwest   Predictions
               Seismic Activity New Madrid   Forecasts
               Fault Lines   Illinois
                                St. Louis

               Enter the search terms in separate CONCEPT
               groups. An 'AND' Search will retrieve
               references with at least ONE TERM from
               each CONCEPT group or column.

               * Press ENTER to continue Search   *
               Help Screens on Concept searching

Ver. 3.30 - 10-1-92   Funded in part by BECKMAN INST for ADV SCI & TECH

Figure 7. IBIS help screen

by the microcomputer interface program. For a single search term or process that will result in the generation of a single search set, program parsing can be disabled. For more extensive native mode activities or to review what has been done so far in native mode, the interface can be "turned off" completely, allowing for a direct native mode session between the terminal and the mainframe.

Finally, allowance has been made in the software for some workstation-specific interface tuning. The IBIS microcomputer interface has the built-in capability to trap for search inputs specific to a particular subject or library clientele and make automatic substitutions before forwarding the search argument to the mainframe BRS/SEARCH implementation (the user is notified on the search term entry screen). Trap/substitution lists used by the interface in performing this function can be both database and workstation specific. (An example of this substitution operation is described below.) Additionally, available interface output options can take advantage of specific, local workstation printing and downloading capabilities. Lastly, the help screens that describe and illustrate the search process can be modified easily for a specific workstation or cluster of workstations.

Figures 8-14 show a sample microcomputer-mediated IBIS search for information about interfaces to online catalogs done in the ERIC database. In addition to performing a keyword search, the hypothetical searcher is also aware of an author writing in the subject area and so wants to add in any works by that author whether picked up in the keyword search or not. Finally, having a fairly large retrieval set, the searcher decides to limit the final search set to conference paper or speech citations.

Figure 8 shows an initial keyword concept term entry dialog box. Note the illustration included in the prompting for term entry. After a user has searched for the first term of a concept, he is given the opportunity to add additional related terms to the concept. Choosing

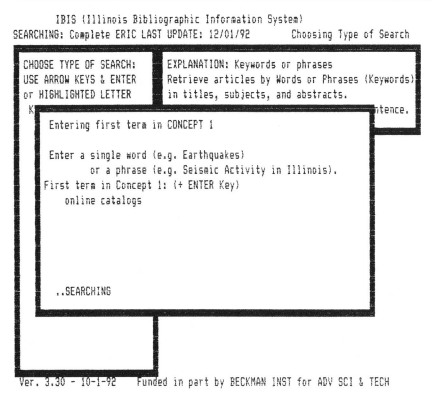

Figure 8. Initial keyword concept term entry dialog box

to do so will bring up the slightly modified search term entry box shown in Figure 9. The user is reminded of the first search term in the concept in the prompt for all later related terms in a concept.

After the user has entered all the terms in a given concept, he is asked if he wants to narrow his search with an additional concept (i.e., do a Boolean AND search), broaden his search with an additional concept (i.e., do a Boolean OR search), or take one of several other actions (see Figure 10). In this example, the user chooses to narrow with an additional keyword search term. (Different types of searches can be combined within the concept building block approach, as illustrated by concepts 3 and 4 described below.) Figure 11 is the dialog entry box for entering the first term of concept 2. Note the automatic substitution for the patron's entry of "interface" as a search term. As mentioned above, this substitution was made using a list of terms particular to the workstation on which the search is being done.

```
SEARCHING: Complete ERIC LAST UPDATE: 12/01/92


Current Concept 1: online catalogs;
  Last Term Entered: online catalogs                    RESULT:   958
┌─────────────────────────────────────────────────────────────────┐
│ K                                                          ntence. │
│   Entering SYNONYMS or RELATED TERMS for CONCEPT 1 terms.         │
│       Other topic ideas should be put in separate Concepts.       │
│                                                                   │
│   Enter ONE TERM (Word or Phrase) AT A TIME   (+ ENTER Key)       │
│   F3 to FINISH this CONCEPT, combine results, GO to NEXT CONCEPT  │
│   F4 to Print or Display Results                                  │
│                                                                   │
│   Another Alternate term for online catalogs :                    │
│       opacs                                                       │
│                                                                   │
│                                                                   │
│       ..SEARCHING                                                 │
│                                                                   │
└─────────────────────────────────────────────────────────────────┘


Ver. 3.30 - 10-1-92    Funded in part by BECKMAN INST for ADV SCI & TECH
```

Figure 9. Modified search term entry box

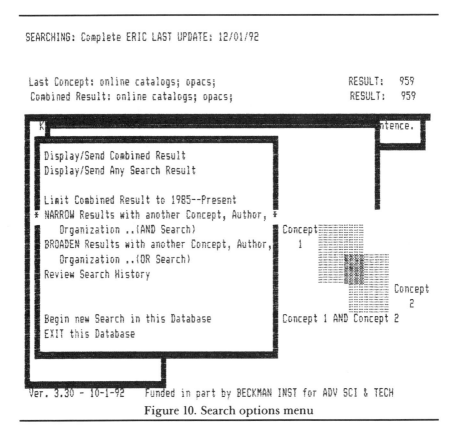

SEARCHING: Complete ERIC LAST UPDATE: 12/01/92

Last Concept: online catalogs; opacs;   RESULT: 959
Combined Result: online catalogs; opacs;   RESULT: 959

K   ntence.

Display/Send Combined Result
Display/Send Any Search Result

Limit Combined Result to 1985--Present
* NARROW Results with another Concept, Author, *
    Organization ..(AND Search)   Concept
BROADEN Results with another Concept, Author,   1
    Organization ..(OR Search)
Review Search History
                                                          Concept
                                                             2
Begin new Search in this Database   Concept 1 AND Concept 2
EXIT this Database

Ver. 3.30 - 10-1-92   Funded in part by BECKMAN INST for ADV SCI & TECH

Figure 10. Search options menu

After adding a second concept, our hypothetical patron next decides to broaden his search by adding in all citations attributed to a particular author. Figure 12 shows an author entry dialog box with entry template. This template removes any ambiguity about order or form of personal name entry. The template is consistent across databases; database-specific syntax and field nomenclature are taken care of behind the scenes by the interface software.

Finally, the patron uses the main IBIS microcomputer interface search menu to narrow his search set to "Speeches, Conference Papers." In response to the menu selection, the interface generates and sends the appropriate publication type search command and displays an already filled in search term dialog box to the user (Figure 13). The resulting retrieval set is 11 documents. An interface-generated summary of the entire search is shown in Figure 14. Contrast this with the summary generated by the BRS/SEARCH native-mode "..d all" command shown

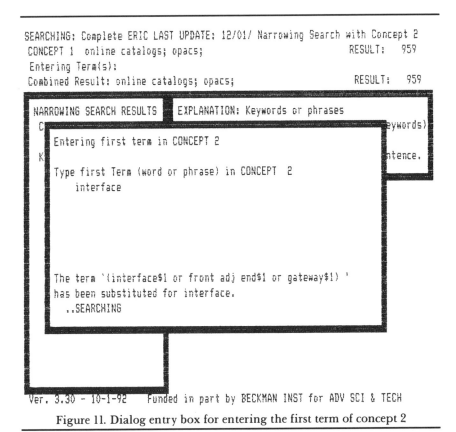

Figure 11. Dialog entry box for entering the first term of concept 2

in Figure 15. Note the work done behind the scenes by the interface software.

Appropriate adjacency and Boolean operators have been inserted by the interface. The automatic substitution of "(INTERFACE$1 OR FRONT ADJ END$1 OR GATEWAY$1)" for the original user input of "interface" has been made (search set 4). The author name has been hyphenated, a preferred form constructed to improve recall, and the name has been searched in both the author field and the abstract field (which in ERIC is usually the only place where authors of individual conference papers are indexed). Finally, the appropriate ERIC-specific publication type code for "Speeches, Conference Papers" has been sent by the program in response to the patron's menu selection. As much as feasible, the burden for knowing proper syntax and database-specific index practices has been shifted from the end-user to the interface software.

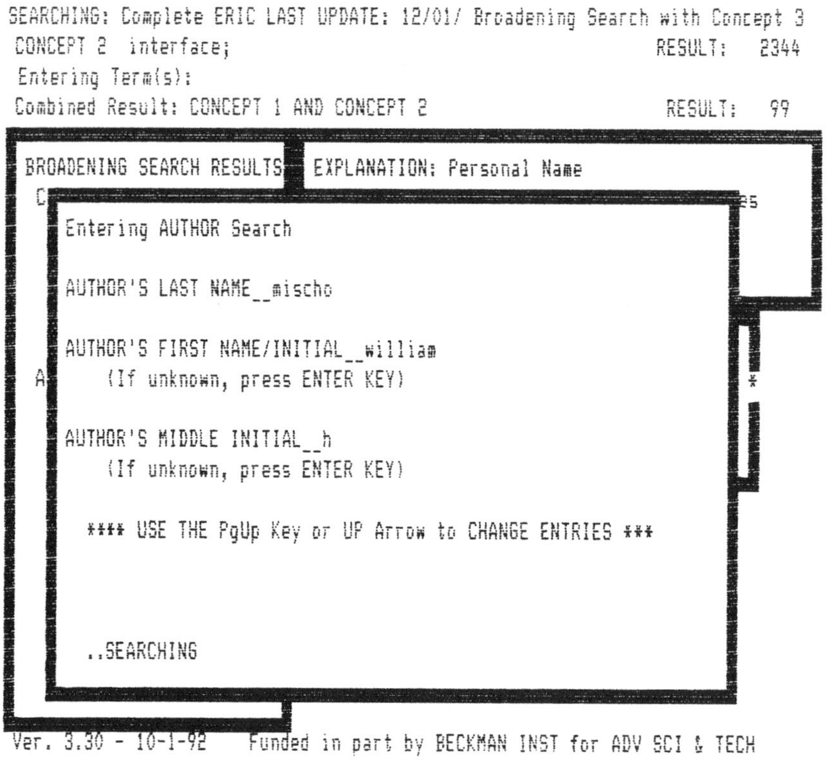

```
SEARCHING: Complete ERIC LAST UPDATE: 12/01/ Broadening Search with Concept 3
CONCEPT 2  interface;                                    RESULT:    2344
Entering Term(s):
Combined Result: CONCEPT 1 AND CONCEPT 2                 RESULT:    99
```

Figure 12. Author entry dialog box with entry template

Having facilitated the patron's search, the interface also simplifies the display/output of search results. Again the intent is to have the user make his or her output selections from a menu and have the interface software interpret those selections and generate an appropriate BRS/SEARCH native mode command. Figure 16 shows the output options available to patrons using the IBIS microcomputer interface including e-mail and downloading of citations to diskette. After selecting the output mode, the user then selects the desired output format as shown in Figure 17. A typical citation printout (from an IBIS search of ISI's Current Contents database) is shown in Figure 18.

Note the full-paragraph labelling and the formatting of the citation printout. This is done on the mainframe by the BRS/SEARCH print-time formatting process. The added line at the end of the citation showing UIUC library call number and three-letter library location

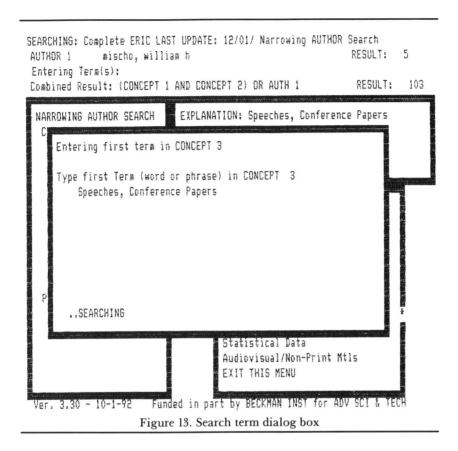

Figure 13. Search term dialog box

code is added by the microcomputer interface software. The interface recognizes the citation source field as it displays or prints the citation and then performs a search of a local database file stored on the workstation hard disk to find the call number of the item (using the same algorithm developed for local database searching and described previously). The fact that this look-up file resides on the workstation easily accommodates the campus-to-campus variations in information about journal availability, call numbers, and location information.

CONCLUSION: FUTURE DEVELOPMENTS

The software functions of the Library Information Workstation have evolved over the course of the project as the various IO+ resources

SET NUMBER	SEARCH TERM	RESULT
01	online catalogs (Keyword)	958
02	opacs (Keyword)	81
03 CONCEPT 1	online catalogs; opacs;	959
04 CONCEPT 2	interface;	2344
05	CONCEPT 1 AND CONCEPT 2	99
06 AUTHOR 1	mischo, william h	5
07	(CONCEPT 1 AND CONCEPT 2) OR AUTH 1	103
08 CONCEPT 3	Speeches, Conference Papers ;	68969
09	((CONCEPT 1 AND CONCEPT 2) OR AUTH 1) AND CONCEPT	11

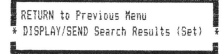

RETURN to Previous Menu
* DISPLAY/SEND Search Results (Set)   *

Figure 14. Interface-generated search summary

have become available. IO+ and the UIUC campuswide information system will continue to expand and add new resources, and the UIUC LIW will add new features and continue to refine its present functionality in response.

Specific work is underway to expand the UIUC LIW to provide enhanced access to a number of new information resources including many outside the UIUC library system itself. In December 1993, the UIUC will open the new Grainger Engineering Library Information Center. The Grainger Center will feature state-of-the-art computing and networking facilities. All LIWs within the center will be able to access campus and Internet network resources. Additionally, several high-capacity, in-house network servers will provide a number of supplemental information access resources and capabilities.

In-house services currently under design and development for the new Grainger Center include networked CD-ROM databases; a

```
                          ERIC            SCREEN    1 OF    2
ERIC LAST UPDATE: 12/01/92
    1 ONLINE WITH CATALOGS
      RESULT                        958
    2 OPACS
      RESULT                         81
    3 1 OR 2
      RESULT                        959
    4 (INTERFACE$1 OR FRONT ADJ END$1 OR GATEWAY$1)
      RESULT                       2344
    5 3 AND 4
      RESULT                         99
    6 MISCHO-WILLIAM$-H$.AU. OR MISCHO-W-H$.AU. OR WILLIAM ADJ H ADJ MISCHO OR
WILLIAM ADJ MISCHO
      RESULT                          5
    7 5 OR 6
      RESULT                        103
    8 150.PT.
      RESULT                      68969
    9 7 AND 8
                          ERIC            SCREEN    2 OF    2
      RESULT                         11
        ****  END OF DISPLAY  ****

BRS SEARCH MODE - ENTER QUERY
```

Figure 15. BRS/SEARCH search summary

```
        ((CONCEPT 1 AND CONCEPT 2) OR AUTH 1) 11 Refs


       ┌──────────────────────────────────────────┐
       │    SELECT DISPLAY/PRINT/E-MAIL OPTION (+ ENTER)    │
       │                                          │
       │ * Display References on Screen         * │
       │   DOWNLOAD References to 3.5 in. Diskettes │
       │   Print to High-Speed Printer (NOT YET AVAILABLE) │
       │   Send Result to Electronic Mailbox      │
       │   Print on Attached Printer              │
       │   EXIT THIS MENU                         │
       └──────────────────────────────────────────┘
```

Figure 16. Output options using the IBIS interface

((CONCEPT 1 AND CONCEPT 2) OR AUTH 1) 11 Refs

```
    SELECT DISPLAY/PRINT/E-MAIL OPTION (+ ENTER)

Display References on Screen
```

```
    FORMATS:
  Author/Title List
  Title, Source & Major Descriptors
  Author, Title, Source & Abstract
* Full Format, including Abstract              *
  EXIT THIS MENU
```

Figure 17. Output formats using the IBIS interface

Grainger Center BRS/SEARCH implementation to support access to databases of interest to Grainger patrons but not of sufficient interest to justify loading on the statewide BRS/SEARCH implementation IBIS; Internet access to online catalogs at other CIC schools; access from all workstations to campus network resources such as the OED, local area weather forecasts and alerts, and campus phone/e-mail directory; state-of-the-art scanning, computer-aided-design, and computer-aided-instruction hardware and software; and coordinated full-text article retrieval and delivery via fax or image transmissions over network connections. Figure 19 provides a preliminary indication of the kind of services that will be available from the Grainger Center LIWs.

The LIW interfaces as well will evolve to incorporate enhanced search techniques such as Best Match and Partial Match algorithms, term query expansion, and knowledge-based query expansion. We are interested in exploring the "find another like this one" approach to

```
        CONCEPT 1 AND CONCEPT 2              22 Refs    SCREEN    1 OF    2
            Record        1  of      22
   Accession number: 9248.
            Author: HUSAIN-S. OBRIEN-A.
  Author affiliation: LOUGHBOROUGH UNIV TECHNOL,DEPT INFORMAT & LIB STUDIES,
                     LOUGHBOROUGH LE11 3TU, LEICS, ENGLAND.
      Article title: RECENT TRENDS IN SUBJECT ACCESS TO OPACS - AN EVALUATION.
    Source (journal): INTERNATIONAL-CLASSIFICATION. 1992, V19, N3, P140-145.
   Cited references: 0043.
  Genuine Article #: JW395.
           Language: ENGLISH (EN).
   Publication type: ARTICLE (U).
    Subject keywords: MACHINE-READABLE-LCSH. ONLINE-CATALOGS.
                     INFORMATION-RETRIEVAL. ELEMENTS.
    Subject category: LIBRARY-&-INFORMATION-SCIENCES (in BEHA).

        Abstract: Research conducted in the early 80's has shown that subject
   access is still one of the most dominant approaches in OPACs. However, while
   some of the subject searches result in no recall, others often retrieve so much
   Call No.: Q.025.41612  LSX




   Next    Prev   NUmber  *Mark*  Change   PRint/Send   TOC    SOrt   EXit
   Mark Reference for Printing/Downloading (NOT E-MAIL)
```

Figure 18. Citation printout from an IBIS search

---

expanding search results. Interfaces will increasingly make use of state-of-the-art multimedia and graphical techniques to accommodate and facilitate more effective user information-seeking behaviors.

The UIUC Library IO+ extended OPAC and campuswide information services provide users with access to a myriad of local and remote information resources. The Library is committed to making these resources available and facilitating their use through the continued evolution of the Library Information Workstation.

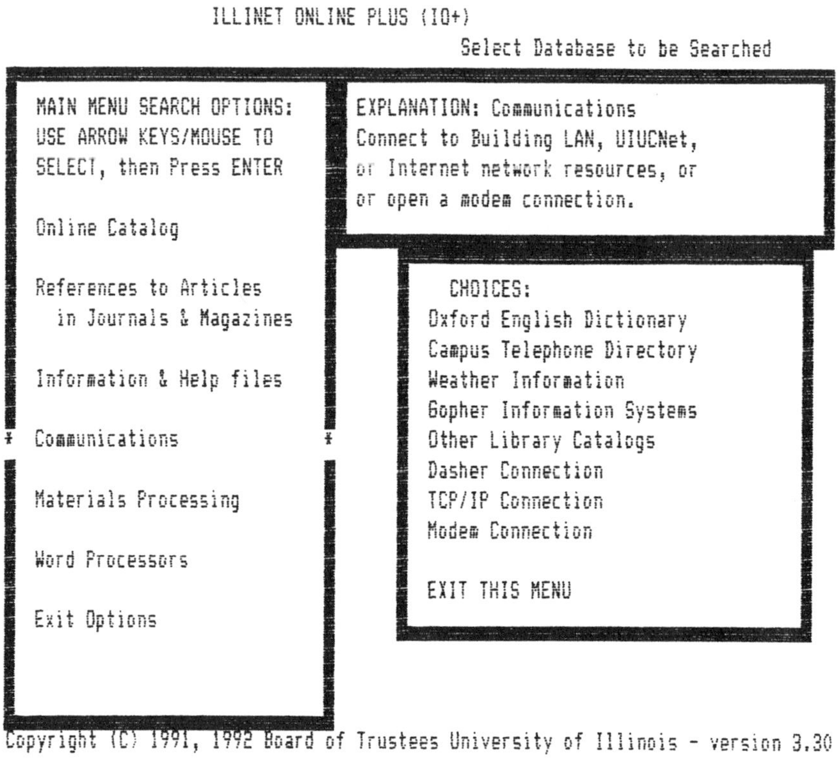

ILLINET ONLINE PLUS (IO+)
                            Select Database to be Searched

```
MAIN MENU SEARCH OPTIONS:        EXPLANATION: Communications
USE ARROW KEYS/MOUSE TO          Connect to Building LAN, UIUCNet,
SELECT, then Press ENTER         or Internet network resources, or
                                 or open a modem connection.
Online Catalog

References to Articles                   CHOICES:
   in Journals & Magazines       Oxford English Dictionary
                                 Campus Telephone Directory
Information & Help files         Weather Information
                                 Gopher Information Systems
*  Communications       *        Other Library Catalogs
                                 Dasher Connection
Materials Processing             TCP/IP Connection
                                 Modem Connection
Word Processors
                                 EXIT THIS MENU
Exit Options
```

Copyright (C) 1991, 1992 Board of Trustees University of Illinois - version 3.30

Figure 19. Future services available from the Grainger Center LIWs

REFERENCES

Ankeny, M. L. (1991). Evaluating end-user services: Success or satisfaction? *Journal of Academic Librarianship, 16*(6), 352-356.

Arms, C. (Ed.). (1990). *Campus strategies for libraries and electronic information.* Rockport, MA: Digital Press (EDUCOM Strategies Series on Information Technology).

Borgman, C. L. (1986). Why are online catalogs hard to use? Lessons learned from information-retrieval studies. *Journal of the American Society for Information Science, 37*(6), 387-400.

Charles, S. K., & Clark, K. E. (1990). Enhancing CD-ROM searches with online updates: An examination of end-user needs, strategies, and problems. *College & Research Libraries, 51*(4), 321-328.

Cheng, C.-C. (1985). Microcomputer-based user interface. [Special section: In depth— The online catalogue of the University of Illinois at Urbana-Champaign]. *Information Technology and Libraries, 4*(4), 346-351.

Drabenstott, K. M. (1991). Online catalog user needs and behavior. In N. Van Pulis (Ed.), *Think tank on the present and future of the online catalog: Proceedings* (pp. 59-83). Chicago: Reference and Adult Services Division, American Library Association.

Fischer, G. (1989). Human-computer interaction software: Lessons learned, challenges ahead. *IEEE Software, 6*(1), 44-52.

Gould, J. D., & Lewis, C. (1985). Designing for usability: Key principles and what designers think. *Communications of the ACM, 28*(3), 300-311.

Grudin, J. (1989). The case against user interface consistency. *Communications of the ACM, 32*(10), 1164-1173.

Guidelines: Search strategy development. (1989). *BRS Bulletin, 13*(3).

Hildreth, C. R. (1987). Beyond Boolean: Designing the next generation of online catalogs. *Library Trends, 35*(4), 647-667.

Hildreth, C. R. (1989). General introduction; OPAC research: Laying the groundwork for future OPAC design. In C. R. Hildreth (Ed.), *The online catalogue: Developments and directions* (pp. 1-24). London: Library Association.

Hildreth, C. R. (1991). Advancing toward the E-3 OPAC: The imperative and the path. In N. Van Pulis (Ed.), *Think tank on the present and future of the online catalog: Proceedings* (pp. 17-38). Chicago: Reference and Adult Services Division, American Library Association.

Hunter, R. N. (1991). Successes and failures of patrons searching the online catalog at a large academic library: A transaction log analysis. *RQ, 30*(3), 395-402.

Large, J. A. (1990). Software developments. In P. T. Bysouth (Ed.), *End-user searching: The effective gateway to published information* (pp. 19-43). London: Aslib.

Locally loaded databases in online library systems [Special issue]. *Information Technology and Libraries, 8*(2), 99-185.

Marcus, R. S. (1981). An automated expert assistant for information retrieval. In L. F. Lunin, M. Henderson, & H. Wooster (Eds.), *The information community: An alliance for progress* (Proceedings of the 44th ASIS Annual Meeting) (Vol. 18, pp. 270-273). White Plains, NY: Knowledge Industry Publications.

Mathews, J. R. (1991). The online catalog: Time to move beyond the boundary of a catalog! In N. Van Pulis (Ed.), *Think tank on the present and future of the online catalog: Proceedings* (pp. 5-16). Chicago: Reference and Adult Services Division, American Library Association.

Mischo, W. H., & Cole, T. W. (1992). The Illinois extended OPAC: Library information workstation design and development. In M. Ra (Ed.), *Advances in online public access catalogs* (pp. 38-57). New York: Meckler.

Mischo, W. H., & Lee, J. (1987). End-user searching of bibliographic databases. In M. E. Williams (Ed.), *Annual review of information science and technology* (Vol. 22, pp. 227-263). New York: Elsevier.

Mischo, W. H., & Moore, A. F. (1989). Enhanced access to periodical literature within an online catalogue environment. In C. R. Hildreth (Ed.), *The online catalogue: Developments and directions* (pp. 107-126). London: Library Association.

Mischo, W. H.; Sandore, B.; Clark, S. E.; & Gorman, M. (1990). University of Illinois at Urbana-Champaign. In C. Arms (Ed.), *Campus strategies for libraries and electronic information* (pp. 117-141). Rockport, MA: Digital Press (EDUCOM Strategies Series on Information Technology).

Nielsen, B. (1986). What they say they do and what they do: Assessing online catalog use instruction through transaction monitoring. *Information Technology and Libraries, 5*(1), 28-34.

Norlin, D. A.; Cardman, E. R.; Davis, E. B.; Dossett, R.; Henigman, B.; Mischo, W. H.; & Troutman, L. (1992a). Interface design and development: The human factor. *Library Hi-Tech, 10*(3), 7-24.

Norlin, D. A.; Cardman, E. R.; Davis, E. B.; Dossett, R.; Henigman, B.; Mischo, W. H.; & Troutman, L. (1992b). Dynamics of interface design and development [Abstract]. In T. Kirk (Ed.), *Academic libraries: Achieving excellence in higher education: Proceedings of the Sixth National Conference of the Association of College and Research Libraries* (pp. 374-376). Chicago: Association of College and Research Libraries.

Peters, T. A. (1989). When smart people fail: An analysis of the transaction log of an online public access catalog. *Journal of Academic Librarianship, 15*(5), 267-273.

Pfaffenberger, B. (1990). *Democratizing information: Online databases and the rise of end-user searching.* Boston: G. K. Hall.

Pollitt, A. S. (1990). Intelligent interfaces to text retrieval systems. In P. Gillman (Ed.), *Text retrieval: The state of the art* (Proceedings of the Institute of Information Scientists text retrieval conferences, "The User's Perspective" [1988] and "Text Management" [1989]) (pp. 192-208). London: Taylor Graham.

Potter, W. G. (1989). Expanding the online catalog. *Information Technology and Libraries, 8*(2), 99-104.

Puttapithakporn, S. (1990). Interface design and user problems and errors: A case study of novice searchers. *RQ, 30*(2), 195-204.

Schultz, K., & Salomon, K. (1990). End users respond to CD-ROM: What users really think. *Library Journal, 115*(2), 56-58.

SearchMate strategy development. (1990). In *SearchMate search manual.* Los Angeles, CA: University of Southern California Health Sciences Library.

Seiden P. (Ed.). (1991). *Survey of libraries providing locally mounted databases.* Chicago: Reference and Adult Services Division, American Library Association.

Shneiderman, B. (1987). *Designing the user interface: Strategies for effective human-computer interaction.* Reading, MA: Addison-Wesley.

Sutcliffe, A. G., & McDermott, M. (1991). Integrating methods of human-computer interface design with structured systems development. *International Journal of Man-Machine Studies, 34*(5), 631-632.

Tiefel, V. (1991). The Gateway to information: A system redefines how libraries are used. *American Libraries, 22*(9), 858-860.

Wilson, J., & Rosenberg, D. (1988). Rapid prototyping for user interface design. In M. Helander (Ed.), *Handbook of human-computer interaction* (pp. 859-875). New York: Elsevier.

Yee, M. M. (1991). System design and cataloging meet the user: User interfaces to online public access catalogs. *Journal of the American Society for Information Science, 42* (2), 78-98.

JEAN ARMOUR POLLY*

Assistant Director, Public Services
Head, Microcomputer Services
Liverpool Public Library
Liverpool, New York

Somebody Knockin':
The Public Library at the Electronic Door

ABSTRACT

A suburban public library with a long history of technological innovation
chronicles its adventures during its first year of Internet connectivity,
including staff use of electronic mail, TELNET, and File Transfer
Protocol (FTP). Future plans include public use from the computer
lab located in the library. A resource section includes information on
how to get on the Internet and how to learn more about it through
user guides.

COMPUTER USE AT THE LIVERPOOL PUBLIC LIBRARY

The Liverpool Public Library, in central New York State, has a
long history of computer use for both staff and patrons. In October
1991, we celebrated ten years of public computing. What had begun
in 1981 with a 48K Apple II+ has grown into a multimedia
lab/playground with seven computers and related peripherals. Over
1,400 hours per month are reserved on two Macintosh LC's, a Macintosh
SE, an Apple IIGS, an Apple IIe, or an IBM compatible. Clients tinker
with their résumés and learn how to use application software like word

---

*The author is now the Manager of Network Development and User Training at
NYSERNet, Inc.

processors, databases, and spreadsheets. Home-schooled students use the computers for drill and practice. Churches produce newsletters; clubs produce mailing labels.

The seventh system is called the Emerging Technologies Workstation. It is a color Macintosh IIci with attached videodisk and CD-ROM players as well as an audio mixer and headphones. This equipment was part of an Apple Library of Tomorrow grant, which the library received in 1990. Currently, we are beta-testing the Library of Congress's American Memory Project interactive videodisks, but more on that later.

About a year ago, our mid-level regional network, NYSERNet, Inc., approached us with a deal that we could not refuse. We accepted a grant from them and became the nation's smallest public library with Internet connectivity. NYSERNet, Inc., is an unusual nonprofit corporation "whose mission is to advance science, education, and research through the interchange of information via computer networks." Affiliates include over 40 academic sites, libraries, nonprofit organizations, and research and government facilities. Their goal is New York Statewide connectivity for everyone. NYSERNet is aggressively bringing new users to the Internet. Recently, a number of sites have come online due to their New Connections grant program. Besides our library, others include the American Museum of Natural History, the Russell Sage Foundation, the New York Public Library, and various K-12 sites.

Under our grant, NYSERNet subsidizes network costs for a trial period of varying lengths. The site must provide its own phone line, 9600-baud modem, and computer (MS-DOS compatible, Macintosh, or Sun system). At the end of the grant period, we can elect to keep the software and pay for our connection, which at this time is about $200 per month.

Sometime during 1992, we hope to offer Internet access to lab clients. It is unclear at this time what form this access will take. Will users have "accounts" and private mailboxes so that they can exchange electronic mail (e-mail) and subscribe to listservs and newsgroups? Or will the front-end be just a screen or two of a "Top Ten" list of interesting places to telnet to?

We also have developed a proposal to provide a "Free-Net-type" dial-in system that would allow up to 64 concurrent sessions via a standard, dedicated Internet connection. The Cleveland Free-Net, described later in this paper, is a wonderful pilot, but it operates under the UNIX operating system. We think that most small libraries will not have a UNIX box nor a UNIX wizard on-site, so we propose to develop this project under the Macintosh operating system. Not that we think most public libraries are able to afford a standard connection and a support staff like ours, either, but we hope to pave the way and show what can be done with these resources.

We think that ALL librarians need access to e-mail right away. They can get this connectivity with a minimum of equipment: a computer, phone line, communications software, and low-speed modem. Average costs are about $20 per month for e-mail only.

LOCAL ELECTRONIC MAIL

Our site uses QuickMail (CE Software) as its in-house mailer. Most full-time staff members have e-mail addresses on our system. They can log in to these mailboxes from any computer on our local area network (LAN). Mail is stored on a server located in the Computer Department. When someone logs in, the server is checked for mail addressed to that person. New mail may be read, stored, forwarded, printed, or deleted. Users can compose new mail and easily send it to individuals, or "groups" of individuals may be set up under one address, like "all Department Heads."

Mail can be carbon copied to others as well as blind carbon copied— meaning the main recipient does not know you have also copied others. Mail can even be "unsent" if it has not been read by the addressee. This function is useful if you change your mind about sending that nasty note!

E-mail has many benefits, although there are drawbacks, too. Some of the good things:

- Saves paper, although not if you print out every message. Most users do not do this, instead storing messages electronically on their computers.
- Improves communication among those on different work schedules and in different work groups. It is time efficient to send an electronic message to many people rather than making one memo, using a photocopier to make many copies, then physically distributing all the copies.
- Avoids face-to-face confrontation. Sometimes this is also more time efficient since meeting with someone to communicate one message may lead to more conversation about other issues, which time management may not allow.

One of the negative things about e-mail is that it allows users to avoid face-to-face confrontation. Everyone likes to distance themselves from conflict, and e-mail is just one more way to do it. Our system even lets you write a memo and time it to be sent after you have left the building and are safely 10 miles away!

Reprimands via e-mail are never a good idea, and many of us have a reminder note taped to our monitors that says "bad news should be delivered only in person."

USE OF THE QUICKMAIL-TO-INTERNET GATEWAY

We have had e-mail throughout our building for many years, and everyone is used to the easily understood interface. Once connected to the Internet, we feared that its users would need to learn another mailer. Fortunately, we use a combination of products that allows our Internet mail to appear in our QuickMail mailboxes alongside our in-house library mail.

QuickMail Administrator runs all traffic through the various mailcenters we have set up. QM Admin takes care of where the mail is, who it is addressed to, who has read what, what has been deleted, etc.

One mailcenter is called Internet. Anything sent to this mailcenter is handled by a third-party product called UMCP QuickMail. This software "gateway" has been configured to grab the 9600-baud modem and a standard phone line every 30 minutes and call out to the local PSI (Performance Systems International) POP (point of presence).

From there it hops to a UUCP (UNIX-to-UNIX Copy Program) mail server located Out There, exchanges mail from and to addresses at lpl.org (our Internet domain name), and logs off.

UMCP QuickMail then releases the line and resets the modem. It goes through all mail received and re-sorts it into the local mailboxes of our users. QuickMail Remote lets our users call in from their home systems and send and receive mail just as they would do at their desks on-site. Our only problem with this is speed—it is much faster at work than at home, and only one person at a time can log on from a remote location.

Readers used to academic computing centers and many incoming lines and modem ports will scoff at the "paper clip and baling twine" method of getting Internet mail to our public library clients—but on the other hand, it's cheap and it works.

TELNET AND FTP

QuickMail will not help us if we want to connect to a remote computer and use its resources using TELNET or if we want to acquire files or software using anonymous File Transfer Protocol (FTP). For that we use Intercon's TCP Connect II. Its graphical user interface is a big step toward making Internet use much less arcane. This program allows us to call the local POP and initiate a SLIP (Serial Line Internet Protocol) connection to the fast network backbone.

Most academic and research sites have a dedicated connection to the Internet and a static numeric address. Our SLIP connection gives us a dynamic address—it changes depending on what modem we have hit on the way in. Once we have been given our address for that particular session, we become what amounts to any other "host" computer on the Internet—but only for as long as we stay connected. Once we log off, we are truly gone, known only to the domain name servers Out There in dataspace.

TCP Connect II's TELNET and FTP tools are easy to use and support the Macintosh interface. But we do not think they are easy enough for the public to use. Getting the assigned dynamic IP (Internet protocol) number slid into the right place is something we do not feel clients in our lab should have to do. We want a macro to log on, get the IP, put it where it needs to go, and then ask what the client wants to do. We have not been able to do this using this product. Many other telecommunications programs allow creation of scripts like this, but none of them works using a SLIP connection—so far. Or if they do support SLIP, they must run under Ethernet at your site—and we are running only PhoneNet/LocalTalk at this point. Remember, I said this was a cheap solution! Nothing is easy on the frontier of telecommunications. . . .

WHAT WE HAVE BEEN DOING WITH OUR INTERNET CONNECTION

In the past year, we have "subscribed" many employees to various discussion groups. Most of these are job related, such as PACS-L (Public-Access Computer Systems) or LIBADMIN (Library Administration), although we do have some "fun" subscriptions such as DOROTHY-L (for mystery readers) and BIRD.EAST, which is the Audubon hotline for announcements of unusual bird sightings. Recently, after receiving one of these hotline reports, we all piled into the van to inspect a rare arctic visitor: a hawk owl who had settled on a tree about 30 miles from the library.

We are disseminating some of this Internet wealth in print form to our library patrons. Our Mystery Readers Club in particular enjoys the information they get from DOROTHY-L. Audubon sightings have been distributed to the local Audubon Club, birdseed boutiques, and other interested birders.

It is estimated that there are now over 12,000 moderated lists/discussion groups on the Internet. The figure does not count the many unmoderated lists available. Lists exist on everything from Arthurian legend to origami. It is true that a good percentage of the communication on these lists amounts to so much "line noise"—that is, unnecessary use of bandwidth, personal flames (tirades), and other distractions. However, MUCH of the information exchanged is solid and useful to our lives as professionals as well as helping us achieve personal growth.

No more are we an isolated, small public library hardly looking beyond our own service area borders. Now we are discussing quality circles, coping with shrinking budgets, and personnel issues with our counterparts all over the world.

We compare notes on computer hardware and software and are able to get personal recommendations of products from real users rather than relying on vendor hype and reviews, if we can find them. We are expressing our views on public library on-ramps to the National Research and Education Network (NREN) and policies that will affect our patrons' use of new technologies. Telecommunicating through the Internet has helped us level the playing field for discussions with government officials, network providers, policy makers, and other users. Now that we have got Internet connectivity, we do not remember life without it.

NYSERNET AND THE NEW YORK STATE LIBRARY

Of course now we want all the other libraries in New York State to have what we have. There is hope. In 1989, the New York Statewide Automation Committee released a report on the telecommunications future of New York State's 7,000 libraries. It proposed the idea of the "Electronic Doorway" through which even the smallest and most remote libraries could access the resources of other libraries around the state.

The New York State Library is the largest state library in the nation, with over 5.5 million items in its collection. In 1992, it will join NYSERNet and make its online public access catalog (OPAC) available to Internet researchers.

The State Library and NYSERNet will collaborate on a joint initiative to begin implementation of the Electronic Doorway concept. They will investigate possibilities for staging a replacement of the New York State interlibrary loan system (NYSILL) and deployment of a statewide e-mail system among libraries and library systems.

Although there are some small New York libraries currently without even telephones, let alone computers, we support this initiative. Herbert

S. White says that the poorer and more remote a library is, the more it needs technology.

Recently, wireless communications technology has taken off, and we see demonstrations of the following:

- wireless LocalTalk networks;
- the wireless equivalent of T1 network speed over a line-of-sight distance of three miles;
- products such as the Mobidem modem, which provides two-way packet radio Internet connectivity;
- products such as the HP 95-LX palmtop computer and the Motorola Newstream pager (dial 1-800-Skyword with your modem, address a friend's personal ID number, and send a message directly to the computer in his backpack; it uses satellites and magic to deliver your instantaneous thoughts for about $40 a month).

All this means is that we will not continue to be dependent on wired, land-based telecommunications infrastructures. This is of particular interest to rural libraries.

MULTIMEDIA ON THE NET?

The Library of Congress's American Memory Project is currently in beta-test at 37 libraries around the United States. Our library is one of the handful of public libraries using it. It is available for use in our public computer lab.

The project brings primary source material "out of the archives and into the streets." In its latest incarnation, it includes three videodisks of material including the following:

- 25,000 postcards of turn-of-the-century American landmarks from the Detroit Publishing Company;
- Nation's Forum audio archives of political speeches and portraits of the speakers;
- films of the building of New York City, boat tours of the harbors, films of the 1901 Pan-American Exposition in Buffalo, New York;
- 18th century broadsides;
- political cartoons.

Eventually, the Library of Congress hopes to make resource material like this available over the NREN. We think their graphic interface is particularly easy to use.

Interesting uses of telecommunications technology were demonstrated at the March National NET'92 Conference in Washington, DC, including packet video. Conference goers saw and spoke to a researcher in North Carolina, who appeared on a color computer screen. The quality was excellent although it works best for "talking heads" teleconferencing and not for full-motion. The video was coming over the Internet, not being broadcast from a satellite.

WHAT USERS NEED

As cheap connectivity and hardware become more ubiquitous in homes and as video dial tones and ISDN (Integrated Services Digital Network) proliferate, will the public library survive? Many copyright-free electronic texts can be downloaded from Project Gutenberg now (get to it via Gophers); some journals now exist in electronic-only editions; publishing books on demand, tailored to the reader's interests, is now a reality. Brian Kahin's new book *Building Information Infrastructure*, published under the Primis imprint by McGraw-Hill, is one of these. Kahin writes, "the chapters can be printed individually or in combination with any other material in the Primis database to create custom textbooks . . . we wanted a Protean publication whose many parts could be assembled and reassembled to fit the interests of many readers" (pp. 3-4).

Users can even telnet to the Stanford University Bookstore (via MELVYL, telnet 31.1.0.11 or telnet melvyl) and electronically peruse the wares. Rumor has it that students at least will soon be able to purchase their books online using a credit card. Although the Rest of Us cannot order books via Internet, we can call the bookstore during normal business hours and place an order (order desk phone: (800) 533-2670, fax: (415) 322-1936).

If library users can do all this from home, will public librarians still have jobs? The answer is yes as long as the Internet remains difficult to use.

Although interfaces are becoming easier, many people prefer to simply ask a human. In our computer lab, we note that people will not read a simple one-paragraph "start-up instructions" note posted at the computer workstation. They much prefer help from another person.

We wonder how automatic teller machines (ATMs) have impacted bank business. Have they lessened traffic through the line inside? Will we see less telephone and walk-up reference as people are empowered to search with Gophers and archies and whatnot from home? Or will we simply see our emphasis shift from a focus less on a facility-based collection to more of an individualized client-based "collection" spread over host computers on many continents? Will we see publicly funded "911 for Information" network information centers, operated around the clock, staffed by librarians who know where the Internet goods are and who's got 'em?

And do we as a profession have the Right Stuff? How do we avoid being caught in traditional library backwaters so we can emerge as librarians surfing the Internet? Training! Training! Training! Get e-mail as fast as you can even if you have to pay for it personally. Join some discussion groups even if you just absorb what others are saying. Get involved somewhere and gopher it!

APPENDIX A

WANT TO GET CONNECTED TO THE INTERNET?

To get connected to the Internet, we recommend talking to your regional network provider first since they may be able to provide libraries, schools, and nonprofits low-cost or subsidized connectivity. If you do not know who your regional is, contact the NSFNet people at 10 Moulton Street, Cambridge, MA 02138; phone: (617) 873-3400. There are many low-cost ways of exchanging global e-mail, including FidoNet and FrEdMail, which are not described here. A few other methods of connecting to the net, which include the ability to use TELNET and FTP, follow.

CERFnet

The California Education and Research Federation (CERFnet) offers DIAL N'CERF USA. It allows access to the Internet from anywhere in the continental United States. Users dial a toll-free number to log in to remote machines, transfer files, and send and receive e-mail. The cost is $20 a month with a $10-per-hour usage fee. There is an installation charge of $50. For more information, contact CERFnet, California Education and Research Federation, c/o San Diego Supercomputer Center, P.O. Box 85608, San Diego, CA 92186-9784; e-mail: help@cerf.net; phone: (800) 876-CERF or (619) 534-5087.

Performance Systems International (PSI)

PSI offers several varieties of network connectivity, including e-mail-only accounts, e-mail and TELNET accounts, dial-up host connectivity on demand, and dedicated connections. Costs are competitive, and performance is reliable. PSILink, e-mail, and delayed FTP are $19 a month for 2400-baud service or below, $29 per month for 9600-baud service. GDS (Global Dial-up Service) includes TELNET and rlogins at $39 a month, 2400-baud, 24-hour access. Host DCS (Dial-up Connection Service), at about $2,000 per year, includes a full suite of Internet activities (mail, news, FTP, TELNET). PSI has POPs in over 40 U.S. cities. For more information, contact Performance Systems International, Inc., 11800 Sunrise Valley Dr., Suite 1100, Reston, VA 22091; phone: (800) 82PSI82 or (703) 620-6651; fax: (703) 620-4586; e-mail: info@psi.com. Entering all-info@psi.com generates an automatic response containing summaries of various PSI products.

The World

Software Tool & Die runs a public access UNIX system called The World. Basic rates are $2 per hour and a $5 monthly account fee. Services offered by The World include Internet e-mail, USENET news, ClariNet (UPI, AP, and satellite news services), real-time chat, UNIX Software, archie, the Online Book Initiative (a publicly accessible repository for freely redistributable collections of textual information—a net-worker's library). The World can also be accessed over the CompuServe Packet Network. You do not have to be a CompuServe subscriber to use this network, but you will be billed for its use.

For more information, contact The WORLD, Software Tool & Die, 1330 Beacon Street, Brookline, MA 02146; phone: (617) 739-0202.

AlterNet . . . "IP Networking for the Rest of Us"

Another twist on low-cost networking is AlterNet. They also lease equipment like routers and modems and will preconfigure "plug and play" hardware solutions for you. They will also deal with getting 56k, T1, or T3 lines run to your site. AlterNet Domestic Service Charges follow (effective 9/13/91):

Type	Monthly Rate	Startup Charge
T1	$2,000	$5,000
T1-LV (Low Volume)	$1,000	$5,000
56k DDS	$1,000	$2,000
Subrate DDS	$ 500	$2,000 (19.2k/9.6k)
Async SLIP/PPP	$ 250	$1,500 (V.32 or V.32bis)

For more information, contact UUNET Technologies, Inc., 3110 Fairview Park Drive, Suite 570, Falls Church, VA 22042; phone: (800) 4UUNET3, (703) 876-5050; fax: (703) 876-5059; Internet: alternet-info@uunet.uu.net.

Netcom

If you are in the San Francisco Bay area, check these folks for connectivity. They provide a complete dial-up and communication service including netnews, e-mail, Internet access, and general computing services. They anticipate expansion of their network to southern California (Los Angeles) and Sacramento by early 1992. Personal accounts are based on a fixed monthly fee without any hourly or connect charges. There are two different pricing schedules: personal account (invoiced monthly), $19.50/month or personal account (auto-billing) $17.50/month. Standard connections and business connections have varying rates. For more information, (408) 554-UNIX; Internet: info@netcom.com.

APPENDIX B

RESOURCES FOR LEARNING MORE

Computer Systems Policy Project

At the March 1992 National NET'92 Conference in Washington, DC, a representative of the Computer Systems Policy Project provided a broader vision of what the NREN could accomplish. An illuminating videotape spotlighted innovative services and health care for seniors, improved education and lifelong learning opportunities, advances in industrial design and manufacturing, as well as broad access to libraries, databases, and e-mail. Copies of the full report, along with the video, are available for $20 from the Computer Systems Policy Project, 1735 New York Avenue, NW, Suite 500, Washington, DC 20006; phone: (202) 628-1700.

Emily Postnews Answers Your Questions on Netiquette

Brad Templeton's (brad@looking.on.ca) piece on how NOT to behave on the net, Emily Postnews is the foremost authority on proper net behavior, giving satirical and hilarious advice. To ftp the most recent update, enter pit-manager.mit.edu. Here is a sample:

> Dear Miss Postnews: How long should my signature be?—verbose@noisy
> A: Dear Verbose: Please try and make your signature as long as you can. It's much more important than your article, of course, so try to have more lines of signature than actual text. Try to include a large graphic made of ASCII characters, plus lots of cute quotes and slogans. People will never tire of reading these pearls of wisdom again and again, and you will soon become personally associated with the joy each reader feels at seeing yet another delightful repeat of your signature. Be sure as well to include a complete map of USENET with each signature, to show how anybody can get mail to you from any site in the world. Be sure to include Internet gateways as well. Also tell people on your own site how to mail to you. Give independent addresses for Internet, UUCP, and BITNET, even if they are all the same.

Hitchhiker's Guide to the Internet

As many Network Information Centers are doing, the CERFnet NIC stores many Internet guides and RFCs (requests for comments), including the famous, if technical, *Hitchhiker's Guide to the Internet*. These may be obtained via anonymous FTP to nic.cerf.net (192.102.249.3). Call the CERFnet Hotline at (800) 876-CERF for assistance. Ask for their Captain Internet and CERFBoy comic, too. For more information, contact California Education and Research Federation, c/o San Diego Supercomputer Center, P.O. Box 85608, San Diego, CA 92186-9784; e-mail: help@cerf.net; phone: (800) 876-CERF or (619) 534-5087.

Library Resources on the Internet: Strategies for Selection and Use

RASD Occasional Paper no. 12, published in 1992, sells for $18 for members, $20 for nonmembers. It can be ordered from ALA Order Services, 50 E. Huron,

Chicago, IL 60611, (800) 545-2433. Electronic versions are available via FTP: ASCII file from host dla.ucop.edu, directory pub/internet, filename libcat-guide; host ftp.unt.edu, directory library; filename libcat-guide. WordPerfect 5.1 file from host hydra.uwo.ca, directory libsoft; filename internet.com.

Mining the Internet

There is a guidebook called *Mining the Internet* available from the University of California at Davis. Here is how the Gold Country Mining Instructions begin:

> Jist durn tuckered o' workin' eight t' five for a salary. ain't you? An' you wanna set out for parts unknown. You're hankerin' for an a'venture. Come'n then go 'Mining the Internet' with me, father of Clementine (that's my darlin'), and I'll tell you some old timey tales and introduce you to a new resource for students, faculty, and staff called wide area networking. . . . 'Taint goin' to hurt you any, and the prospect looks good for a lucky strike.

Mining the Internet and *Using the Internet A&B* are available from Computing Services, University of California, Davis, CA 95616-8563; phone: (916) 752-0233; or electronically by anonymous FTP from ucdavis.edu (128.120.2.1) directory ucd.netdocs/mining.

New User's Guide to Unique and Interesting Resources on the Internet 2.0

Available from NYSERNet (New York State Education and Research Network), it is over 145 pages and lists some 50 sources—OPACs, databases, information resources, and more. May be obtained electronically by anonymous FTP from nysernet.org directory /pub/resources/guides. The cost is $25 or $18 for NYSERNet members.

Beyond the Walls: Networked Information Kit

Linda Carl of NYSERNet describes this as "an excellent introduction to the possibilities of 'The World of Networked Information'. This instructional package, of use in presenting the possibilities and benefits of electronic networking to groups, consists of a videotape and an instructional notebook package." The cost is $99 (price includes postage and handling) and $49 for NYSERNet affiliates. Send a check (made out to NYSERNet) or purchase order. Send with your name, U.S. mail address, and phone number to NYSERNet New User's Guide, NYSERNet, Inc., 200 Elwood Davis Rd., Suite 103, Liverpool, NY 13088-6147; phone: (315) 453-2912; e-mail: info@nysernet.org.

NorthWestNet User Services Internet Resource Guide

NorthWestNet offers a 300-page guide to the Internet, covering e-mail, file transfer, remote login, discussion groups, online library catalogs, and supercomputer access. Copies may be purchased for $20 from NorthWestNet. NorthWestNet, 15400 SE 30th Place, Suite 202, Bellevue, WA 98007; phone: (206) 562-3000; fax: (206) 562-4822.

NSF Internet Tour HyperCard Stack

This guide includes net history, net maps, and net poetry and lore and is free. The NSF Service Center also publishes a very complete *Internet Resource Guide* ($15). Many items, including the HyperCard Tour to the Internet, are freely available by anonymous FTP from nnsc.nsf.net. For more information, contact NSF Network Service Center (NNSC), Bolt Beranek and Newman Inc., 10 Moulton Street, Cambridge, MA 02138; phone: (617) 873-3400; e-mail: nnsc@nnsc.nsf.net.

Special Internet Connections

Compiled by Scott Yanoff, this indispensable list of network resources is available using TELNET and FTP and is updated weekly. It includes a few OPACs, chat lines, weatherservers, campuswide information systems, and reference resources. Send e-mail to the list manager (Scott Yanoff) at yanoff@csd4.csd.uwm.edu or FTP to csd4.csd.uwm.edu, and the filename is inet-services.

There's Gold in Them Thar Networks! or Searching for Treasure in all the Wrong Places

Written by Jerry Martin at Ohio State University, this document is available via Internet message to infoserver@nnsc.nsf.net. Once inside the message area, give the following commands to retrieve the document:

REQUEST: NSFNET
TOPIC: NETWORK-TREASURES
REQUEST: END

Zen and the Art of the Internet

This guide is the BEST and unfortunately hardest to get unless you are connected. This will be published in book form sometime in spring/summer 1992. Contact the author, Brendan Kehoe, Sun Network Manager, Widener University, Chester, PA; e-mail: brendan@cs.widener.edu. Electronic editions at ftp.uu.net (137.39.1.9) in /inet/doc; ftp.cs.toronto.edu (128.100.3.6) in pub/zen; ftp.cs.widener.edu (147.31.254.132) in pub/zen as zen-1.0.tar.Z, zen-1.0.dvi, and zen-1.0.PS; ftp.sura.net (128.167.254.179) in pub/nic as zen-1.0.PS. If you are limited to UUCP, you can get it anonymously by dialing UUNET at 900-GOT-SRCS and get the file /inet/doc/FILES.

A Cruise of the Internet

This guide is a new, free Internet HyperCard stack from Merit. Merit is also a treasure trove of Internet information and resources, including Internet use statistics. For more information, contact Merit Network, Inc., 2901 Hubbard Ave., Ann Arbor, MI 48109-2016; phone: (313) 936-3000; e-mail: nsfnet-info@merit.edu.

APPENDIX C

INTERNET RESOURCES

Besides our use of discussion lists, we have been exploring resources available for TELNET and FTP visits, with an eye toward their usefulness to public library audiences. Here are some of the ones we like.

Cleveland Free-Net

Free-Nets are the brainchild of Tom Grundner, Director, Community Telecomputing Laboratory, Case Western Reserve University, 303 Wickenden Building, Cleveland, OH 44106; phone: (216) 368-2733; fax: (216) 368-5436; Internet: aa001@cleveland.freenet.edu; BITNET: aa001%cleveland.freenet.edu@cunyvm; and the folks at National Public Telecomputing Network (NPTN), Box 1987, Cleveland, OH 44106; phone: (216) 368-2733; fax: (216) 368-5436; e-mail: aa622@cleveland.freenet.edu.

Free-Nets use a city metaphor, complete with schools, hospitals (for people AND pets), the Cleveland Public Library, the courthouse, and other public services. Free-Nets also provide weather, news, and gateways to other resources, including other Free-Nets. To access the Cleveland Free-Net, simply telnet to freenet-in-a.cwru.edu 129.22.8.82 or 129.22.8.75 or 129.22.8.76 or 129.22.8.44 and select "visitor" at the login menu.

MELVYL

MELVYL includes the union catalog of monographs and serials held by the nine University of California (UC) campuses and affiliated libraries. It represents nearly 11 million holdings at UC, the California State Library, and the Center for Research Libraries. The MELVYL catalog also provides access to MEDLINE and Current Contents as well as a gateway to many other systems. Access to some databases is restricted under a license agreement to the UC faculty, staff, and students; telnet to melvyl.ucop.edu or any of four Internet addresses (31.1.0.1, 31.0.0.11, 31.0.0.13, 31.1.0.11). For more information, contact the University of California MELVYL Catalog, Division of Library Automation, University of California Office of the President, 300 Lakeside Drive, 8th floor, Oakland, CA 94612-3550; phone: (415) 987-0555 (MELVYL Catalog Helpline); e-mail: lynch@postgres.berkeley.edu.

CARL

CARL is a gateway to academic and public library online catalogs, as well as resources like UnCover and Magazine Index, the *Academic American Encyclopedia,* and *Internet Resource Guide.* Access to some items is limited; telnet to pac.carl.org or 192.54.81.128. For more information, contact Colorado Alliance of Research Libraries, 777 Grant, Suite 306, Denver, CO 80203-3580; phone: (303) 861-5319; e-mail: help@carl.org.

North Carolina's bbs.oit.unc.edu

Read USENET newsfeeds, use LibTel, a scripted TELNET gateway to access both U.S. and international libraries plus such things as Data Research

Associates Library of Congress catalog, the Ham Radio Call Book, the National Science Foundation, the Weather Server, Webster's dictionary and thesaurus, and more. For more information, telnet to bbs.oit.unc.edu or 152.2.22.80 to connect to the bulletin board system.

Services

For information on American University's gateway to many interesting sites, telnet to wugate.wustl.edu or 128.252.120.1 using the login services.

NYSERView

Travel to the resources described in NYSERNet's *New User's Guide to Useful and Unique Resources on the Internet.* For more information, telnet to nysernet.org or 192.77.173.2 to try these. The login is nysrview; password is nysrview.

Liberty High

This is a pilot project linking secondary education students with college campuses. NYSERNet plans to expand this service to every campus in New York State. To try it out, telnet to nysernet.org or 192.77.173.2 and log in as librtyhi with the same password.

APPENDIX D

NAVIGATING THE SEA OF 700,000 HOSTS

Recent estimates of host computers on the Internet have exceeded 700,000. Many of these hosts offer files, data, graphics, audio files, and more for transfer to local computers. The notion of sifting through these millions of files looking for one particular item gives even ALA lifetime members the shakes! Fortunately, various projects are underway that simplify this search process.

Archie

Peter Deutsch, of McGill's Computing Centre, describes the archie server concept, which allows users to ask a question once yet search many different hosts:

> The archie service is a collection of resource discovery tools that together provide an electronic directory service for locating information in an Internet environment. Originally created to track the contents of anonymous FTP archive sites, the archie service is now being expanded to include a variety of other online directories and resource listings.
>
> Currently, archie tracks the contents of over 800 anonymous FTP archive sites containing some 1,000,000 files throughout the Internet. Collectively, these files represent well over 50 gigabytes (50,000,000,000 bytes) of information, with additional information being added daily. Anonymous FTP archive sites offer software, data, and other information that can be copied and used without charge by anyone with connection to the Internet. . . . The archie server automatically updates the listing information from each site about once a month, ensuring users that the information they receive is reasonably timely, without imposing an undue load on the archive sites or network bandwidth. (Deutsch, *CERFnet News*, Nov.-Dec. 1991, vol. 3, no. 7)

For more information, contact UNIX Support Group, Computing Centre, McGill University, Room 200, Burnside Hall, 805 Sherbrooke Street West, Montreal, Quebec, Canada H3A 2K6; phone: (514) 398-3709; e-mail: peterd@ cc.mcgill.ca. Some archie server sites to telnet to include archie.rutgers.edu or 128.6.18.15 (USA), archie.sura.net or 128.167.254.179 (USA), archie.mcgill.ca or 132.206.2.3 (Canada), archie.funet.fi or 128.214.6.100 (Finland/Mainland Europe), archie.au or 128.184.1.4 (Australia/New Zealand), archie.doc.ic.ac.uk or 146.169.3.7 (Great Britain/Ireland).

Gopher

A gopher (or go-fer) is a little furry creature who tunnels through the ground or someone who fetches necessary items from many locations. Telnet to consultant.micro.umn.edu or 134.84.133.255, log in as gopher, and enjoy having your very own gopher. Gopher includes fun and games, humor, libraries (including reference books such as *The New Hacker's Dictionary*, *Roget's 1911 Thesaurus*, and the *CIA World FactBook*), gateways to other U.S. and foreign Gophers, news, and gateways to other systems. There is also an archie server.

WAIS

Wide Area Information Servers (WAIS—pronounced wayz) allows users to get information from a variety of hosts by means of an electronic "client." This may be the new world order of automated librarianship. The client searches various WAIS servers around the globe. The user tells the client how relevant each hit is, and the client can be sent out on the same quest again and again to find new documents.

WAIStation is an easy to use Macintosh implementation of a WAIS client. It can be downloaded from think.com as well as a self-running MediaTracks demo of WAIStation in action.

WAIS developer Brewster Kahle also moderates a thoughtful WAIS newsletter and discussion group, often speculating about the future of libraries and librarians. For more information, contact Brewster Kahle, Project Leader, Wide Area Information Servers, Thinking Machines Corporation, 1010 El Camino Real, Menlo Park, CA 94025; phone: (415) 329-9300, ext. 228; e-mail: brewster@think.com.

WorldWideWeb

Tim Berners-Lee describes his Web this way:

> The WWW project merges the techniques of information retrieval and hypertext to make an easy but powerful global information system. The WWW world consists of documents, and links. Indexes are special documents which, rather than being read, may be searched. The result of such a search is another ("virtual") document containing links to the documents found. The Web contains documents in many formats. Those documents which are hypertext (real or virtual), contain links to other documents, or places within documents. All documents, whether real, virtual, or indexes, look similar to the reader and are contained within the same addressing scheme. To follow a link, a reader clicks with a mouse (or types in a number if he or she has no mouse). To search an index, a reader gives keywords (or other search criteria). These are the only operations necessary to access the entire world of data.

To get there, telnet to 128.141.201.74 or info.cern.ch. For more information, contact Tim Berners-Lee, WorldWideWeb Project, 1211 Geneva 23 Switzerland; phone: +41(22)767 3755; fax: +41(22)767 7155; e-mail: tbl@cernvax.cern.ch.

APPENDIX E

MUST-HAVE VOLUMES FOR THE INTERNET SURFER

Kehoe, Brendan P. (1993). *Zen and the art of the Internet: A beginner's guide* (2nd ed.). Englewood Cliffs, NJ: Prentice Hall. The first edition is available for free from many FTP sites. This version has about 30 pages of new material and corrects various minor errors in the first edition. Includes the story of the Coke Machine on the Internet. For much of late 1991 and the first half of 1992, this was the document of choice for learning about the Internet. ISBN 0-13-010778-6. Index. $22.00.

Krol, Ed. (1992). *The whole Internet user's guide & catalog.* Sebastopol, CA: O'Reilly & Associates. Comprehensive guide to how the network works, the domain name system, acceptable use, security, and other issues. Chapters on telnet/remote login, File Transfer Protocol, and electronic mail explain error messages, special situations, and other arcana. Archie, Gopher, NetNews, WAIS, WWW, and troubleshooting each enjoy a chapter in this well-written book. Appendices contain information on how to get connected in addition to a glossary. ISBN 1-56592-025-2. $24.95.

LaQuey, Tracy, & Ryer, Jeanne C. (1993). *The Internet companion: A beginner's guide to global networking.* Reading, MA: Addison-Wesley. Beginning with a foreword by Vice-President Elect Al Gore, this book provides an often-humorous explanation of the origins of the Internet, acceptable use, basics of electronic mail, netiquette, online resources, transferring information, and finding e-mail addresses. The In the Know guide provides background on Internet legends (Elvis sightings is one), organizations, security issues, and how to get connected. Bibliography. Index. ISBN 0-201-62224-6. $10.95.

Tennant, Roy; Ober, John; & Lipow, Anne G. (1993). *Crossing the Internet threshold: An instructional handbook.* Berkeley, CA: Library Solutions Press. A cookbook to run your own Internet training sessions. Real-world examples. Foreword by Cliff Lynch. Library Solutions Institute and Press; 2137 Oregon Street, Berkeley, CA 94705; phone (510) 841-2636; fax: (510) 841-2926; ISBN 1-882208-01-3. $45.00.

DAVID V. LOERTSCHER

President
Hi Willow Research and Publishing
Castle Rock, Colorado

Electronic Information in School Libraries

ABSTRACT

Microcomputers have progressed from toys to tools in managing school libraries. Equipment inventory, circulation, online catalogs, acquisitions, and serials management/check-in have all been affected. In addition, high technology has presented new possibilities for educating young people, and school librarians are faced with a role change as they rise to meet this challenge.

INTRODUCTION

Picture the faculty of the College of Education at the University of Arkansas in 1979 gathering for a symposium that is to explore the possibilities of the microcomputer in education. Since almost none of the faculty has seen a microcomputer, they are anxious to attend and see what this new technology has in store for education. The presenter is introduced to this august body—an expert from out of town—a person with as much experience with microcomputers as about anyone in the country. (Remember, it is 1979 and the Apple microcomputer has just made its appearance on the market.) Our expert is Bryan Burdick from Kansas City. He is 10 years old. The professors come unglued.

As the era of high technology has dawned upon education in the past 13 years, three phenomena are evident:

1. Microcomputers and high technology have progressed from toys to tools in managing school libraries.
2. New possibilities for educating young people with high technology have developed.
3. School librarians are faced with yet another role change as they rise to meet the potential that high technology brings to the education of young people.

The purpose of this paper is to explore these three areas of interest from the perspective of the school library as it fits into the larger perspective of education.

MICROCOMPUTERS AS A TOOL
FOR MANAGING SCHOOL LIBRARIES

Educators in virtually every school in the country have adopted the microcomputer as an administrative tool for the three basics: word processing, databases, and spreadsheets. Such things as mass letters to parents, inventory, scheduling, and budgets are commonplace. School librarians have been a little slower to adopt these same tools partly because administrators innovated first, but also because librarians tended to purchase computers for instructional purposes first and only learned of management possibilities second. Betty Costa was one of the first to produce a handbook for the school librarian about using microcomputers as a management tool, and her book remains a classic in the field (Costa & Costa, 1991). Standard uses of microcomputers as tools in school libraries in 1992 include equipment inventory, circulation, online catalogs, acquisitions, card catalog production, serials management/check-in, and general management.

Equipment Inventory

Librarians/principals use both homegrown databases and sophisticated programs to track audiovisual equipment and furniture owned. Sophisticated programs track original vendors, equipment description, model and serial numbers, location of the equipment, maintenance records, lists of replaceable parts (such as lamp numbers for overhead projectors), and equipment condition. Such programs provide information for security and insurance purposes including projected costs of equipment repair and replacement.

Circulation

Librarians used microcomputers early to circulate equipment and specialized materials such as periodicals. Homegrown overdue systems were also popular in the early 1980s. The earliest commercial programs for school libraries were those designed to circulate books using a bar code system. Hundreds of systems were sold to school libraries that tracked patrons, books in circulation, and overdues. Today, the early adopters of circulation systems are envious as they see the features of the fully developed online catalogs for the school library. These people face automating twice with all the attendant problems of school politics, new equipment and software costs, and in some cases, the reinputting of an entire collection.

Online Catalogs

Online catalogs utilizing mainly MS-DOS systems are now common in school libraries. Popular system names include Follett, Winnebago, Mandarin-Media Flex, and Dynix. Systems generally use the MARC format, are individually school based (they do not share data with other schools or libraries), and contain catalog, circulation, and acquisition components. Catherine Murphy (1992), who has conducted one of the few dissertation studies to date about online systems in school libraries, has recently pulled together some of the most current articles that describe these systems and ways to select, implement, and evaluate them. As she was collecting the articles on school library automation, each article had to be sent back to the original author for a major update, even when the article had been published the previous year—an indication of the rapid rate of change in this area.

A typical online public access catalog (OPAC) for a school library provides author, title, and subject searches plus Boolean searching of all data fields. A few systems are beginning to provide such things as "interactive search assistance, error-correction features, and additional information about the contents of materials" (Hooten, 1992, p. 145). Catalog records for these systems are being purchased from vendors or downloaded from commercial CD-ROMs.

Two major issues for school OPAC systems are the quality of subject access and user friendliness for the child. When catalog records are downloaded into a school library catalog, a number of quality control problems emerge. Many commercial retrospective conversion companies have not cleaned up their databases. This means that classification numbers and subject headings reflect only the editions of Dewey and Sears/Library of Congress (LC) used at the time of cataloging. Thus, conflicting classification numbers and a mix of LC or Sears or AC subject headings are transferred into the OPAC, making it no better than its card form counterpart. Only if the system has global change capabilities and if the school librarian has enough expertise to recognize and deal with consistency does a better product emerge. Sloppy data delivered by computer are still sloppy. Boolean and keyword searching helps by locating common terms that children know, but subject searches with high recall rates are the exception rather than the rule, and shelf order is not improved at all. It is not surprising to sit at a school OPAC and find an author's name spelled several different ways requiring that the user look in several places to track an author's works. Errors abound if a combination of local input and downloading from commercial services has been utilized.

Vendors of OPACs for schools are making plans for higher quality cataloging data now that basic automation features are refined. For example, a program could be written to automatically present changed numbers from one Dewey edition to another, allow the librarian to accept/reject the change, print out a bibliography of those changes, and print the spine labels that could be applied to books in a few minutes. As the librarian approved these global changes, she could override national suggestions in favor of local preferences. Thus, sports biographies could be classed with the biographies or with the sport, and if with the sport, each sport would have a consistent number.

In subject cataloging, troublesome headings such as NEGROES, BLACKS, or AFRO-AMERICANS could be easily changed to a consistent term. Modules creating a cross-reference structure for the OPAC could be created and sold as add-ons so that consistency could be assured. Consistency in information systems is more important to children than it is to adults. Adults have a higher developmental level, are more flexible, and, one hopes, are more tolerant.

Early studies of children using OPACs are quite negative. Children do not seem to be able to use computer catalogs any better than printed ones. Edmonds, Moore, and Balcom (1990, 1992) found that Piaget's concrete operations probably apply to the use of OPACs just as they apply to other information or learning tasks. Thus, designers of screens and searching procedures for OPACs need to constantly investigate and utilize the research dealing with how children see and interpret information. Much needs to be done with picture subject searches and automatic transfer from misspelled words to the correct word form or to a "kid-known" synonym. Voice requests to OPACs need to be designed. If a child asks the computer for a Dr. Seuss book, the computer might print out a map showing the shelf location and pictures of some of Seuss's book covers and their spine labels.

As results of experiments with young children are forthcoming, many potential improvements will become apparent. Then again, perhaps it is too much to expect a child under age 9 or 10 to navigate a complex information system without the assistance of an older child or an adult. Are commercial companies willing to design information systems with children in mind? Librarians must demand such features and be willing to pay for them.

One of the more exciting aspects of quality cataloging for school libraries is the sharing of in-depth analysis of books. For example, one high school on Long Island analyzed every one of its play collections and made the amplified cataloging records available to all libraries in the area. Online indexes not only to plays but to poems, collective biographies, and songs are but a few of the possibilities that make small collections serve patrons to their full potential.

One barrier to school library automation is the lack of a networking capability that would connect schools and libraries to other schools and libraries. Although a few states such as Pennsylvania have produced statewide CD-ROM catalogs of holdings in school libraries, generally school libraries have yet to become a part of national systems such as OCLC (there are exceptions).

Acquisitions

Although OPACs may contain acquisition modules, these systems are not usually sophisticated enough to do any type of collection analysis and acquisition assistance based on collection segments. This author has proposed a simple system of collection mapping that chunks the collection into segments that support the curriculum of the school. Thus, a school library would have a general collection (providing breadth) and several to many specialty collections (providing depth) designed to serve special topics studied by the students. Even if the designer of the system has not planned for collection segmentation, the librarian can "cheat" the system. Using any field that has some form of user control, the librarian can control collection segments through a coding system.

For example, suppose the librarian wishes to build an in-depth collection of dinosaur books because the topic is studied by several classes and grade levels of students each year. The librarian assigns a code in a controllable data field to the "dinosaur collection," scans all materials relevant to that collection (both print and audiovisual), and then maintains this special collection in the OPAC or automated circulation system. Items deleted from the collection are automatically deleted from the emphasis collection. Each time the topic is studied, the librarian prints out the dinosaur collection bibliography, assigns the dinosaur code to any new materials, scans and deletes any irrelevant materials, and in a few moments has complete control of this emphasis collection. Use/circulation statistics can be analyzed easily helping with decisions such as when to add duplicate titles and when to discard outdated or unused titles. This information can also be used as the basis of collection building in that emphasis area. The author's book *Computerized Collection Development for School Library Media Centers* describes this system of collection building using manual, simple database managers or OPAC systems (Loertscher & Ho, 1986).

Card Catalog Production

Librarians still using card systems can purchase quite sophisticated programs that will produce card sets from original input data or will print out card sets from CD-ROM databases. Catalog cards, spine labels, circulation cards, and card pockets can all be printed from these programs.

Serials Management/Check-in

Several commercial programs exist to manage a periodical collection that would not only be used in check-in but in claiming, weeding, subscription renewals, and circulation.

General Management

Popular programs such as AppleWorks or Microsoft Works are used by school librarians to write letters, generate reports, keep statistics, track and prepare budgets, keep address files of suppliers, and manage a myriad of other files that are better kept on computer than in card files.

School librarians have been quite slow to become computer literate enough to make the computer a useful management tool. The same fear and trepidation that confront a generation of people who grew up in the manual world prevent librarians from taking advantage of the computer. At our company, we still get many calls from persons who cannot use the ubiquitous Print Shop program and the graphic disks we market. We are amazed at the number of people who don't know how to turn a computer on or accomplish even the simplest of tasks electronically.

Both the word processor and the database manager are the school librarian's best friends. Once these programs are mastered, school librarians are extremely creative in using these tools to save time and to manage their centers more effectively. Every year, Libraries Unlimited publishes a number of products, usually indexes created by these "hacker" librarians. Examples are indexes to multicultural projects, science projects, or specialized bibliographies of wordless picture books or reference books about Indians.

Librarians who want to succeed with computers in managing their libraries must not only become computer literate, they must learn several major programs in depth. Whether it requires being tutored by a knowledgeable person, taking computer classes, or teaching oneself, the time investment in learning about computing pays major dividends. Librarians must keep current with developments in computing including hardware and software. A few suggestions include the following:

- Read several popular computing journals each month such as *MacUser* or *PC World.* If you don't understand the articles, at least read the ads.
- Read several library-oriented computing journals such as the *ALUG Newsletter* (free from Apple Computer, Inc.), *Library Hi Tech,* or *Computers in Libraries.*
- Find a friend who is interested in computers and "talk shop" on a regular basis.
- Share computer stories and concerns with other librarians facing similar problems. Ideas and solutions to common problems can save hours and days of frustration.
- Attend computer sessions at conferences. If vendors conduct the session, don't believe all you hear.
- Never buy a computer software package or hardware without comparing features with other programs/machines that will do similar tasks. Be careful about being one of the first to try out a new "library package." We would never have good systems for libraries without those willing to experiment, but one can always expect new applications to have problems that will take a great deal of time and effort to fix.
- Companies go in and out of business in the computer software and hardware business. Try to choose the most solid companies that support their sales and are likely to be in business for a few years.
- Discussions about computers with other school, public, and academic librarians will provide news on developments both local and national.
- Don't overlook the expertise of students who are knowledgeable about computers. They will often provide hundreds of hours of assistance in exchange for the excitement of building a system that makes a positive contribution to the library.
- Invest in a computer for the home and use it daily. Many software packages require constant practice if they are to be mastered.
- Finally, developing political contacts with administrators will provide opportunities to update equipment and software as funds become available.

Like their counterparts in business, school librarians cannot sit back and wait for computerization to solve their management problems like magic. They must continually increase their skill and computer knowledge if the payoff is to come.

TECHNOLOGY AND EDUCATION

Since the appearance of Edison's motion picture projector in 1910, there has been a great deal of interest in technological devices that could be used in education. Wave upon wave of interest has been given to each new technology, and many have been labeled the saviors of education. The motion picture projector, the filmstrip projector, the opaque projector, the 8-mm single concept loop projector, the overhead projector, radio, television—all and more have had their "day in the sun." The history of this entire movement is best documented in Saettler's (1990) *The Evolution of American Educational Technology.*

The major drawback with technology is that none has been developed specifically for education. Generally, a technology has been created for a business or scientific purpose, then educators try to figure out how students can benefit. The cart has always been ahead of the horse. After a technology is created, a company will try to market that technology to schools. Modifications to suit students' needs are often made after some period of adoption in the education market. Such modification is expensive and time-consuming thus limiting the spread of the technology.

For example, the motion picture projector was developed as an entertainment technology first and as an educational one second. School teachers hated 16-mm projectors because they were never easy to thread, they were tricky to handle when they malfunctioned, and they required total environmental control to use in the normal classroom.

In the past few years when videotape, also an entertainment technology, became cheaper to own than 16 mm, teachers rushed to adopt a technology they could operate both at school and home, and a technology that did not require a darkened room. Teachers did not care that the picture size, color, and clarity were inferior; they wanted a technology that worked and one they could operate without help. Today, film companies are having a hard time staying in business, not because they cannot produce videotape instead of film, but because of unit pricing. Consumers are so accustomed to buying a videotape in the store for $30, they think educational videos should be comparatively priced. Film companies have usually charged $300 to $900 per film print, and films were purchased only by school districts or film libraries. It takes sales of thousands of prints at $30 to individual schools to recoup the production costs film companies need to stay in business.

A second problem with technology in education is that producers generally have made outlandish claims for the contribution of their particular technology to learning. The 16-mm film was going to replace teachers. So was educational television. So were teaching machines. Research projects by the thousands documented the power of these media to teach. Sometimes research results were positive in favor of the particular technology; most of the time, research results showed "no significant difference." Students learned equally well no matter the medium. It seems logical to assume that a fact can be learned from a book or a film or a microcomputer screen with equal ease.

What the research did not test was the amount of learning from the unique characteristics of each medium. For example, since a film uses motion, it should teach certain things as well as a book and other things better than a book when a concept is motion oriented. Conversely, the book should be superior to the film under certain circumstances— for example, for browsing. Today, educational technologists generally agree that a teaching medium should be selected based on its unique characteristics as well as its content. Teachers, however, usually choose a technology based on convenience first, content and characteristics second.

The research on educational technology does show that new or different technologies are popular with learners. Students who use a computer for the first time find it exciting, and they tend to learn more. Since students' primary objection to schooling is boredom, teachers and school librarians can exploit this novelty effect if they provide a wide variety of technological or media experiences rather than concentrating on a few. Variety is the spice of teaching and learning.

Because education is such a labor-intensive industry, the costs of educating a nation of students have risen astronomically in the past 20 years. Theorists have been trying to make the case that technology could replace some of the teachers and thus lower costs (Molenda, 1992). Within the past 10 years, a number of schools have been created that use banks of computers that provide hours upon hours of drills, tutorials, and simulations. These schools employ lower paid adult aides and a few teachers who are instructional managers. The computer system in these schools employs a technique of mastery learning where students must achieve criterion levels of learning before they can progress onto the next level of work. Such schools have high costs of investment in technology, support, and software and are not less expensive to establish and maintain. For example, WICAT Systems in Provo, Utah, has such a school. The tuition is comparable to an exclusive private school. They do advertise, however, that their students perform much better on standardized tests than students in traditional schools.

Generally, technology is an add-on cost to schools. That is, the school will employ enough teachers to teach in the conventional 1-to-30 or 1-to-25 ratio and then provide technology as tools for the teachers to use. In this case, technology enhances what a human is able to provide. Such a plan provides a tremendous challenge to a school district where 90% of the money for education goes to teacher salaries. Technology must compete for a very small piece of the budget pie. If teachers do not adopt a technology in such a manner that students are benefiting from it in a demonstrable way, the technology is considered a frill.

Technology carries with it a tremendous temptation to use it as a "filler." The teacher may rest and let the machine take up some time. Then the teacher will attempt to compress the human teaching content into a smaller time frame. In the past few years, teachers have been assigned a greater and greater amount to teach in the same or decreased amount of time. These teachers reassess the time that a technology takes: Does it really teach as well as I can? Does it cover the content as fast as I can? Can I get relevant learning materials for the technology the school owns? Are the materials to be used on a technology of only peripheral value to the objectives currently being taught?

Many teachers are not comfortable using technology. They may not be able to operate the equipment. They may fear that when a piece of equipment fails, it will do so right in the middle of a class, and they will lose control of the presentation and the students. Many teachers opt not to use machines. They view technology as either an add-on responsibility or as irrelevant to the specific task at hand. They laugh when someone provides a single computer and no software for their classroom of 30 students and expects something magic to happen.

In an attempt to make technology and materials much easier to use, schools have been and are being designed around teaching stations. For example, in Chesterton, Indiana, the new high school building has been designed around technology. The building has been completely wired with optical cable. There is a telephone in each classroom. Each classroom has a computer/technology station complete with at least two large classroom television monitors. Teachers can command any number of technologies coming into their rooms at a moment's notice. They can call up a film at will, connect into a computer network, call pictures, text, or sound from a CD-ROM to illustrate their lectures, or use amplified telephone to talk with their class to experts anywhere in the world. If a malfunction occurs, they can send a message to the central media center operator on their computer, or they can call the person on the telephone.

This dazzling array of technology is impressive, but it is an add-on. The community is investing more dollars in each student's educational experience than in a comparable school using the textbook-lecture method. Currently, taxpayers are struggling. They are wondering how much to invest in education when scores on national exams are declining or at least are not improving significantly. There is no rush toward technology as "the answer."

THE SCHOOL LIBRARY AND TECHNOLOGY

During the 1960s, when technology first became available to education on a grand scale, school librarians were resistant to change. The 1960 Standards for School Libraries advocated the adoption of a multimedia center concept. At first, many schools hired audiovisual specialists to handle nonprint media, but with the passage of time, librarians became more comfortable with a wide range of formats and generally were put in charge of all media.

When microcomputers came along, many school librarians saw these machines as learning tools, were early adopters of the technology, and became computer leaders in their schools. Other librarians ignored computers, and so others were hired to set up and manage computers for both computer literacy coursework and computers as instructional tools. Without the benefit of a national survey (data will be collected in 1994), this author would guess that a minority of school librarians are considered to be microcomputer specialists in their buildings. With the advent of online technology and other high-tech equipment, school librarians again stand on the threshold of a role choice. Immersion into the high-tech world of information and media will provide new frontiers of information use/access for the youth of the nation. School librarians have a chance to prepare young people for an emerging information society, but only if they become leaders in the information technology that has and will appear.

To get a better picture of the potential of the new information technology as an education tool, let us explore the technology, not by type of hardware, but by the educational/information functions that it can provide to young people. Although we may briefly describe a specific piece of technology and what it does at this moment in time, the function that it performs is likely to outlast the current model of whatever gizmo is available.

Access to Bibliographic Information

Currently, bibliographic data are a well-known commodity being handled by all types of libraries. At first, data such as magazine indexes, bibliographies, and other indexes were available principally via telephone lines; now much is available through CD-ROM or through locally created databases. Citations of articles or books are only helpful to a young person if there is easy access to hard copy through local public or academic libraries. Another problem concerns who pays for the bibliographies produced from remote online databases. A number of high schools have budgeted funds for online searching and do not pass these costs on to students. This policy limits the amount of searching that is done and requires extensive planning before searches are conducted (not a bad practice).

Still another problem is the relevance to children and young people of information on large commercial databases. In the past 10 years, the availability of databases has proliferated to such an extent that more and more is available for the younger set. That trend should continue. Of particular use are information systems containing abstracts of the books or articles indexed. This format helps students choose a few relevant articles, and at times the article can be cited in a research paper when the abstract contains an appropriate fact.

When the school library is connected to a local, regional, or national network, access to bibliographic data is very useful to young people. If they know that another school, public, or academic library in the community has a magazine or book they need, they can usually find a way to obtain the needed materials for their research. Through the school OPAC or a separate terminal, the young person can query the libraries in the area. In Denver, Colorado, any home or school that has a modem and a computer can access the CARL system. The user can dial into many libraries on the front range to check bibliographic citations and do keyword searches of collections throughout Colorado and beyond. The system is so simple that anyone who can read can use it.

Another example of networking for young people is Access Pennsylvania. The collections of hundreds of school libraries in Pennsylvania have been stored on several CD-ROMs. Young people can find specific titles or do subject searches and locate materials in their own school, neighboring schools, regional libraries, or the state as a whole. Access to distant libraries takes time—a commodity that young people often do not plan for.

School librarians are wise to seek the technology needed to connect their library to collections other than their own. They should teach young people how to access other collections and create a simple system of interlibrary loan. These are the same challenges faced by libraries of all types and come with the same attendant problems: How can we provide access? Who will pay? How can we support interlibrary loan? When shall we own an item or just borrow?

The Locally Produced Database

A number of school librarians have discovered database managers such as AppleWorks, Microsoft Works, Claris Works, and others. They begin to realize that many bibliographies and indexes to local collections can be created to make certain materials extremely useful. Examples might include the following:

- A song index
- A play index
- An index to science experiments
- A poetry index
- A biographical index to collected works
- A local newspaper index
- A speaker's index
- A famous person's address index

Libraries Unlimited has created a number of databases and bibliographies that can be used as local databases. For example, Mary Ann Pilger's (1992) *Science Experiments Index for Young People* is an index to over 2,000 science experiments books. This index is available in traditional print form or can be purchased as a database for use on Apple, Macintosh, or IBM computers. The print form of Pilger's database has the same drawbacks as other print indexes—first you find the experiment you want, but then you must try to locate the book in your own or some other library's collection. The database version has an advantage. The librarian searches which of the 2,000 titles the library owns, deletes the rest, and prints out the result. The new index becomes an index to the in-house collection. User success rates jump to near 100%. The master database can be kept so that titles can be added or deleted as the collection evolves or as an interlibrary loan source. Young people and student helpers can be taught how to add or delete from such an index. In this way, students can understand how an index is created and how it can be searched to advantage.

If a student can create an index, that student can use many types of electronic indexes easily and can begin to comprehend what electronic indexes can and cannot do, how they are built, and how they can be searched. Although some care must be taken when allowing young people to save and delete information in a master index, much good training can accrue. Both library and user benefit.

A second example of a local database is the book and database by Vandelia VanMeter (1992) entitled *World History for Children and Young Adults*. This source contains an annotated bibliography of all books reviewed in the past 10 years for world history. The printed version is interesting, but the database is much more valuable from a collection-building perspective. Comparisons between what is currently owned and what is wanted can be done quickly, and purchase lists can be printed out. Better access to the books is also available through keyword searching rather than through the traditional subject index available in the print version. Bibliographies, both of owned materials and other sources, are easily printed out or included in reference lists for teachers for use in printed articles or lesson plans. For example, consider the request, "I need a list of books about the Vietnam War that have been published in the past 10 years that have been reviewed positively." Such a request takes moments to prepare either in print form or in data form that can be pulled into another document.

A third example of a locally owned database is one in which factual or narrative information is stored for instructional use. Such databases are available from commercial sources on CD-ROM or as databases that can be used with common database managers. Examples might be data about presidents, facts about endangered animals, weather data, address files, or astronomical data. Such databases are used by students to extract facts but also to do higher level thinking and for data manipulation. A few examples and their use include the following:

- In a database about the states, which states have the cardinal as their state bird?
- In a database containing weather information, what are the top 10 temperatures recorded in the United States, and where and when did these temperatures occur?
- In two databases, one containing incidents of communicable diseases and the other weather data, is there any relationship between the weather and the occurrence of certain diseases?
- In a database containing demographic statistics, do certain states have predominant religions? Are predominant religions regional in nature? What are the historical reasons for predominant religions being located in a region?

Students can be expected to use an electronic database in the same way they would use a reference book. The advantage of the electronic version is usually both speed and the type of questions that can be answered/computed in the electronic version. In printed reference works, the authors and editors must decide how the user is going to approach the data. In an electronic source, the designers can allow numerous approaches to the data without allowing the size of the data pool to increase exponentially.

Young children can learn how to search databases for answers they need to certain questions, but it is even more educational if young people can participate in database construction. There are numerous articles in the literature that describe the process of creating a database with children. Ron Martin (1992) in Alaska recently described a database he had children create about dogs. Each child did research on a different dog, entered that data into a database Ron had created, and then the class used the database to help make decisions on what type of dog each of them might like to own, how dog breeds compare, and what breeds of dogs are common to certain areas of the country.

Children who learn to construct databases have many advantages. They learn to research certain facts; they must check those facts to see that they are as accurate as possible; they must learn how a database is structured; they must learn how data are entered into a database; they must learn quality control principles and how to think ahead as data are entered (do we enter the surname first or the given name?); and they must learn how to search a database to answer questions of varying degrees of difficulty. Such classroom activities provide simultaneous growth in subject competence and in information literacy. There are few better ways to teach young people the concept of databases.

Databases can be constructed on any microcomputer, even an old Commodore 64. Happily, database managers simple enough for even young children are readily available at affordable prices. It does not require a major investment to reap excellent results.

Children who can create databases can also learn how to chart the data they enter (budding Edward Tuftes?). Many programs allow a wide variety of charts and graphs to be constructed from simple data entered from a database manager or in its cousin, the spreadsheet. Because children are constantly tested to see if they can interpret chart and graph data, they can leap forward in standardized test scores if they know how to create their own understandable charts and graphs using a computer.

Data Gathering, Exchange, and Analysis

The American Association for the Advancement of Science is encouraging teachers to involve young people in more realistic science experiences. If the school librarian is informed about both data-gathering opportunities and high-tech possibilities, she can assist the science faculty in creating marvelous learning experiences. A few sample scenarios might be the following:

- Students gather data on acid rain as a part of National Geographic Kid Net. They can examine and analyze data from students in all regions of the country, make comparisons, look for cause and effect, and pose possible solutions to problems they observe.
- Students can gather data from their local streams and rivers as a part of a major statewide effort sponsored by a university to chart water availability, usage, and quality. Such cooperation can cultivate

student/expert relationships, provide career information, and help students participate in real-world and current scientific problem solution.

- Students might collect data in a cooperative agreement with another school somewhere in the world. Data can be sent by fax or electronically mailed back and forth for comparison and analysis.

A school librarian who is comfortable with numerous high-tech possibilities becomes a valuable team member as data-rich instructional experiences are designed and carried out. Not only can students gather data from their local environment, they can enter data from library reference sources for verification or comparison with the data collected locally. For example, does the sun rise when the almanac says it should? Why or why not? Data comparison, analysis, and criticism are the newer types of information skills students can experience as part of a high-tech library media center program.

Student Creative Output

In the past 13 years, a whole new world of production has emerged. Through the word processor, the video camera, CD-ROM, and digital audio/video, both adults and students can express their ideas and channel creative energies through a wide variety of media. When students were limited to transcribing ideas by pencil and paper or by using the typewriter, only the best students produced any sizable volume of work. Now, using the new technology, students can produce much more than they did in the same amount of time. Two factors account for this phenomenon: a high rate of efficiency and higher motivation through novelty. A few comments about the various forms of technology that stimulate student production are illustrative of these factors.

Word Processing
Research shows that students using word processors will write longer and better reports/papers. Students will revise more because of the ease of machine revision and the presence of spelling and grammar checkers, and thesauri allow students to create a higher quality product. These machine assists actually improve a student's grasp of the language because spelling, wording, and grammar changes must be approved by the user; they are not automatic. At first, teachers were hesitant to accept student work done on word processors because there was some feeling that, like a calculator in math, students might be getting an unfair advantage or might be cheating a bit. Most of this fear has been erased as teachers themselves have become processors of words. There are many good word processors for children and young adults. Some

of these programs can be used just as soon as a child can recognize letters and how they are used to create words. Many schools require word processing of all students as a part of their computer literacy classes. Typing teachers, who were at first very nervous about kids learning poor keyboarding habits, have resigned themselves to a new world.

Desktop Publishing

In the past five years, desktop publishing software has become available for children and young adults. One of the most popular programs is The Children's Writing and Publishing Center. If students can handle a very simple word processor, they can automatically handle a publishing program that allows them to create layouts and add graphics to their reports. The finished product can be so professional looking that students become interested in the creation of high-quality printed products. Young children can produce books, magazine articles, advertisements, posters, and illustrated reports and term papers. The school librarian who can envision the potential of desktop publishing should work with the teacher to plan research or topical studies, have a plentiful supply of relevant graphics, and provide an open lab for the creation of products. Students can be required to write more and better pieces complete with proper citations to print or electronic sources. Layout requirements can be accomplished through the use of templates or can be designed by the student depending on the sophistication level.

Desktop Everything Else

In the past three years, a wide variety of new technologies have emerged that link to a computer to produce not only print but sounds and images. Perhaps the first move in this direction was the creation of hypertext. Products like HyperCard for the Macintosh and Linkway for the IBM allow the user to create databases with buttons. These programs create something like a box of 3×5 cards that can either be viewed in sequence, or by adding "buttons" (places on the card to click with a mouse), the user can be linked to any card in the box. In addition, the user could be linked to both sound sequences and to pictures.

Even more recent technology allows students to link words to film clips or video clips or even to other databases by connecting the computer to a CD-ROM, a VCR, or a tape recorder. Multimedia reports can be created by young children with a minimum of instruction as long as the proper equipment, software, and materials are available. It is interesting to read or hear the technospeak that accompanies the descriptions of such technology:

Multimodality. The new media are translatable. Words, images, and sounds can be placed in one document or can be edited from any other document to any other document. Information can be presented in text, graphic, animation, natural voice, music, and special effects on the same platform. Moreover, multimedia software provide for linking a segment of information, represented in any mode, to any other chunk of available information. Hypermedia allows for an omnidirectional search of information, a part of which may be stored on a CD-ROM or laser disc. The microcomputer drives the disc player to search and display the information. However, computers with advanced microchips and internal optical drives provide an even more powerful platform to designers and producers. Media computers provide an integrated hardware/software platform for production and display of instructional information. Digitized audio, video, and text can be stored and retrieved for the production of new instructional materials on the same system. Using total digital systems, such as DVI (Digital Video Interactive), educators are able to represent information in any mode on demand. Optical scanners and video cameras enable them to transform information from analog to digital form for editing into multimedia documents. Using image processing software, visuals can be edited, enhanced, and transformed products in a matter of seconds. Conducting such procedures in analog photography remains only in the purview of professionals in a fully equipped darkroom. Music[al] Instrument Digital Interface (MIDI) provides the same freedom of expression for music and sound effects. A keyboard puts composing, interpreting, and performing power of a full symphony orchestra, a jazz quartet, or a single instrument at the fingertips of instructional designers and media producers. (Saba, 1992, p. 129)

The advantages to students in this new multimedia world are quite simple to understand when a real-world example is given. A report on the Civil War can contain facts or narrative with accompanying pictures, stories with accompanying sound effects, or reenactments of battles complete with animated battle maps and simulated battle sounds.

There is a new term for this manipulation of media—re-purposing. That is, a student can take materials created in one medium for a single purpose and then edit or merge them into a new product with a new purpose—re-purposing. Although questions of copyright immediately emerge, the fair-use clause of the copyright law is generally thought to cover this manipulation as long as the product is created by students for educational assignments and the resulting product is not sold or used in public performance.

Teachers and librarians are likely to embrace such products because these products require the student to spend more time and effort and require much greater mastery of a topic than was true using either a pencil or a typewriter. The idea is that students become mini-experts about a topic as they create a very exciting high-tech product.

An example might be illustrative of the potential. Last year was the 25th anniversary of Fox-Fire, the oral history project done in the hill country of Georgia. Using high technology, students can now create, not only the magazine articles for which the students of Rayburn, Georgia, are famous, but they can combine commercial or original videotape, commercial or live-recorded sounds, and still photographs to create their final product. One can imagine the impact of a multimedia oral history report on killing a hog or attending a mountain country funeral or even reporting a family reunion—country-style.

IMPLICATIONS FOR SCHOOL LIBRARIANS

In the age of high technology, school librarians must be very familiar with the storage, retrieval, and the production of information, sound, and pictures. This expanded literacy allows them, with teachers, to be catalysts in a whole new world of educational possibilities. Many school librarians are already living in this new world. Others are not even aware that a new world exists.

Librarians in public and academic libraries can easily recognize students who are comfortable with this new high-tech world. They will come into the library, look around, and then ask where all the technology is located. If the library does not have the technology they like, they will stomp out complaining about "this rinky-dink place." Students of this breed will not only be reluctant to use conventional technology, they may not know how. Being reduced from desktop publishers to pencil and paper or to the typewriter can be a humiliating and jolting experience. These students will want instant access to data, full-text articles, and easy access to fax or quick interlibrary loan. They will demand current data from the most authoritative sources. They will want access, not just to words, but to extensive collections of pictorial and audio material. They will have little patience with librarians who plead ignorance or poverty as an excuse. Those in academic and public libraries should be prepared.

In all our enthusiasm for high technology, however, we must be realistic. Technology must pay its own way if it is to be adopted widely. We can only expect taxpayers to pay for these expensive tools if

- students learn more than they would have by using traditional teaching and learning techniques;
- the technology releases students to be more creative;
- students are more information literate and can navigate and use information technology wisely.

There are lots of reasons not to use technology:

- its cost;
- the frustration it causes teachers, librarians, and users;
- the temptation to just be glitzy;
- the increased ability for children to waste time on an expensive machine.

School libraries are on the forefront of the information technology world. They are laying the groundwork for a whole new generation of information literate persons. Because they are often alone in a library media center, without help, they must be superhuman in their breadth of knowledge, their leadership skills, their technology skills, and their ability to make a technology pay a true educational benefit. Some of them complain that there is too much to know. Others dig in and are constantly refreshed by the excitement and challenge.

If we are truly creating an information society, then we all have a stake in what goes on in the schools of the nation. The college years are much too late to begin to build the information skills our society will demand.

REFERENCES

Costa, B., & Costa, M. (1991). *A micro handbook for small libraries and media centers* (3rd ed.). Englewood, CO: Libraries Unlimited.

Edmonds, L.; Moore, P.; & Balcom, K. M. (1990). The effectiveness of an online catalog. *School Library Journal, 36*(10), 28-32.

Edmonds, L.; Moore, P.; & Balcom, K. M. (1992). The effectiveness of an online catalog. In C. Murphy (Ed.), *Automating school library catalogs: A reader* (pp. 181-190). Englewood, CO: Libraries Unlimited.

Hooten, P. A. (1992). Online catalogs: Will they improve children's access? In C. Murphy (Ed.), *Automating school library catalogs: A reader* (pp. 144-149). Englewood, CO: Libraries Unlimited.

Loertscher, D. V., & Ho, M. L. (1986). *Computerized collection development for school library media centers.* Castle Rock, CO: Hi Willow Research and Publishing. (Distributed by Libraries Unlimited, Englewood, CO.)

Martin, R. (1992). Dogs and databases. *School Library Media Activities Monthly, 8*(5), 39-42.

Molenda, M. (1992). Technology and school restructing: Some clarifying propositions. In *Educational media and technology yearbook* (pp. 153-158). Englewood, CO: Libraries Unlimited.

Murphy, C. (Ed.). (1992). *Automating school library catalogs: A reader.* Englewood, CO: Libraries Unlimited.

Pilger, M. A. (1992). *Science experiments index for young people, update 91.* Englewood, CO: Libraries Unlimited.

Saba, F. (1992). Digital media: A platform for converging educational technology 'preparadigms'. In *Educational media and technology yearbook* (pp. 127-133). Englewood, CO: Libraries Unlimited.

Saettler, P. (1990). *The evolution of American educational technology.* Englewood, CO: Libraries Unlimited.

VanMeter, V. (1992). *World history for children and young adults: An annotated bibliographic index.* Englewood, CO: Libraries Unlimited.

RUTH V. SMALL

Assistant Professor
School of Information Studies
Syracuse University
Syracuse, New York

Principles and Strategies for Designing Effective Computer-Mediated Instruction

ABSTRACT

Information professionals are increasingly asked to assist instructional designers or to be designers of computer-mediated information systems including the online instruction that facilitates their independent, skillful use by information consumers. This paper provides some guidelines for information professionals asked to create effective computer-mediated instruction. It begins with a discussion of a number of issues to consider both before and during the design process, describes a simple yet powerful instructional design model that forms a framework for making design decisions, and presents a wide range of design strategies for implementation.

INTRODUCTION

The overwhelming acceptance of computer technologies as instructional delivery systems requires designing instruction that considers the unique interactive capabilities of computers as a medium for providing effective, efficient, and appealing instruction to users. As more and more information services and resources go "online," information professionals are increasingly asked to assist instructional designers or to be the designers of computer-mediated information systems, including the online instruction that facilitates their independent, skillful use by information consumers.

Whether designing drill-and-practice programs in which the objective is the memory of simple skills, tutorials that teach concepts or rules, or simulations and games that integrate concepts, skills, and problem-solving activities (Bunderson, 1981), designers find a variety of creative options through computer-mediated instruction. This paper is intended to provide some guidelines for information professionals who are designing or adapting instructional programs or who are serving in an advisory capacity in that regard. It begins with a discussion of a number of issues to consider both before and during the design process, presents a simple yet powerful model that forms a framework for making design decisions, and concludes with a host of related design strategies to select based on specific needs and preferences. Figure 1 provides a graphic overview of the issues and model to be presented in this paper.

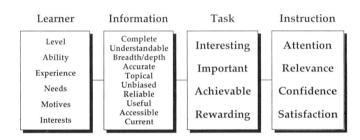

Learner	Information	Task	Instruction
Level	Complete Understandable	Interesting	Attention
Ability	Breadth/depth		
Experience	Accurate Topical	Important	Relevance
Needs	Unbiased Reliable	Achievable	Confidence
Motives	Useful		
Interests	Accessible Current	Rewarding	Satisfaction

Figure 1. Design considerations for computer-mediated instruction

COMPUTER-MEDIATED INSTRUCTIONAL DESIGN ISSUES

Learners

The first issue to consider is always an information professional's primary concern—the users or, in this case, the learners. Who will receive the instruction? Who is the target audience? What do I know about them?

There are a number of important learner characteristics to consider before beginning the design process. When designing computer-mediated instruction, these characteristics become even more critical because the learning process is often an independent activity where the information professional or instructor serves in a facilitative or advisory capacity rather than as the source or provider of knowledge.

The level and ability of learners are important characteristics related to cognitive knowledge of the subject matter and psychomotor computer skills. Levels and abilities may range from remedial to gifted, from beginner to advanced, and from entry level to expert. In most cases, users of computer-mediated instruction represent a mixture of levels and abilities requiring a range of options to accommodate them. Other characteristics such as age and physical limitations may also affect the design of computer-mediated instruction.

In addition, learners approach the learning experience with a range of experiences both with the technology and the subject matter. If learners must possess specific entry behaviors or skills in order to successfully learn (e.g., English language skills, keyboarding skills, basic reading skills) and the computer program does not teach them, where and how will they get them? This is an additional consideration when planning computer-mediated instruction.

The second group of important learner characteristics relates to attitudes—both toward the subject matter and the technology. Attitudes encompass individual needs, motives, interests, and preferences. What do your users need or want to know or do?

There are several ways to determine learner characteristics, including reviewing the professional literature, consulting academic records, observing, testing, or interviewing. Although a careful analysis of the target learner population is recommended before beginning the design process, it is important to continuously evaluate the design with selected members of that population to be certain that it continues to be responsive to their needs and abilities (Marchionini, 1991).

Information

The second issue for consideration is the information itself. How do you judge the quality of the information (both the subject matter and the interface) for learning? This is often an overlooked dimension when designing instruction. If, for example, one designs a motivational, instructionally sound program in which the information is incomplete or inaccurate, that instruction becomes at best useless and at worst dangerous. For instance, if one is designing computer-mediated instruction that trains nuclear power plant workers to interpret online information, a change in the function of a key command that is not reflected in the instructional interface may result in learners becoming frustrated and not using the system. Furthermore, consider the potential consequences if the information itself is incorrect or out-of-date.

Taylor's (1986) Value-Added Model identifies a number of dimensions for evaluating the quality of information. In some cases, this type of evaluation may require consultation with a subject matter expert. The information may be evaluated on the following dimensions:

- *Complete.* Does the information provide comprehensive coverage of the topic for achieving predetermined learning goals?
- *Understandable.* Are the terms, language, and vocabulary used comprehensible to the intended users? Does it avoid unnecessary technical jargon and explain necessary complex or interrelated concepts?
- *Breadth/Depth.* Is enough information provided for learners to achieve predetermined learning goals?
- *Accurate.* Is the information error-free so learners can trust the system?
- *Topical.* Is all of the information directly related to the subject matter? Is there any peripheral or potentially distracting or irrelevant information that should be eliminated?
- *Unbiased.* Is issue-related information presented in a manner that includes more than one point of view?
- *Reliable.* Is there a consistent use of terms? Are the directions and rules consistent throughout the instruction?
- *Useful.* Is all of the information potentially useful to learners?
- *Accessible.* Are important content and instructions available at any time throughout the program?
- *Current.* Is the information the most recent and up-to-date required to attain predetermined learning goals?

Including a large amount of information allows the learner access based on individual needs, interests, or time available (Schaefermeyer, 1990). Winn (1990) suggests using task analysis and field testing procedures to determine the breadth and depth, completeness, and accuracy of the information.

Task

The third issue for consideration is the learning task. What are learners expected to know or do when they are done? Is the program functionality transparent or self-evident enough that learners can quickly turn their attention to the learning task rather than concentrating on how to use the program? For, what the task itself does not provide, the instruction must.

The first determination about the task is if it has intrinsic interest to learners. For example, it is probably unnecessary to spend much time designing strategies that motivate third graders to learn during a lesson on dinosaurs. On the other hand, it is unlikely that college freshmen find instruction on online searching equally intrinsically stimulating.

Another determination about the learning task is its importance to learners. If college freshmen must learn online searching techniques in order to complete a required history assignment, it is likely that the learning task will be important. If, however, online searching skills are taught isolated from any required or desired learning goal, the learning task may not be perceived as relating to learner needs or interests, and therefore the task does not, on its own, take on a sense of obvious importance to the learner.

A third task-related concern is whether the task is perceived as manageable or achievable by all learners. If learners lack the prerequisite skills or knowledge or if there are external constraints that prevent learners from successful achievement (e.g., not having enough time to complete the program), the task may be perceived as unattainable. Low self-esteem or feeling a lack of personal competence may also interfere with learning success. Finally, if the task is too complex or abstract for the target audience to comprehend, the likelihood of learning success will be greatly diminished unless prerequisite knowledge or skills are taught first.

The final task characteristic is whether accomplishing the task is, in and of itself, rewarding. What will learners gain from successful achievement? Most people need some type of reward for their efforts. Some rewards take a tangible form, such as grades or the proverbial "Christmas bonus." Other rewards are more intangible, for example, praise or when success at one level allows a learner to progress to a more advanced level. Although the ultimate goal of "learning for learning's sake" might be desirable, most learners require other types of rewards. Therefore, if the task is not perceived as intrinsically interesting, rewarding, and valuable, or if the task is complex and abstract, then specific instructional design strategies will need to be systematically included.

THE ARCS MODEL

Once the characteristics of the learner, the information, and the task have been identified, the design process may be initiated. Although there are a number of models that provide effective approaches to the systematic design of instruction, one model that is both powerful and easy to apply will be presented in this paper. The ARCS (Attention, Relevance, Confidence, Satisfaction) Model was developed by Dr. John M. Keller, Professor of Instructional Systems at Florida State University. The ARCS Model is based on a number of psychological theories, but its foundation is expectancy-value theory (Keller, 1983, 1987).

Most of the research on expectancy-value theory was conducted in the workplace to determine how to increase performance on the job. It is only within the past 15 years, through the work of Keller and others, that the theories developed for the workplace have been adapted to applications in education and training.

Therefore, in these latter contexts, expectancy-value theory may be described in the following manner—for learners to put forth the effort to reach a learning goal, they must (a) value the learning task and (b) believe that they can successfully accomplish the learning task. Both must be present. If either or both are absent, the likelihood of learner effort toward the task is low.

ARCS is a systematic approach to design that addresses both of these two criteria, as well as the issues previously described. There are a variety and range of design strategies that relate to each of the four ARCS principles. Although the ARCS Model may appear to be largely intuitive, its power lies in its organization and the ability to apply this intuitive knowledge.

As each of these strategies is described, it may be useful to reflect on computer-mediated instructional programs used in the past, whether they were effective or ineffective, and how the strategies presented in this paper might have improved or enhanced them. They may also suggest applications to meet current or future design needs.

Attention

The first ARCS principle is to gain the learner's attention and to sustain it throughout the instruction (Keller, 1987). To gain attention, consider that variety is "the spice of life." Variety can refer to multimedia formats selected on the basis of how best to represent the information. For example, if the information intends to convey motion, a sequence of events or time-lapse animation may be the appropriate strategy.

Format strategies that may be selected to provide this type of variety are

- text that includes expository information, examples, and practice items;
- graphics (illustrations, figures, diagrams, charts, maps);
- sound;
- animation;
- photographs;
- full-motion video.

There are other ways of providing variety. When a concept is complex or abstract, providing both a textual and visual representation offers useful redundancy of the concept to the learner because visuals convey ideas faster and easier than words, emphasize target information, and provide an alternative representation to satisfy visual learning styles (Hazen, 1985). Interspersing information presentation screens with interactive screens also provides variety (Keller & Suzuki, 1988). When information is varied with clear, familiar examples and performance activities and feedback, learners do not seem to tire of the activity as quickly (Dick & Carey, 1985).

Variety may also describe a number of attention-focusing techniques that are relatively easy to activate in computer-mediated instruction. These include

- *Flashing* (or blinking). This alerts the learner to important information or that some action is required.
- *Borders.* Borders can be used to set apart important information and draw the learner's eye to that information. They must be kept separate from the information they contain (Jones, 1988).
- *Colors.* They not only add aesthetic appeal but also may be used to facilitate readability or to indicate functionality. Color may also facilitate subtle discriminations within complex displays (Shneiderman, 1987). Colors should not be used in a way that contradicts common expectations (e.g., using red to indicate go forward and green to indicate exit) (Galitz, 1985).
- *Shapes.* They may be used to quickly indicate similar functional or navigational command keys or content areas (e.g., a text or graphics window). Both colors and shapes may be used to delineate areas on a screen, thereby helping the learner find needed information quickly and easily.
- *Highlighting.* This may be used to indicate important concepts or rules.

A number of other attention-focusing devices that draw the learner's attention to the most important aspects of the information have been identified (Carson & Curtis, 1991). These include

- type size or font and upper- and lowercase that may be used to emphasize or discriminate information;
- mnemonics and other memory devices that may be used to help organize information for long-term memory;
- humor, such as a well-placed cartoon (it must be noted that because humor is a subjective strategy—i.e., what one person finds humorous, another may not—it should be used judiciously);
- novel, surprising, or incongruous information that may attract learner interest and stimulate curiosity.

With all of these attention-focusing devices available to provide variety and enrich information, the designer may be tempted to infuse as many different strategies into the instruction as possible. However, although too few strategies may result in learning boredom, too many strategies may cause learning anxiety. The optimal number of design strategies is dependent on all of the issues discussed and, therefore, must be customized to the specified learning requirements. It is likely, however, that a design that specifies a menu with 20 flashing items, all in different colors and type fonts, will cause learning anxiety. Selection of attention strategies for variety must be purposeful, without sacrificing stability and structure. Designers should avoid dysfunctional attention-getting effects as they can be distracting and annoying (Keller & Suzuki, 1988). The use of too many attention strategies has been likened to driving down "The Strip" in Las Vegas—for many an assaulting rather than pleasing experience (Jones, 1988).

Furthermore, learners must have their attention refreshed throughout the instruction (Marchionini, 1991). That is, the strategies suggested above may be used to gain the learners' attention, but others must be implemented in order to sustain their attention thereby stimulating a deeper level of curiosity and higher level of interest throughout the instruction (Curtis & Carson, 1991).

An excellent method for sustaining attention is the inclusion of activities that require learner participation in the learning experience known as "interactivity"—a particularly relevant strategy for computer-mediated instruction. Interactivity maintains interest and involvement in the learning process. It may be accomplished through use of navigational and functional commands or keys in the interface and strategies such as practice items or embedded questions.

Two useful types of embedded questioning are "overt" and "subtle" questions. Overt questions typically require a verbal response, either by the learner typing it or selecting among a choice of responses. Subtle questioning does not necessarily require an immediate, physical response from the learner but is intended to promote active thinking by posing a problem that the learner must mentally ponder, generating alternative solutions as he proceeds through the program.

A third strategy for maintaining attention relates to making complex or abstract concepts more concrete. This may be accomplished by using examples of the concept, personal anecdotes, analogies, or visual representations.

Relevance

The second ARCS principle is concerned with helping the learner to understand the relevance of the learning task (Keller, 1987). Anyone who has worked with teenage children has probably heard occasional comments related to subjects such as algebra or earth science, "Why do I have to learn this? I'm never going to use it!" The importance of the learning task must be clearly articulated whenever it is not obvious to the learner.

One relevance strategy is providing familiarity—when learning about or doing something new is similar to something the learner already knows or does. This may be accomplished through the use of recognizable examples or anecdotes from the learner's realm of experience or by relating content to learners' prior experience or maintaining individual progress records within the program and referring to these at various points as the learner proceeds through the computer-mediated instruction (Keller & Suzuki, 1988).

Another method of providing familiarity is through the use of powerful metaphors or analogies to explain complex content making it easier to relate new ideas to those with which the learner is familiar (Curtis & Reigeluth, 1984). In a recent project to design multimedia case studies for learners enrolled in an international executive education program, the metaphor of a journey was used, and specific navigational tools strengthened the metaphor. For example, the menu was a "map," screens were organized into "regions," and individual screens had specific "locations" (Curtis & Gluck, 1992).

A second strategy for providing relevance is informing the learner of the purpose of the learning task at the very beginning of the instruction and reinforcing its usefulness throughout the instruction— that is, stating what the learner will know or be able to do after completing the instruction and linking achievement of the task to both learning goals and real-world applications. Game and simulation formats are useful for making somewhat obtuse subject matter seem more relevant.

Another relevance strategy is allowing learners to make choices that meet their individual needs and interests such as menus and submenus, varying amounts and sequences of accessible information, flexible entry and exit options, branching, on-screen notetaking capability, printing capability, "sound off" options, and full-screen or zooming capability. Options that include competitive or collaborative teamwork activities also allow further opportunities for meeting learner needs.

Confidence

The third ARCS principle considers ways to build learners' confidence levels (Keller, 1987). Instructional strategies that provide enough learning support for learners to succeed will help to build learning confidence, competence, self-esteem, the desire to persist at a learning task, and the motivation to continue learning.

Most learners tend to seek out challenging learning tasks as long as they believe they are attainable (McClelland, 1965). Most learners sincerely want to learn, to become competent at the learning task (White, 1959). Learning activities that seem either too easy or too difficult tend to be avoided because they are not perceived as linked to one's effort. When a task is perceived as too difficult to learners, it is unlikely that they will persist because the cost of success is seen as too high. Conversely, when a task is perceived as too easy to learners, it is unlikely that they will persist because it is seen as not worth the effort.

Specifying prerequisite skills, attitudes, and knowledge and clearly presenting the objectives and overall structure of the program at the beginning of the learning session allow learners to know whether they are adequately prepared to successfully complete the task (Keller & Suzuki, 1986). Providing feedback that links successful achievement with personal effort helps prevent perceptions that the results were due to luck or that the task was easy (Weiner, 1980). Novice computer users require more "user-friendly" programs and guidance than more expert users (Keller & Suzuki, 1988).

Confidence-building strategies provide both access to an appropriate level of difficulty and, when needed, to instructional aides such as pretesting and placement, accessible online help screens, and control over type and number of examples and practice items. In addition, orienting navigational headings and other cues that let learners know where they are, where they have been, and where they are going, as well as how long it will take, are desirable (Shneiderman, 1987).

To aid in learning, Carson and Curtis (1991) suggest the use of alternative, redundant representations of textual information (e.g., graphic overviews, diagrams, flowcharts), the use of divergent examples that proceed from simple to complex, matched nonexamples that are similar to the example and presented simultaneously to illustrate common errors, and embedded questions.

Although embedding overt questions within instruction offers a method for monitoring learning progress, in classroom settings instructors typically allow their students very little time to respond to those questions (usually no more than one second). Research indicates that providing slightly more time (3-5 seconds) results in a greatly increased likelihood of student responses (Rowe, 1986). Yet instructors seem to feel uncomfortable with silence and often blurt out an answer to avoid it. Although the response may be in the instructor's short-term memory (on the "memory surface") because the instructor has been thinking about it, it is likely to be in the learner's long-term memory, thereby requiring additional time for the learner to retrieve the information. Computer-mediated instruction is especially "patient" in providing the appropriate amount of wait-time, based on the learner's required or preferred pace, which permits the learner to retrieve relevant information from long-term memory, organize that information, and respond to the question posed—greatly increasing the opportunity for a successful response.

Some additional useful strategies that help to build learning confidence are

- graphic overviews that provide the learner with a context for organizing information;
- chunking textual information into short, meaningful, and manageable segments (Keller & Suzuki, 1988) according to the age level of learners, complexity of material, type of learning taking place, flexibility of the activity, and learning time requirements (Dick & Carey, 1985);
- scheduled synthesizers that relate ideas within or across lessons and integrate new material with old and summaries that follow presentation of significant chunks of information throughout the instruction, reviewing what has been learned (Reigeluth & Stein, 1983);
- divergent examples and content that range from easy to difficult, known to unknown, and simple to complex;
- learning cues or prompts that can "jog" the learner's memory (Cohen, 1983);
- menus so that learners do not have to recall or type terms or phrases in order to access needed information; and
- more explanation or guidance for those with little or no previous knowledge of the topic and a fast track for those who wish to move quickly through the instruction.

Galitz (1985) recommends a number of confidence-building strategies including recovery options for retracting or undoing an action, commands that use familiar, obvious, or common commands, function keys for frequent actions (e.g., page forward), and labels that provide information that clearly describes a function key's purpose. Providing supplementary print materials such as quick reference cards, manuals, job aids, and keyboard templates allow learners to choose alternative formats that best match their learning styles and preferences (Cohen, 1983).

Consistency, another confidence-building strategy, may be implemented by setting consistent standards for achievement that are fully and adequately described to the learner at the beginning of the instruction and reinforced by the way the information is presented and learning is evaluated. For example, instruction that requires the learner to recall or recognize information would be presented and evaluated differently than instruction that requires the learner to apply newly learned information to a new situation (Carson & Curtis, 1991).

Consistency may also be provided through logical organization of content and use of color, shapes, terms, and key functions, which aid in screen location. Consistent screen designs that have an orderly, well-spaced, clutter-free, and clean appearance, and transparent functions; that use plain, simple English, large enough fonts to read easily, and clear labeling; and that cohesively group relevant elements on a screen help to cue appropriate cognitive behavior (Schaefermeyer, 1990; Hannafin & Hooper, 1989; Hooper & Hannafin, 1988; Jones, 1988; Galitz, 1985). An instructional interface that provides consistent selection methods, window layout, and positioning of important text and buttons is also desirable. Consistent location, structure, and terminology should be preserved, with only occasional variations (Shneiderman, 1987; Keller & Suzuki, 1988).

Another strategy for building confidence is feedback. Duffield (1991) defines the three basic steps in human-computer interactions as (a) the computer receives a response, (b) the computer processes the response, and (c) the computer provides feedback to the learner. Feedback can also be used as guidance when the learner uses inaccurate or inappropriate strategies, immediately following response to a question or completion of a practice item.

Reinforcing feedback is useful to encourage and support learning as long as it is used sparingly and is always linked to effort. The most effective type of feedback is corrective feedback that presents a message immediately after the learner has made an error. Corrective feedback not only provides the learner with a simple, concise, and nonthreatening error response and directs the learner to the error, but also includes the steps involved in the correct solution (Wager, Wager, & Duffield, 1989; Cohen, 1983; Tosti, 1978). In this way, the feedback becomes part of the learning experience.

Satisfaction

The final ARCS principle promotes learning satisfaction (Keller, 1987). One method for doing so is to show or explain the consequences of successfully achieving the learning task; for example, pointing out that the learner can now do something she was unable to do previously, understand something new and difficult, or use something in a new way.

Extrinsic rewards used in computer-mediated instruction such as motivational feedback linked to effort may take the form of animated sequences, sound effects, or verbal praise. These are useful as long as learners have control over receiving feedback and opting out of it (Keller & Suzuki, 1988). Although some tasks require extrinsic rewards to motivate learners, the ultimate goal of instruction is to develop an intrinsic motivation to learn.

Another way to link learning to its consequences is by providing opportunities for learners to use their newly learned knowledge or skills in real or simulated, meaningful applications (Keller & Suzuki, 1988). Opportunities to immediately apply what is learned to a real problem such as a class assignment or job responsibility promote learning satisfaction. As new instructional technologies such as multimedia and virtual reality develop, learners will be exposed to exciting new ways of simulating life experiences that are either too difficult, too expensive, or too dangerous to experience in reality.

Another strategy for promoting learning satisfaction is by providing an environment of "learner control" in which the learner perceives a sense of learning empowerment over the learning experience. Computer-mediated instruction lends itself extremely well to developing this sense of learner empowerment by allowing, to a greater or lesser degree, control over the pace of the presentation, the sequence of content, and options such as returning to a desired screen or module, choosing when and where to enter and exit the program, reentering where the learner left off, selecting additional examples or practice items, saving completed work, printing completed work, or deciding which information to engage and which to ignore or bypass. However, the amount of learner control provided must be carefully determined based on the various design issues presented in this paper. Research indicates that learner control does not assure greater learning (Steinberg, 1989) and may, in fact, result in an unintentional lack of access to critical information. This is an important consideration when making decisions regarding learner control.

A final strategy for promoting learning satisfaction is through equity. Equity assures that the goals and evaluation criteria for learning set and stated at the beginning of the instruction are the same at completion of the instruction, that the instruction does what it was purported to do, and that the objectives, content, and test items are consistent so that learning success is attributable to the effort the learner has put into the learning activity (Curtis & Carson, 1991).

CONCLUSION

This paper has outlined several learning inputs to consider in the design of effective computer-mediated instruction. Issues to consider are learner characteristics, quality of information, and task characteristics. The ARCS Model, in consideration of these issues, proposes four design principles and a variety of related strategies for the creation of effective, efficient, and appealing computer-mediated instruction. The resulting outcomes are improved learning performance and increased motivation to learn.

REFERENCES

Bunderson, C. V. (1981). Courseware. In H. F. O'Neil, Jr. (Ed.), *Computer-based instruction: A state-of-the-art assessment* (pp. 91-125). New York: Academic Press.

Carson, C. H., & Curtis, R. V. (1991). Applying instructional design theory to bibliographic instruction: Micro theory. *Research Strategies, 9*(2), 60-76.

Cohen, V. B. (1983). Criteria for the evaluation of microcomputer courseware. *Educational Technology, 23*(1), 9-14.

Curtis, R. V., & Carson, C. H. (1991). The application of motivational design to bibliographic instruction. *Research Strategies, 9*(3), 130-138.

Curtis, R. V., & Gluck, M. (1992, March). *Multimedia case studies.* Paper presented at Focus on Instruction: Multimedia Conference. Syracuse, NY: Syracuse University.

Curtis, R. V., & Reigeluth, C. M. (1984). The use of analogies in written text. *Instructional Science, 13*(2), 99-117.

Dick, W., & Carey, L. (1985). *The systematic design of instruction* (2nd ed.). Glenview, IL: Scott, Foresman.

Duffield, J. A. (1991). Designing computer software for problem-solving instruction. *Educational Technology Research and Development, 39*(1), 50-62.

Galitz, W. O. (1985). *Handbook of screen format design.* Wellesley Hills, MA: QED Information Sciences.

Hannafin, M. J., & Hooper, S. (1989). An integrated framework for CBI screen design and layout. *Computers in Human Behavior, 5*(3), 155-165.

Hazen, M. (1985). Instructional software design principles. *Educational Technology, 25*(11), 18-23.

Hooper, S., & Hannafin, M. J. (1988). Learning the ROPES of instructional design: Guidelines for emerging interactive technologies. *Educational Technology, 28*(7), 14-18.

Jones, M. K. (1988). *Human-computer interaction: A design guide.* Englewood Cliffs, NJ: Educational Technology Publications.

Keller, J. M. (1983). Motivational design of instruction. In C. M. Reigeluth (Ed.), *Instructional-design theories and models: An overview of their current status* (pp. 383-434). Hillsdale, NJ: Lawrence Erlbaum Associates.

Keller, J. M. (1987). Development and use of the ARCS model of motivational design. *Journal of Instructional Development, 10*(3), 2-10.

Keller, J. M., & Suzuki, K. (1988). Use of the ARCS motivation model in courseware design. In D. H. Jonassen (Ed.), *Instructional designs for microcomputer courseware* (pp. 401-434). Hillsdale, NJ: Lawrence Erlbaum Associates.

Marchionini, G. (1991). Psychological dimensions of user-computer interfaces. *ERIC Digest.* (ERIC Document Reproduction Service No. ED 337 203)

McClelland, D. C. (1965). Toward a theory of motive acquisition. *American Psychologist, 20*(5), 321-333.

Reigeluth, C. M., & Stein, F. (1983). The elaboration theory of instruction. In C. M. Reigeluth (Ed.), *Instructional-design theories and models: An overview of their current status* (pp. 335-381). Hillsdale, NJ: Lawrence Erlbaum Associates.

Rowe, M. B. (1986). Wait time: Slowing down may be a way of speeding up. *Journal of Teacher Education, 37*(1), 43-50.

Schaefermeyer, S. (1990). Standards for instructional computing software design and development. *Educational Technology, 30*(6), 9-15.

Shneiderman, B. (1987). *Designing the user interface: Strategies for effective human-computer interaction.* Reading, MA: Addison-Wesley.

Steinberg, E. R. (1989). Cognition and learner control: A literature review, 1977-1988. *Journal of Computer-Based Instruction, 16*(4), 117-121.

Taylor, R. S. (1986). *Value-added processes in information systems.* Norwood, NJ: Ablex.

Tosti, D. T. (1978). Formative feedback. *NSPI Journal, 17*(8), 19-21.

Wager, W.; Wager, S.; & Duffield, J. (1989). *Computers in teaching: A compleat training manual for teachers to use in their classrooms.* Cambridge, MA: Brookline Books.

Weiner, B. (1980). *Human motivation.* New York: Holt, Rinehart, and Winston.

White, R. W. (1959). Motivation reconsidered: The concept of competence. *Psychological Review, 66*(5), 297-333.

Winn, W. (1990). Some implications of cognitive theory for instructional design. *Instructional Science, 19*(1), 53-69.

JOE C. RADER

Head, University Archives
University of Tennessee Libraries
Knoxville, Tennessee,

The Development of Computer-Based Training in a Systematic Staff Training Program

ABSTRACT

In 1990, the Libraries of the University of Tennessee, Knoxville, successfully developed a seven-unit program of computer-based training (CBT) for library staff under a Department of Education grant. The program's development and its implementation mark a first in libraries for systematic CBT for staff. Named *New Horizons in Library Training,* the program has been distributed widely to other libraries. Although expensive, this pioneering work has promise for further development and refinement as a staff training tool and for joint utility with computer-based programs of user instruction.

BACKGROUND

Since 1990, a program of computer-based training (CBT) for library staff, developed using HyperCard at the University of Tennessee, Knoxville (UTK), has received wide publicity in the library press and has been acquired by more than 75 institutions that are known. Others who are not known may have downloaded the files via File Transfer Protocol (FTP) over the Internet since the entire program has been available to the world on the UTK Libraries' VAX (address: utklib.utk.edu or 128.169.202.177). To date, 211 people have made direct inquiries about the program by electronic mail, phone, or other means to the CBT project directors, Pauline S. Bayne and Joe C. Rader. It is named *New Horizons in Library Training: Computer-Based Training for Library Staff,* and the following is a discussion of the program, the process of its development, its reception and implementation, and some conclusions about the experience.

Since HyperCard became available to the public in 1987, librarians of all degrees and stations have been exploring its use in the construction of interactive, computer-based training for library users. The result has been many programs with widely divergent degrees of sophistication, thoroughness, and implementation success. Some have been one-librarian attempts to create something helpful for users of the reference room. Others have been team efforts with significant institutional support that were designed to be implemented in a programmatic way. Project F.O.R.E. (or Focus on Research and Evaluation) from Utah State University is a good example of this effort (Piette & Smith, 1990). And there is the multilibrary joint effort called HyperCard Library Instruction Project (HLIP) (Talan, 1992); that product is to be available in the fall of 1992. All these projects have the common goal of using technology to solve a library challenge of human interaction that is both labor intensive, from an administrative perspective, and highly repetitive, from the individual staff member's perspective. Computer software packages like HyperCard (and there are several available now) have placed into librarians' hands the capability of creating self-paced, interactive CBT without requiring the expensive services of programmers, who must write reams of code to create even simple forms of interactive CBT as had been the case in the past.

THE TENNESSEE CBT PROJECT

In general terms, the project at UTK had as a primary goal the application of technology to help solve a library challenge: systematic training of library staff. Despite the widespread enthusiasm for HyperCard to create library instruction for users, the UTK developers found no evidence in the literature of the use of CBT in libraries for staff training (other than a few reports of using some application-specific programs to teach certain computer skills like DOS or a particular software like WordPerfect). Yet, among librarians and in the literature, one encounters much discussion of the training needs and skill requirements for all levels of library employees.

In reality, the research library of today presents a large, highly complex environment in which the information needs of users are met increasingly through technology-mediated processes. The people who work in this environment must be trained and retrained constantly, but this is rarely done systematically—or, if it is, it is not reported.

Often the training of the new employee is left totally to the supervisor in the employee's department with little if any coordination from unit to unit—except perhaps for a general welcome and orientation to the institution given to groups of new employees. Where training does occur, it is collectively expensive in staff time although staff may be largely unaware of its cost librarywide. A Carnegie Foundation report has suggested that industrial corporations spend $40 billion per year in the training of employees. No one knows what libraries spend.

Into this environment stepped the team of librarians at UTK to see if they could develop a partial remedy to this management problem. They proposed CBT with these characteristics:

- the program would be accepted by staff and administration;
- the program would ensure instruction for all library employees (student, part-time, full-time) in fundamental, basic library operations;
- the materials would be machine-based (no need for human intervention after an introduction);
- the machines would track trainees' progress;
- the materials would be transferable with little effort from institution to institution.

It was an ambitious proposal and required support beyond that which a single institution could readily afford. Backing came from the Department of Education in a $67,000 grant and, later, from Apple Computer, Inc., in training, encouragement, and additional equipment. The project also required much support from the University of Tennessee Libraries as well since this major project drew people away from their normal positions to work on various aspects of the project, officially and unofficially, for 15 months. The official "Final Performance Report" to the Department of Education, available as an ERIC document, contains details of the activities of the project as well as appendices of forms, surveys, and other documents used (Bayne & Rader, 1991).

One of the first matters to be decided was who was to be responsible for developing the instructional units. The grant specified a team of seven librarians plus two as directors. Team members were solicited by the codirectors on the basis of instructional experience or interest in HyperCard applications. To the extent possible, the members were chosen also to represent a cross section of the libraries. This prevented the burdening of any one area too heavily by having multiple staff members away from their normally assigned duties, and it gave a widespread base of interested parties who, it was hoped, would "infect" others in their areas with their enthusiasm for the project. Later, team members were paired with codirectors to create pairs of coauthors, each of which was responsible for a specific instructional unit. (For those doing arithmetic on the division of labor among the team, one topic had three persons assigned to it, and all the others had two each.)

Topic Selection

Another thing to be decided early on was which topics out of all those that might be addressed would be treated in the CBT. Two surveys, one local and one national, gave guidance. A quick and easy survey of library supervisors and department heads at the UTK Libraries gave the developers their initial guidance on subject matter to consider for inclusion in the program. A more extensive questionnaire was mailed to all directors or personnel officers of the 119 members of the Association of Research Libraries in late autumn of 1989. An interesting outcome was that high priority topics from the national survey were among those that had been ranked high in the local survey also. At the top were the following:

1. Service Attitudes and Behaviors
2. Orientation to the Academic Library
3. Access to Journal Literature
4. Integrated Online Systems for Libraries
5. Introduction to Reference Work
6. Resource Sharing
7. Acquiring and Processing Library Materials
8. Preservation of Library Materials
9. Introduction to Government Documents

The list was modified somewhat. Number 1 on service attitudes was omitted because no one could figure out how to develop an effective unit with the medium that was to be used. Orientation was to be included but with institution-specific information; it was thought that to be effective this unit would have to contain local, highly specific information. It was developed for two reasons: it would be used at UTK, but it also could serve as a model for other institutions. All other units were to be designed to present generic information so that they could be readily used in different libraries. Number 4 on the list, "Integrated Online Systems for Libraries," became "Computers in Libraries." Six new units—besides a revamped prototype unit introducing the Library of Congress classification system—were the limit called for in the grant; therefore, the cutoff dropped preservation and government documents for purposes of the project.

Besides gathering information on topics to be developed, the surveys also served to plant initial expectations locally—and nationally to some degree—for a CBT staff training product "one fine day." It was a stimulus to people in libraries to think about the possibility of such, at the very least.

Preliminary Decisions

At the outset, considerable analysis led to the decision to use HyperCard and the Macintosh platform. For one thing, there were not many options in terms of easily accessible hypertext software at the time, and HyperCard was a relatively simple and highly intuitive tool in the hands of a Macintosh user of only moderate expertise. A second consideration was the cost of HyperCard in 1989: free and bundled with new Macintoshes or $49 if purchased otherwise. And, finally, the Macintosh, plain and simple, was thought to be the most widespread kind of computer found in libraries after the IBM and clone PCs.

While waiting for equipment and software, the CBT development team had much to do. The planning of the content of each unit began. Each pair of coauthors had to determine exactly what information was to be conveyed, and, even more difficult, what was the most economical way to convey that information. To get a group of logocentric people to use as few words as possible in instruction without sacrificing important information was a formidable task. This was necessary, however, for CBT to work effectively; it is not a mechanism that allows wordy presentation if it is to hold the trainee's interest.

Considerable training was necessary for each team member to be brought up to speed in the use of HyperCard for development and in other areas. A two-day intensive HyperCard tutorial taught by Apple representatives brought the entire team up to the level of doing simple programming using HyperTalk. A seminar on basic graphic design and another on the fundamentals of instructional design introduced the team members to concepts and areas for further individual reading and exploration. Resource books on HyperCard were made available, and such standard texts as Gagné, Briggs, and Wager's (1988) *Principles of Instructional Design* and Dick and Carey's (1985) *The Systematic Design of Instruction* were recommended for further self-education.

Development Activities

When their Macintoshes were available, team members began the design of "storyboard" stacks that were forerunners of the actual stacks that would be developed. They created "draft" narration screen-by-screen. Then reinforcing or presentation ideas for each segment of text were noted on the screen on which the text was recorded: graphics, sound resources, special effects, animation, or other production ideas.

In this way, an outline of content was being created, and the outline could mimic the actual features of the ultimate presentation using, for instance, such devices as loops or other hypertextual connections. This early conceptualization of the instruction to be presented and the metaphors and devices of presentation to be used was an important step on the road to production.

Although team members were topically assigned, the team met as a group at least once each month for the duration of the project to review the work done by the pairs of coauthors and to decide matters of common concern such as the design of screen templates, fonts to be used, and other questions that affected the consistency of all units of the series. Team members circulated for comment drafts of texts and other plans—in print and in HyperCard formats—so that reciprocal reviewing could take place as work was being done. This meant that any creation went through a kind of "pretest" since it was reviewed by seven other team members before the first review by anyone not a part of the team.

Evaluation Techniques

Evaluation of the CBT products created was extensive and based on the Dick and Carey (1985) model for the design of instruction. First, two or three selected library employees viewed a unit in the presence of one of the developers of the unit. Discussion between the reviewer and the developer gave important feedback to the author, who was able also to observe the interaction of reviewer and material. Authors made many notes for consideration when revising the instruction. Next what was termed an "expert review" occurred. All nine team members reviewed each unit completely and made specific comments and notes in a screen-by-screen fashion. The coauthor teams then revised their units based on the information gathered from these evaluation processes.

A second phase of evaluation occurred when 13 library employees who had not seen the materials reviewed the material. Each examined all units and made comments on each unit on prepared forms. Again coauthors made revisions in either instructional content or presentation. Among the changes made were adjustments to drop the average length of time to go through a unit from a range of 30 to 50 minutes to 15 to 45 minutes. If trainees are truly learning from the concentrated instruction presented in CBT, 45 minutes is a long and tiring time for one sitting.

Late in the year in 1990, the CBT program was ready for one last "field test." In this phase, library supervisors and new employees went through the instruction under circumstances that anticipated those in effect during full future implementation. A total of 49 persons participated in this evaluation.

After final adjustments and minor changes, the CBT program was ready for implementation at the UTK Libraries. The main library had a training room equipped with six Macintoshes, and each branch library had a Macintosh dedicated to training purposes. Since January 1, 1991, *New Horizons in Library Training* has been a part of the training that all new employees receive. For the first time, perhaps in the history of the institution, there is a program that ensures that all employees receive the same basic core of instruction about the libraries, their roles, and major functions.

Structure of Instruction

Some specific information about the structure of the CBT instruction might be helpful in understanding both the scope of the program as it was initiated and how it worked for trainees. The developers had started with the premise that each trainee would be issued his or her personal "trainee diskette" that would both control progress through the program according to a predetermined route and would be the vehicle by which data on the trainee's progress were recorded. This information would be used by supervisors to follow a trainee's progress through the program and would be used for analysis and evaluation of the program itself. Trainees were to pick up their diskettes before they started a unit and turn them in again when finished.

Analysis of this procedure soon made it evident that another system would have to be devised. Keeping up with scores of trainees and their diskettes would have taken enormous effort. Moreover, the transferring of files from the individual trainee diskettes to administrative machines, combining and manipulating the data, and then getting appropriate information to supervisors in departments throughout the libraries would have been an even larger personnel administration burden.

At this point, a sound educational principle that had guided the planning of instruction in the individual units also provided the inspiration for designing trainee access to the program: namely, "Give the learner as much choice as possible while learning a set of materials." Or put another way, "People have a better attitude toward learning and, therefore, learn more when they can feel that they are in control." The access solution was simply to provide a menu that offered buttons for all topical units. Trainees would choose options and have the responsibility for proceeding through the program as they and their supervisors determined what was best for them in their particular situations. Central administrative control, generally resented by employees, was diminished by shifting the responsibility to the individual trainee and his or her supervisors.

This decision meant that another means of data tracking, gathering, and consolidation was necessary, however. Scripting in the individual HyperCard stacks caused certain data to be captured unobtrusively as a trainee went through the program. At the start of a unit, the trainee must enter his or her name and the department of employment; after indicating whether a student employee or full-time employee, the trainee is not asked for further input of information. But the program automatically records information on the trainee's performance, for instance:

- the date,
- the unit being worked on,
- the time work began,
- times when the trainee passes certain markers in the unit,
- the identifying numbers of questions missed and a score,
- any comments the trainee wanted to volunteer when prompted at the conclusion of the unit,
- the time the unit was completed.

The computer writes this information to a text file each time the trainee uses a "quit" button to exit from the CBT program. Not using a trainee diskette meant that these data text files would have to remain on the hard disks of the machines the trainees used until there was some human intervention to remove them. At UTK, the Library Personnel Office assumed the responsibility for gathering and massaging the data. Each Friday, the text file from each training Macintosh is copied to a diskette and removed from the hard disk, and a "fresh" empty text file is put on the hard disk to replace the one just removed. These gathered files are consolidated in the personnel office, extraneous data (from "false starts" and similar errors) edited out, and reports generated that are sent to the trainees' supervisors for whatever action might be appropriate. Supervisors have lists of review and test questions, for example, so that they can analyze those missed by their trainees and pursue correction, remediation, or further training. If a book shelver appears still not to understand the Library of Congress classification system after going through the CBT module on that topic, the shelver's supervisor had best take further action either to train the employee fully or see that he or she is transferred to another position.

The CBT project directors at UTK did the preliminary analysis of what data were desired and the programming to capture the pertinent data and put that data into reports needed for administrative purposes. These programming requirements had to be integrated with the menu access decision already made. The directors also had responsibility for other "front-end" items such as a sequence of "help" screens available on demand throughout the program.

Experience has shown that the menu approach to providing trainee access to the CBT program and the consequences of its administration at UTK have yielded a serendipitous benefit. The cost, formatting, control, and manipulation of the many diskettes that would have been necessary with a trainee diskette approach are not necessary. Although it takes time to gather data and generate the weekly reports, most of that work would have been necessary anyway, and it is far less time-consuming to download data from nine machines than it would have been to download data from—potentially—scores of trainee diskettes each week. That both trainee and supervisor, with a sense of control in their access to and use of CBT, have more of a feeling of "ownership" is certainly a boon, though *New Horizons in Library Training* is, in fact, an activity mandated by central administration.

Supervisors were introduced to the CBT program early. Then, knowing the contents of the program, they determined the sequence of units for trainees from their individual departments to follow and the desired pacing. This information is the basis of a departmental, paper checklist that is created by the personnel office and maintained by that office and the trainee or supervisor. Having supervisors who are responsible for the rest of a new employee's training also responsible for the CBT portion seemed, in the end, eminently sensible and appropriate to the developers of the program and the library administration at UTK.

If for some reason a trainee does not pursue CBT in the time recommended on his or her checklist, the personnel office sends a reminder to the department head about the lack of anticipated progression through the program. At the conclusion of the CBT, a trainee's supervisor sends the checklist to the personnel office for record-keeping purposes, and the Dean of Libraries sends the trainee a letter of congratulations for having successfully completed *New Horizons in Library Training,* an important part of library employees' training and orientation.

Although the emphasis here is on the development of machine-based training and learning, a few comments on human relations issues might serve to illustrate the relative success of the CBT program at UTK. The developers are working on a more detailed piece on this topic that will be published later if all goes well. The assumption was that for a new and "foreign" training program to work successfully in a large organization, it is not enough for an administration to mandate its use; it might, in that case, very well be viewed as merely some administrative requirement to be gotten around or negated as much as possible. Nor is it enough for the program to be innovative and attractive. Rather, to be successful, the program must be understood by the people who are to use it and be viewed by them as something that will help them to do their jobs more successfully, easily, or confidently. In business jargon, a program must be "sold" to the actual users.

In the prolonged planning, development, and implementation of CBT at UTK, both the developers and the library administration paid considerable attention to the notion of "buy in" by rank-and-file employees and supervisors. The following succinct list of the major techniques and activities to promote "buy in" illustrates that effort.

1. Even before actual development began, a questionnaire asked selected staff and supervisors to rank topics thought to be suitable and *desired* for development in a CBT program. They understood that their input would help to shape the content of the proposed program.
2. The project directors negotiated with colleagues about becoming team members on (among other considerations and characteristics) the basis of distributed representation throughout the libraries. This became a "grapevine" means of generating continuing curiosity about and interest in the project.
3. As units reached a semblance of their intended shape and content, the development team used every opportunity to stage demonstrations of the project to different representative groups: administrators group, department heads council, staff meetings, etc.
4. At the developers' request, staff members of various levels and in different combinations were asked to evaluate units as they reached some degree of completion. Evaluative comments were treated with total seriousness, and the participating staff members recognized that they were contributing to the project. In due course, such participants received letters of thanks for their participation.
5. Supervisors, a key group to win over in any library enterprise, were apprised of plans and progress throughout the project and were introduced to the various units of instruction early in the final stages of development. Their familiarity with the project was essential for any fruitful discussion of implementation planning and acceptance.
6. As both veteran staff and new trainees experienced the program and then returned to their departments, they became de facto emissaries of the CBT program. It was helpful that the vast majority had had a very positive reaction, according to their comments and responses gathered by machine and paper mechanisms.
7. Finally, the fact that the project enjoyed complete administrative support from the highest levels from inception of the idea through implementation must be acknowledged. Announcements in the *Dean's Newsletter* and individual memos to affected staff on various

topics throughout the development and implementation of *New Horizons in Library Training* served to promote internalization of a project that otherwise might have been viewed as something largely external or peripheral to the everyday life of the UTK Libraries. It may have also been significant that even university administrators expressed respect and congratulations for the project.

Obviously other libraries who choose to implement the UTK-developed CBT program could not imitate completely such techniques and devices for consensus-building for acceptance, but the UTK techniques should provide some advice in ways to achieve institutionwide acceptance of programs that otherwise might meet with resistance. The "top-down" introduction of a new way to train staff is a particularly sensitive issue since any such program automatically sets up a situation in which the methods that have been used to train staff are contrasted with the new way, and individual staff egos, consequently, are sure to be touched.

THE UNIVERSITY OF KENTUCKY REPLICATION

Despite apparent success and ready acceptance by the staff of the UTK Libraries, the original directors of the project and the UTK personnel librarian wanted an opportunity to introduce *New Horizons in Library Training* in a research library setting where the staff had not been "contaminated" by direct exposure to the program or by publicity about it either in a presentation or from bits and pieces of information gathered informally. The basic goal was to be able to pretest a group of trainees to determine whether what appeared to be learning, as inferred from data on UTK trainees, was indeed occurring because of the CBT.

Since the libraries of the University of Kentucky and the University of Tennessee were cooperating on some projects already, the respective deans approved another project. A team of librarians from both institutions were to adapt the HyperCard stacks created at UTK to fit Kentucky's local circumstances and introduce the CBT program there. In essence, in exchange for assistance in creating appropriate local information for Kentucky, the staff there would administer a paper pretest to trainees, gather data on them while they went through the CBT, and forward that information to the UTK team for analysis. Coincidentally, additional work had to be done before starting the Kentucky project because Claris had released a new version of HyperCard after the UTK project's development had ended, and Kentucky was running the latest version (2.0) on their machines where the program was to be mounted. All stacks had to be converted to the new version and checked for any flaws or discrepancies that resulted from the conversion.

The Kentucky study has not been concluded at the moment, but preliminary examination suggests comparable results in terms of trainee performance. There was apparently some significant difference, however, in general receptivity to the program. Trainee acceptance at Kentucky under the circumstances that obtained during the time of the data gathering was not so positive as that among trainees at UTK.

One readily identifiable problem was the availability of machines for Kentucky trainees to use. There the CBT program was mounted on machines in student computer laboratories, placing trainees in the situation of having to compete with students and others for use of the machines. There was clear resentment among some library trainees at the "waste" of their time waiting to get a machine on which to do some CBT assignment about which they were not too sure in the first place. That the activity was part of a study being conducted by the University of Tennessee rankled others. Publication of a formal study of the Kentucky findings is planned soon.

PRESENT AND FUTURE

Funding for UTK Libraries has not been good in the past two years. Consequently, morale has been low for everyone: jobs were eliminated, and services, acquisitions, and even operating hours were reduced to balance the libraries' budget. In this milieu, no one proposed further development of CBT units, although the developers had thought that, once the trail had been blazed, others would follow, quickly, with the creation of additional units either to enhance the general program or to supplement it with training units for departmental activities. Only in the spring of 1992 has this expectation shown signs of being realized, for development of both kinds of units is now proposed.

One person wants a departmental unit on advanced Library of Congress classification training designed for stack attendants. The head of the acquisitions department is developing CBT units to teach more routine tasks to student workers in her department. And the two directors of the original project have received encouragement from the Commission on Preservation and Access to prepare a unit on preservation issues. If developed, the unit would be added to the menu of the general program. Or it could be distributed as a stand-alone unit promoting preservation awareness. Reference librarians have begun studying sections of the CBT designed for staff with an eye toward modifying it for user training, either as computer-assisted instruction in group presentations or library self-instruction devices.

Some successful experimentation has occurred in the UTK Libraries in the conversion of the CBT HyperCard stacks to run on a DOS platform. Required to accomplish this are the software products Convert It and Toolbook and someone competent in both environments, besides a Macintosh with HyperCard and a DOS/OS machine with lots of memory. The process does not convert every aspect of the HyperCard product, and it does not convert without some programming intervention and other tuning and tweaking. It does work, however, although some things are lost such as some font varieties and sound resources; these can be supplied from other sources, just not converted directly from HyperCard. Because of this experimentation with converting stacks, current planning for the preservation unit calls for it to be made available in both formats, thus extending its applicability to many more sites than one version alone would.

There is additional study at UTK of the opportunities multimedia's inclusion offers in the realm of staff training. The product QuickTime has inspired thinking about the mix of real-time video segments in a general CBT presentation. The prospects are exciting for developers, but the cost of development rises with the addition of the multimedia dimension. And the widespread availability of machines capable of running the product in whatever form it might ultimately take is also an important question to be answered. All this must be weighed in the balance of cost-benefit analysis.

CONCLUSIONS

What conclusions can one draw, then, after this long narrative of design, development, and implementation of a systematic CBT program for library staff in an academic library?

In the design of CBT, the developers at UTK learned that some assistance from persons whose expertise was in the practical areas of art, instructional design, and programming would have been more efficient than training the team members responsible for content, to do all work in those areas. They also learned the vital importance of team effort. Not only was the opinion of many rather than few (or one) advantageous for the development team in their freewheeling sessions of brainstorming for ideas, metaphors, or appropriate graphic representations, but the idea proved beneficial to the development process throughout. This included extensive use made of reviewers of various degrees of experience, training, and positions within the libraries. The testing of instruction was found to be absolutely critical to success; even more so was this true for review and test questions. The developers found that it is, indeed, an area of expertise itself to fashion questions that truly test the information intended to be tested and to do so with clarity and without betraying bias.

Another challenge was for developers to understand the medium in which they were working, to understand how conveying information was different in HyperCard from what it was in print or orally. Among the following concerns the team developed, one can see the differentiating characteristics of this instructional medium.

Economy of expression became a foremost concern. A HyperCard presentation is not the place for wordy expression. Related to this is the necessity for including small amounts of text on a given screen— or at least having it appear to the trainee in small segments. Otherwise, a hypertext medium begins to look like a print medium that has been moved to a computer screen.

The quest for potent graphics became obsessive as the importance of the visual element in holding the trainee's attention was realized. And sometimes when the "perfect" graphic had been found, successfully scanned, and imported into HyperCard, it had to be excluded because of copyright considerations. (Or there was not time enough to obtain permission for use.)

Although time-consuming to construct, movement on the screen or outright animation became a powerful tool for punctuating text or graphic representation.

The design of instruction so that the trainee is in control was an important concept that was learned. Even when the learning of certain information is essential and, therefore, required by the instructional design, it should be presented with as much choice as to sequence as possible and with as many options as is reasonable. The use of alternate loops and other devices can assure coverage while allowing for a diversity of routes through the material. In short, involving the trainee, requiring some action on his or her part, is vital for successful interactive instruction.

Trainees found the review or testing after short intervals of instruction to be helpful and complained during evaluation when it was not present. They also preferred immediate feedback as to why their answers to questions were right or, more importantly, wrong; this in itself can be a powerful teaching and learning device.

To the surprise of developers, trainees liked sound resources even if they were overly simple or trite. Similarly, trainees appreciated the humorous or light-hearted style of presentation even though the fundamental instruction was serious.

The developers heard from reviewers and "field test" trainees or otherwise learned these points from actual development and evaluation experience, regardless of whether they had encountered them in their preparatory studies of instructional design or not.

The distribution of the CBT program at little or no cost as had been promised in the original proposal to the Department of Education yielded a surprise or two. Librarians from other institutions sometimes found that what was intended by author teams to be "generic" instruction about library procedures was biased by local practice at UTK. Corollaries to this are that actual details of library practice vary widely from institution to institution even when the libraries seem comparable, and these local customs and traditions are important to librarians when they train employees to work in their institutions. This raises certain questions: How important are these differences in the delivery of library and information services to the clienteles of institutions? Or might the community of libraries—or at least those similar in size and mission— move toward standardization of practice in the same way that many cataloging idiosyncrasies have been lessened over the years since the advent of shared cataloging? Such standardization might make training all staff easier (and perhaps using the libraries easier in the long run). Finding answers to these questions was beyond the scope of the CBT project at UTK, however, and would, no doubt, raise even further questions. (There is also the suspicion—not a clearly stated opinion yet—that there is little interest in truly generic instruction for training staff that is not modified to take into account variant local practices.)

Another conclusion the UTK developers reached is that CBT is an effective technique for staff training (and one that may bring a consistency to basic training for library staff that does not exist without CBT), but it is undeniably expensive to develop—if developed well. Furthermore, libraries collectively are not a big enough market apparently or are not rich enough, or the diversity of practice mentioned above is too great to warrant the development and marketing of staff training by private sector vendors. And the expense of development is often too great for one institution to bear the cost totally for the creation of an effective program. But two possible solutions to this dilemma are emerging. One is the development of materials that may be used commonly to educate the *users* of libraries about practices and to train library *employees*. Distributing the expense of development between user education and staff training would spread the cost burden. The other is the group-based project, in which several libraries pool their resources to create a CBT product useful to all member libraries for staff training. This would follow the HLIP model, mentioned at the beginning of this paper. Or, perhaps, a combination of these approaches might well put CBT development in the realm of the possible for interested libraries.

An indirect outcome that may occur in the activity of considering the development of a CBT program for staff is the focusing of attention on the cost of training staff in nonautomated ways. In fact, recognition of that cost might become a factor in a commitment to an efficient and effective program of staff training as a mechanism for improving quality and efficiency of service to users, the ultimate raison d'etre for libraries after all; that is, a systematic approach.

The CBT project at UTK and its implementation have generally been deemed a success, and the attention generated nationally—and even internationally—has been noteworthy. Clearly there is interest, and one presumes a need behind the interest, in this area of computer applications to library problems. But the project at UTK only broke the ground of a new library management territory. Full exploration is yet to take place; and as with any good research or project, it may have pointed a way to move, but it also raised as many questions as it answered in the process. Perhaps others now will join in pursuing them.

REFERENCES

Bayne, P. S., & Rader, J. C. (1991). *Computer-based training for library staff: A demonstration project using HyperCard. Final performance report.* Knoxville: University of Tennesse Libraries. (ERIC Document Reproduction Service No. ED 333 902)

Dick, W., & Carey, L. (1985). *The systematic design of instruction* (2nd ed.). Glenview, IL: Scott, Foresman.

Gagné, R. M.; Briggs, L. J.; & Wager, W. W. (1988). *Principles of instructional design* (3rd ed.). New York: Holt, Rinehart, and Winston.

Piette, M. I., & Smith, N. M., Jr. (1990). *Focus on research and evaluation: HyperCard library instruction.* Logan: Utah State University, Merrill Library.

Talan, H. (Project Director). (1992). HyperCard library instruction project. San Francisco, CA: San Francisco State University, Leonard Library.

RONNIE PETERS

Art Director
Dynamic Diagrams
Providence, Rhode Island

Designing for the Computer Screen

ABSTRACT

Designing for the computer screen poses new challenges for the designer. While some of the issues are new such as time, motion, and sound, other aspects such as the readability of typography, the separation and combination of image and type, and the general issues associated with projecting the three-dimensional world onto a two-dimensional surface are part of a complex design tradition. When designing for this new medium, the designer is faced with the problem of organizing a large amount of information in a small area and must establish the most orderly arrangement of information, determine the hierarchic scale of importance, arrange the easiest accessibility of information, and design the appearance accordingly.

THE COMPUTER SCREEN AS A DELIVERY PLATFORM

While we still get a great deal of information from looking at the printed page, more frequently the computer screen is the end delivery platform for information. Computer users are not just using the computer screen as the environment on which elements are composed and created in a preview mode for later production as a printed document. The computer screen is more often the reading surface on which the interplay of images, type, and sounds is projected and intended as their final reading and listening form. Hypertext or hypermedia software is one of the first kinds of software to exploit the computer screen as a presentation platform. Hypermedia refers to kinds of linked information and can be various media besides text. Many software systems include some hypermedia capabilities.

Display terminals are proliferating as information delivery platforms in many areas of our daily lives. This new reading surface poses its own set of unique issues and presents new challenges and opportunities for visual design. While some of the rules are similar, designing information for this picture surface is different from the printed page, sign, or billboard. The high resolution and frozen structure of the printed page are gone, and the coarse resolution of the screen, the projected rather than reflected light of the printed page, and the elements of time, motion, and the addition of sound are the qualities of the computer screen.

The medium of the computer screen and the qualities of that surface are new, but the issue of projecting a three-dimensional space onto a two-dimensional surface remains the same. Projection on a two-dimensional plane allows objects to be rendered that are impossible to build in three dimensions and are hard to conceive of without rendering (Figure 1).

What is perceived on the screen of the computer is combinations of pixels (Figure 2). One pixel represents a point; it is one-dimensional. Dragging a point forms a line. Dragging a line forms a plane, which is two-dimensional, and dragging a plane forms a volume, or the illusion of volume, which is three-dimensional.

RULES OF THE VISUAL WORLD

Designing information on and for the two-dimensional plane of the computer screen is a new field; however, the computer screen is a two-dimensional plane, and designing for that space is part of the graphic design tradition. Within this field, the designer is faced with using two basic strategies to project information onto the picture plane: representation and symbol.

Representation is a projection of the world as we literally see it. The understanding that we have of this image is based on the information we have stored in our memory. We identify elements in the image with the elements we remember. For example, we recognize the features of someone's face in a photograph and construct an image of the person we associate with the face in our mind.

Using symbol, the designer represents the world in the form of elements that resemble, imply, or otherwise suggest what we see. Symbol allows the designer to compress information into a small space and eliminate unnecessary detail (Figure 3). Five equally sized rings in a certain configuration become the symbol for the Olympic Games. Each

Projection on a two-dimensional plane allows objects to be rendered that are impossible to build in three dimensions and are hard to conceive of in the mind.

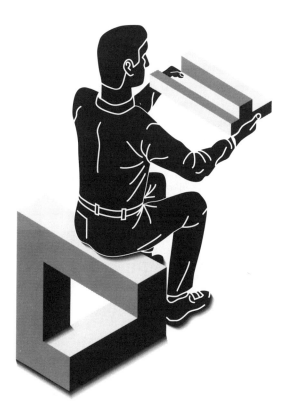

Figure 1. Two-dimensional projection

ring and its color represents one of the five continents. With each compression, the information that passes through our visual channel is reduced. We expand the information carried by the symbol in our mind, constructing its relationship to the world in our associative imagination.

Mixing symbol and representation (Figure 4) can be used by the designer to great effect. In this image of a Dutch treadmill crane by

RONNIE PETERS

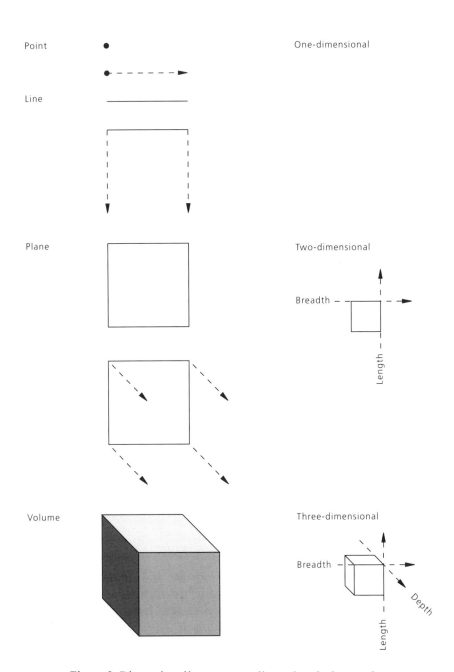

Figure 2. Dimensionality on a two-dimensional picture plane

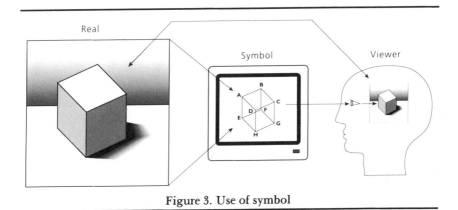

Figure 3. Use of symbol

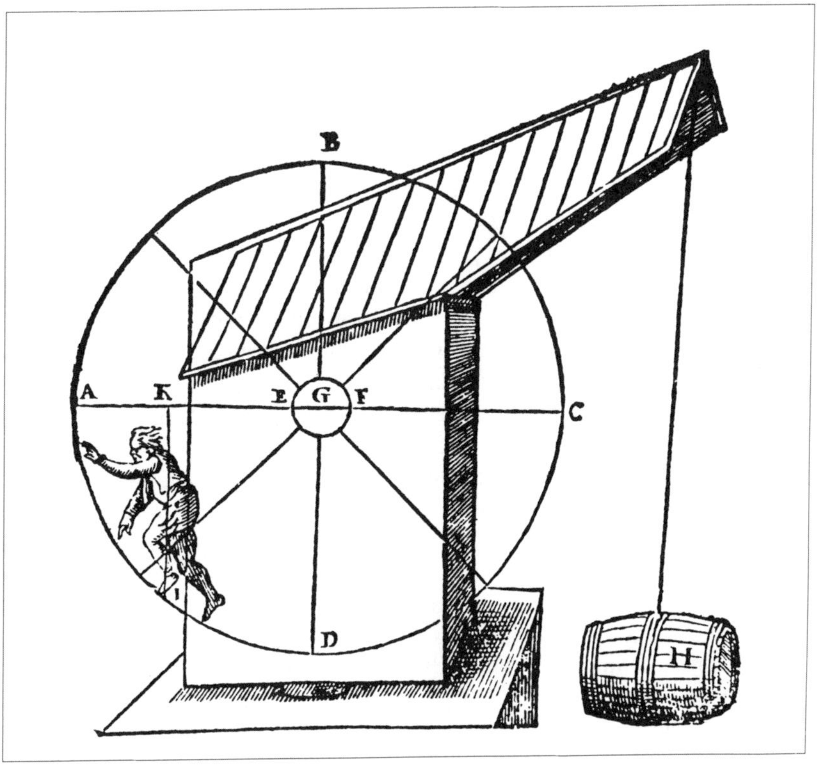

Figure 4. Mixing symbol and representation

Simon Stevin, the *representation* of the figure, the building, and the barrel is integrated with the *symbolic* rendering of the wheel mechanism, which when drawn in a representational manner would be hidden within the building.

LIMITED SPACE

The computer screen for ease of navigation and accessibility is the best place to store information, but it is also the computer's most limited resource. The amount of storage space required on the computer memory is rapidly becoming smaller, but the delivery platform, the computer screen, is increasing in both size and resolution at a much slower pace. The limited space of the computer screen and the coarseness of the resolution leave little room for embellishment and decoration.

To make simultaneous information available on the screen requires a clear and orderly structure. The reader has to be able to differentiate and retrieve in the easiest possible manner.

MULTIDIMENSIONALITY

The desire to simultaneously represent many aspects of an idea has been with us for centuries. Various projection methods have been developed that effectively allow the simultaneous display of views. This technique of simultaneously projecting views of three dimensions onto a two-dimensional surface can be used as a device by the designer of the interactive screen (Figure 5). When compared with the printed page, the resolution of the computer screen is very coarse. The density of detail possible on the printed page is many times greater than what is currently possible on most computer screens. The designer is faced with having to find alternative methods for projecting images and compressing information. These two examples demonstrate how visual techniques can be effectively used to condense information into a small area.

There are a number of projection techniques, each with its own advantages and drawbacks (Figure 6). Orthogonal or orthographic projection is when the various views of the object are projected parallel to the picture plane. The true measures are retained and can be measured.

Oblique projection methods include oblique, axonometric, and isometric projection. With oblique projection, the frontal plane is drawn in orthographic projection, and the top or sides are drawn at an angle of 30° or 45°. With an angle of 30°, the true measures of the sides are retained. If an angle of 45° is used, the measures of the sides are halved in order to retain the correct optical distortion.

An axonometric drawing shows the plane view in orthographic projection and the side elevations drawn at angles of 30° and 60° or

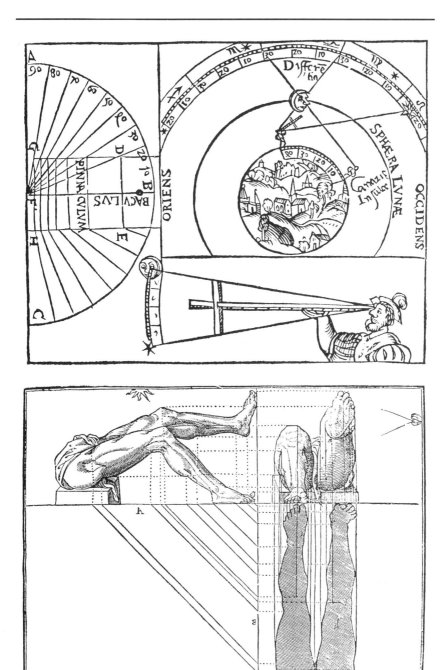

Figure 5. Simultaneous projection of views

both at angles of 45°. The horizontal measures retain their lengths, and the verticals are foreshortened.

Isometric projection shows the lateral angles drawn at identical angles, and the true measures are retained.

Perspective that implies deep space is bound by a horizon line and one or more vanishing points. The viewer of the perspective image is outside of the picture frame looking in, his eye being drawn to the vanishing point. At this point on the plane, all the distorted parallel lines within the image converge. This image is one point in time; there is no motion in the still perspective picture.

Flat projections preserve the parallel condition of lines. Flat projection methods often give the designer more freedom to express and explain, without being faithful to a horizon line or vanishing point. They are particularly useful when designing diagrams where elements of space and time must be projected and cannot be distorted or lost because of the rules of perspective. Multiple events or processes can be projected simultaneously and understood by the viewer. These techniques often allow the designer to describe space and form from a multitude of angles and positions without being hindered by the vanishing point or horizon of the perspective image.

Excellent examples of flat projection techniques are found in pre-Renaissance and Asian art (Figures 7 and 8). Flat projection allowed the artist to create enormous spaces and project figures and continuous narrative over space and time within one image. Often a sequence of events will take place across the picture plane, and the same figures appear more than once in the same image. British painter and photographer David Hockney (1988) describes the difference between the Asian and the Renaissance approach:

> The great difference between the Chinese scholar-artist and Renaissance scholar-artist is this: if the Chinese scholar-artist had a garden . . . he would want to walk in it, so he would make his path so that he'd have a longer walk. So he walks up the path of his garden and then goes and makes a picture of that garden, or the experience of walking in it. But the Renaissance scholar sits in a room and looks out of a window, and then makes his picture.
>
> He is fixed there with the window picture, and therefore he thinks of perspective. The Chinese wouldn't because their experience is moving, flowing, as time is flowing. And so they both start off with very different locations; one is seated and the other is not. (p. 37)

The arrangement of windows and the layout of the computer screen are similar to the manner in which the Chinese painting is rendered, a flat projection. The screen is a flat picture plane on which rectangular windows are projected. The contents of windows scroll up and down and left to right, as if continuous in one plane. Windows appear as though they are lying one on top of the other in plain view. The windows underneath do not proportionately decrease in size as they would if

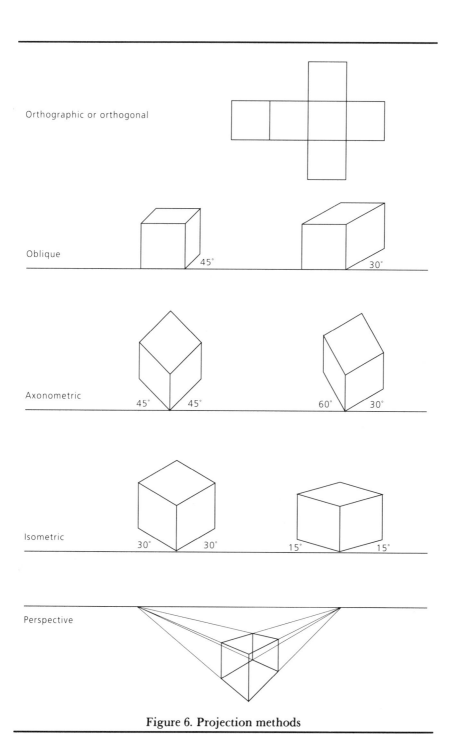

Figure 6. Projection methods

Figure 7. Example of flat projection in Asian art

the screen were rendered in a perspective projection. The effect of placing photographic images and perspective projections within the windows is like mixing the Renaissance perspective image with the flat Chinese projection.

DESIGN FOR THE COMPUTER SCREEN

Any notion that design for the computer screen is merely decorative is a misunderstanding. Good computer screen design does not decorate; it clarifies.

In designing for the computer screen, the designer is for the first time faced with the problem of organizing such a large amount of information in such a small area that there is the chance of creating complete visual chaos. For the best and most persuasive functioning of the computer, it is necessary to establish the most orderly arrangement of information, determine the hierarchic scale of importance, arrange the easiest accessibility of information, and design the appearance accordingly.

Figure 8. Example of flat projection in pre-Renaissance art

Rudolf Arnheim (1971) has described the importance of visual order:

> Order is a necessary condition for anything the human mind is to understand. Arrangements such as the layout of a city or building, a set of tools, a display of merchandise, the verbal expression of facts or ideas, or a painting or a piece of music are called orderly when an observer or listener can grasp their overall structure and the ramification of the structure in some detail. Order makes it possible to focus on what is alike and what is different, what belongs together and what is segregated. When nothing superfluous is included and nothing indispensable is left out, one can understand the interrelation of the whole to its parts, as well as the hierarchic scale of importance and power by which some structural features are dominant, others subordinate. (p. 1)

MULTIPLE WINDOWS

Maximizing the amount of information within the limited area of the computer screen has led to the use of some interesting display methods. Defining information by separating it from its surroundings has led to the development and use of a windowing system. The concept of multiwindows is not new; wonderful examples of windowing techniques can be found in Persian miniatures and manuscripts from the Middle Ages. Windows allow their contents to be separated from their surrounding while still remaining visible.

The windows create the illusion of a slightly three-dimensional space on the picture plane of the computer screen (Figure 9a). The illusion is created by the apparent overlapping of the windows, defined by their borders. The reality is that they are all projected on the same two-dimensional picture plane (Figure 9b). By adding frames to the windows, a layering effect is produced. The windows that are only partially visible behind the top layer are often distracting to the window currently being read. While their position in the stack gives reference to the order in which they were viewed and their existence allows ease of accessibility, their continued brightness on the screen only serves as a distraction. Controlling the relative brightness of the windows and having the possibility of staggering their positions will give a sense of hierarchy to the stack while retaining accessibility and place emphasis on the current window (Figure 9c). The illusion of the third dimension on the screen is more prominent; it helps clarify a structure and gives order to the documents. Having a photograph or image or even a moving image within one of the windows can have the effect of creating a depth hole in the midst of the layer illusion (Figure 9d).

Mixing windows that contain images and areas of high contrast can create a problem. It is important to clearly define contrast between foreground and background elements. Understanding how to control contrast, relative brightness, and color on the screen can be effectively used to unify, layer, and separate elements (Figure 10). This series of buttons and icons demonstrates some of the spatial depth and contrast illusions created by using contrasting shades of gray and black to show foreground, background, raised, and depressed elements.

THE STRUCTURE OF TYPOGRAPHY
ON THE COMPUTER SCREEN

"Typography is the art of using black to bring out the whiteness." The high resolution of the printed page allows for a much denser display of information than the stubborn resolution of the computer screen (Figure 11). Type for decent quality commercial printing is resolved between 1,000 and 2,500 lines to the inch, laser printers usually image at 300 dots to the inch, and most computer screens currently project at about 72 pixels to the inch.

Type of 8.5 points that might be quite readable on a printed page at a resolution of 1,270 lines to the inch is not acceptable in a readable form on the screen of the computer. At less than 12 points, the spaces between characters become random; some too tight, so that characters

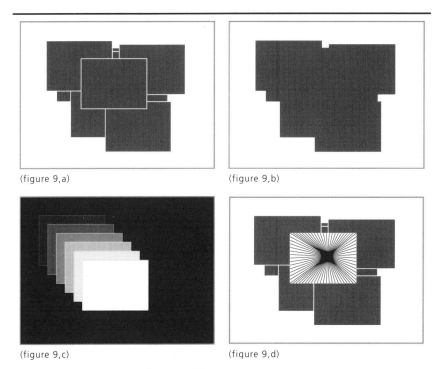

(figure 9,a)

(figure 9,b)

(figure 9,c)

(figure 9,d)

Figure 9. The computer screen

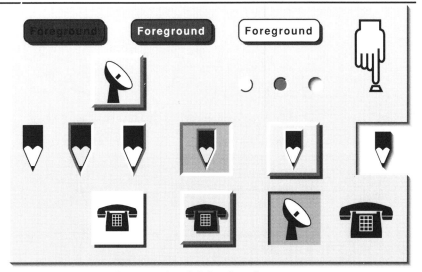

Figure 10. Spatial depth and contrast

10pt Helvetica

Lb ra.ry

10pt Times

Library

14pt Helvetica

Library

14pt Times

Library

1270 Lines to the inch, digital typesetting output

Library   Library

The bitmapped fonts are shown at about 220% of their actual size. At small point sizes, the resolution of the computer screen does not allow for the correct character forms or character spacing to be generated.

Character spacing

very loose	Character space	Character space
loose	Character space	Character space
normal	Character space	Character space
tight	Character space	Character space
too tight	Character space	Character space

Space that may be saved by using tight character spacing may create readability problems. Words with overlapping characters are hard to read.

Figure 11. Pixel distortion and fonts

appear to be overlapping, others too loose. The effect is that words bunch together or break up, and as a result readability is poor. Serif typefaces, which should be used for large areas of text, become harder to read than sans serif fonts.

Line spacing or leading should be set proportionately to both the amount of text that is being displayed and the length of the line of type. If leading is too tight, it is more difficult for the reader's eye to find the next line in the paragraph. Leading that is to loose has the effect of breaking up paragraphs into lines of text and also uses up valuable screen real estate.

Margins around text within windows are important to help readability when text windows overlap (Figure 12).

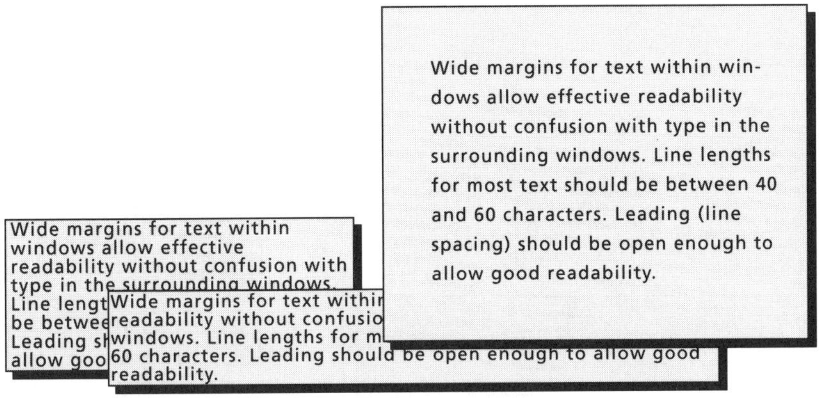

Wide margins for text within windows allow effective readability without confusion with type in the surrounding windows. Line lengths for most text should be between 40 and 60 characters. Leading (line spacing) should be open enough to allow good readability.

Wide margins for text within windows allow effective readability without confusion with type in the surrounding windows. Line lengt be betwee readability without confusio Leading s windows. Line lengths for m allow goo 60 characters. Leading should be open enough to allow good readability.

Figure 12. Margin examples

CONCLUSION

The pixel is the smallest element on the surface of the computer screen; it is the element that combines to form a line or a plane; it is the unit that combines to make up a photographic image or a single letter. It is one point on the plane of the computer screen; it indicates a position in space; it is static, centralized, and directionless.

Designing for the surface of the computer screen poses new and interesting challenges for the designer. While some of the issues are new such as time, motion, and sound, other aspects such as the readability of typography, the separation and combination of image and type, and the general issues associated with projecting the three-dimensional world onto a two-dimensional surface are part of a deep and complex tradition. When designing for this new medium, it is important to be aware of what has already been done and what can be used and applied from the rich history of art and graphic design.

The successful designer of interactive multimedia must understand how to establish a clear visual language on the computer screen. The designer must be able to separate information into frames while separating information within the frames from the information about the frames. Devices such as the use of an overlaying grid can be effectively employed while organizing information on the screen (Figure 13). The grid can prevent random placement and create a good visual sense of structure while saving significant amounts of screen space.

This is a very basic overview of some of the issues faced by the designer of the computer screen. As the development of computer software and hardware continues to become more refined, the designer will be faced by new and varied issues, but the role of design and the goal of the designer as the clarifier of information will continue.

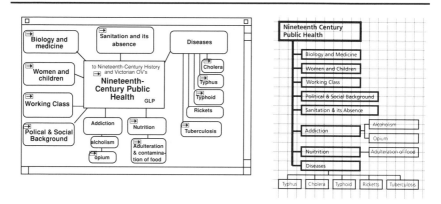

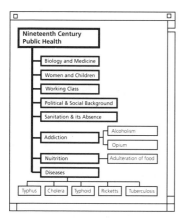

The example above left lacks an overall visual structure. The position of the boxes, the space between the boxes and the type within boxes is randomly spaced. The hierarchical intent of the contents is lost. The diagram is too close to the left edge of the window. The diagram above right is the same information with a more logical and hierarchical structure applied. Using weight of line and size and body weight of type can help create a clear sense of hierarchy. Using an overlaying grid while composing the structure helps to define a visual order and save valuable screen space.

Figure 13. Visual structures for the computer screen

Two-dimensional design, three-dimensional structures, the surface of the computer screen, space, and environments do not exist on their own, separate from one another. They influence each other and extend into each other's territory, and by doing so, they create the world of design.

REFERENCES

Arnheim, R. (1971). *Entropy and art: An essay on disorder and order.* Berkeley, CA: University of California Press.

Hockney, D. (1988). *Hockney on photography: Conversations with Paul Joyce.* New York: Harmony Books.

PETER SCOTT

Small Systems Manager
University of Saskatchewan Libraries
Saskatoon, Saskatchewan, Canada

Hypertext . . . Information at Your Fingertips

ABSTRACT

Hypertext is an alternative to traditional linear text and has been used successfully to create useful indexes on various types of computers. HyperRez, from MaxThink, is discussed in detail, as is the creation of the major Internet index, HYTELNET. Reference is also made to hypertext utilities currently under development that make use of the HyperRez software.

HYPERTEXT DEFINED

Simply put, hypertext is the nonlinear representation of text and graphics. In other words, it is information that is organized in such a fashion that a user can jump from topic to topic easily and quickly.

Good hypertext allows a user to find, browse, and comprehend information by indexing ideas and concepts, not merely words. With just a series of keystrokes, a user can instantly see the relationships between topics within a given hierarchy. Information is only useful if it is well organized and accessible. A reader of traditional, linear text may not be able to comprehend the ideas being propounded by the author since his ideas may appear unstructured if merely read from beginning to end. Hypertext, on the other hand, clearly shows those concepts.

164

HYPERTEXT SOFTWARE

Generally speaking, hypertext is best suited for use on computers. There are many hypertext programs running on many different types of computer platforms. Most people will have heard of HyperCard, which runs on Macintosh computers, and many of those people will, indeed, equate hypertext with HyperCard. However, the Amiga computer has its own hypertext program, The Thinker; the Atari has Spectre 128; and the Apple II has Tutor-tech. Hypertext systems are also available for the IBM personal computer family. These include such programs as Black Magic, EMPOWERment, HyperPad, HyperSprint, and PC-Browse.

This paper will concentrate its efforts on describing just one hypertext system, HyperRez,[1] written by Neil Larson of MaxThink in 1988. This particular system has been chosen since it is the one with which this author is most familiar, and it has been used to run a number of utilities including HYTELNET,[2] which recently won the Research and Education Networking Application Award.

HYPERREZ

Here are a few facts about HyperRez. HyperRez was released in 1988. It is an easy to learn and use program, which remains resident when loaded into the computer's random access memory. It can be invoked at any time by depressing a hot-key sequence, which a developer may customize, and can be returned to memory by pressing the Escape key.

HyperRez makes rapid jumps to pure ASCII files and certain types of graphics files with the keyboard's arrow and page up/page down keys. The program may be used royalty-free for any utility created by a developer. To construct a hypertext utility, a developer need only write files on a word processor that can save files as pure ASCII. This includes all the major MS-DOS packages such as WordPerfect, Word, and QEdit. The key to making jumps is to embed angle-bracket links within the ASCII files. Jumps can be made to the first page of a file, a specified screen of a file, a specified screen and line, or a specified word within a file. A developer can create customized help files for other software packages. For example, it would be possible to embed a link in a database program, one screen of which could contain an angle-bracket link. Once that screen is displayed, HyperRez could be invoked and the appropriate file presented.

For all the reasons stated above, this author chose HyperRez as the hypertext utility of choice. Many utilities have been designed with the software, for example, HYDOS,[3] which gives instant access to all known DOS commands; HYPERVAX,[4] which is a browser for getting help with VAX electronic mail commands; and HYENVOY,[5] which is a browser for finding help with the Canadian telecommunications software ENVOY100. These utilities are freely available to Internet users and may be downloaded from various sites.

HYDIRECT, a hypertext version of *The Directory of Electronic Journals, Newsletters, and Academic Discussion Lists,* published by the Association of Research Libraries, is in the process of development. The paper version has entries for 769 scholarly lists, 36 journals, 80 newsletters, and 17 as yet unclassified titles. It is an ideal candidate for hypertext treatment since new titles are being announced on an almost daily basis. A user should not have to wait for a new paper version to be published to keep up with this rapidly changing information resource.

Perhaps the most popular of this author's utilities is HYTELNET, a browser that gives a user almost instant access to all known Internet sites that can be reached with the TELNET utility. For those of you not familiar with TELNET, it is a program that allows an Internet user to make remote connections to library catalogs, bulletin boards, campuswide information systems, Free-Nets, and a host of useful databases and full-text resources. TELNET can be run on most mainframes, Macintoshes, and IBM personal computers.

The number of diverse sites currently accessible is enormous. The number of potential sites is staggering. The challenge is to organize the information necessary to access the sites in as simple and straightforward a fashion as possible.

HOW TO CREATE HYPERTEXT

To explain and demonstrate the creation of a hypertext utility that can be run with HyperRez, let us look at the design of HYTELNET. Fortunately, HYTELNET is merely a hypertext index—there is no philosophy here, no abstract notions that need to be linked—so the descriptions will be easy to comprehend.

To create a hypertext utility with HyperRez, a developer needs to set up a new subdirectory that will house the files. Then two major ASCII files need to be written: START.TXT and HELP.TXT. Figure 1 shows the START.TXT file. These files are essential since HyperRez needs to load them first in order to operate properly. As soon as the HyperRez hot-key is invoked, START.TXT will be displayed on the screen, covering any existing display.

Let's analyze the START.TXT file. Notice the terms surrounded by angle brackets. These are the initial hypertext jumps. To access one

```
┌─────────────────────────────────────────────────────────────────┐
│        ┌──────────────────────────────────────────┐             │
│        │ Welcome to HYTELNET  version 5.0         │             │
│        └──────────────────────────────────────────┘             │
│                                                                   │
│                 What is HYTELNET?    <WHATIS>                     │
│                                                                   │
│   Telnet-accessible library catalogs  <SITES1>                   │
│                                                                   │
│        Other telnet-accessible sites  <SITES2>                   │
│                                                                   │
│       Help files for on-line catalogs  <OP000>                   │
│                                                                   │
│               Internet Glossary      <GLOSSARY>                  │
│                                                                   │
│             Cataloging systems       <SYS000>                    │
│                                                                   │
│           Understanding Telnet       <TELNET>                    │
│                                                                   │
│          Key-stroke commands         <HELP.TXT>                  │
│   ┌──────────────────────────────────────────────────────────┐  │
│   │       HYTELNET 5.0 was written by Peter Scott,           │  │
│   │ U of Saskatchewan Libraries, Saskatoon, Sask, Canada. 1992│  │
│   └──────────────────────────────────────────────────────────┘  │
└─────────────────────────────────────────────────────────────────┘
```

Figure 1. The START.TXT file

```
┌─────────────────────────────────────────────────────────────────┐
│      ┌──────────────────────────────────────────────┐           │
│      │ HYTELNET...... Program Description.....       │           │
│      └──────────────────────────────────────────────┘           │
│   HYTELNET is designed to assist you in reaching all of the     │
│             INTERNET-accessible libraries, Freenets, CWISs,     │
│             Library BBSs, & other information sites by Telnet.   │
│   HYTELNET is designed specifically for users who access        │
│             Telnet via a modem or the ethernet from an          │
│             IBM compatible personal computer.                   │
│   HYTELNET, when loaded, is memory-resident. Once loaded hit     │
│             Control + Backspace to activate the program. To     │
│             leave the program temporarily hit ESC. To remove    │
│             from memory hit ALT-T while in the program.         │
│                                                                   │
│   For information on customizing the program see <CUSTOM>       │
│   For accessible Library on-line catalogs see <SITES1>          │
│   For other information sites see <SITES2>                       │
│   ┌──────────────────────────────────────────────────────────┐  │
│   │ For extra information on loading the program and how to   │  │
│   │    contact the author go to the <READ.ME> file           │  │
│   └──────────────────────────────────────────────────────────┘  │
└─────────────────────────────────────────────────────────────────┘
```

Figure 2. The WHATIS file

of these files, a user merely moves the cursor with the down arrow key then hits the right arrow key. The WHATIS file is shown in Figure 2.

Notice that the WHATIS file also contains links. Hitting the link for accessible library online catalogs brings up the SITES1 file, as shown

in Figure 3. This file is a listing of all the countries that have online
catalogs available.

```
╔═══════════════════════════════════════════════╗
║   Library Catalogs arranged by country        ║
╚═══════════════════════════════════════════════╝

          <AT000>      Australia
          <CN000>      Canada
          <FI000>      Finland
          <GE000>      Germany
          <HK000>      Hong Kong
          <IR000>      Ireland
          <IS000>      Israel
          <MX000>      Mexico
          <NE000>      Netherlands
          <NZ000>      New Zealand
          <ES000>      Spain
          <SW000>      Sweden
          <SZ000>      Switzerland
          <UK000>      United Kingdom
          <US000>      United States
```

Figure 3. The SITES1 file

If we select Sweden, we are presented with a list of Swedish sites,
as shown in Figure 4. Arrowing down and selecting SW001, we are
presented with the file for Lund University, as shown in Figure 5.

The SW001 file is a typical site file. It contains all the information
a user needs to connect and log in to this particular site. As an added
bonus, there is also information regarding which cataloging system is
used at the site. In this case, it is VTLS. Before logging into a site,
a user may wish to know which search commands will have to be issued.
Notice that OP017 is a link file. Depressing it brings up the help screen
for the VTLS system (Figure 6).

Let's return for a moment to the START.TXT file. Notice that
there are links to other files, which, in turn, make links to further files.
SITES2 will link a user to a file that lists other types of resources available
on the Internet. OP000 is a list of help files for online catalogs.
GLOSSARY is a file containing terms relating to various aspects of
the Internet. SYS000 lists the many different cataloging systems being

```
┌─────────────────────────────────────────────────────────────────┐
│                            Sweden                                 │
│                                                                   │
│  <SW003> Karolinska Institute                                     │
│  <SW001> Lund University                                          │
│  <SW004> Royal Institute of Technology,  Stockholm               │
│  <SW002> University of Umea                                       │
└─────────────────────────────────────────────────────────────────┘
```

Figure 4. The SW0 file

```
┌─────────────────────────────────────────────────────────────────┐
│                       Lund University                             │
│                                                                   │
│  To access:                                                       │
│                                                                   │
│  1.      Type TELNET LOLITA.LU.SE                                 │
│  2.      Select terminal type 10.  If you have a terminal         │
│          that supports Scandinavian 7-bit ASCII, select 4.        │
│  3.      Enter 100 as the location code                           │
│  4.      Type /LANG 1 to select English                           │
│                                                                   │
│  OPAC = VTLS <OP017>                                              │
│                                                                   │
│  To exit:                                                         │
│                                                                   │
│  1.      Type /QUIT.                                              │
│  2.      Enter Y to confirm.                                      │
└─────────────────────────────────────────────────────────────────┘
```

Figure 5. The SW001 file

used in libraries and makes deeper links to the sites that use those systems. TELNET is a file containing a description of that program, plus various tips and tricks to help make remote sessions successful. Finally, HELP.TXT describes the actions of the arrow and page keys. It can also be invoked by depressing the F1 key. All of the files shown so far are written in pure ASCII and are, therefore, easy to edit with any word processor. Much of the information gathered to create the files was found in the Internet sites themselves and captured with a telecommunications program. Many already existed in other documents freely available for downloading.

The current version of HYTELNET contains hundreds of small, discrete ASCII files, so the chore of updating existing files and adding new ones is not burdensome. Traditional linear indexes, with which we are all familiar, are extremely tedious to update, especially if they contain page references that have to be altered each time information is added or deleted. There is also a tendency with linear indexes not to update on a regular basis. It is just too much trouble and far too

```
                           Using VTLS

Advanced User Search System:

Author searches:To search for a particular author, use the A/ searc
                command followed by the author's name.

                     Example:   A/Hemingway, Ernest

Title searches:  To search for a particular title, use the T/ search
                 command followed by the title.  Omit any leading
                 articles such as THE, A, AN, LA, ...

                     Example:   T/Sun also rises

Subject searches:    To search for a particular subject, use the S/
                     search command followed by the subject.

                     Example:   S/Metals

Keyword searches:    To search for a keyword, use the W/ search
                     command followed by the subject.

                     Example:   W/Computers

Boolean Keyword:     To search for keywords with boolean operators,
                     use the B/ search command followed by a
                     keyword, then an operator, and then the second
                     keyword.

                     Example:   B/Ocean and Island
                                B/Dog or Cat
Help:                To see help, type /HELP.

Previous Screen:To see previously displayed screens, type PS.

Next Screen:    The next screen is usually displayed by typing NS.
```

Figure 6. The VTLS file

frustrating. Hypertext indexes, on the other hand, are a joy to update. When changing information in HYTELNET, it is generally only necessary to alter one or two files. Also, when a particular category of information begins to grow too large to fit on one or two screens, it can be split into smaller files and those files renamed. It then becomes necessary to rename any links to those files. Again, this is not an onerous task.

The number of accessible Internet sites continues to grow on an almost daily basis. Keeping current on all the additions has been made easier by the formation of the LIB—HYTELNET[6] mailing list. The list currently has over 350 members from around the world. When a new site is discovered, all members of the list are informed. They may, if they wish, add those new files to their copy of the HYTELNET program so that it is as up to date as possible. Members freely share information regarding sites that may have changed their login procedures or that have added new and interesting databases. Some members have completely rearranged the information in certain files. For example, one user moved the United States entry to be the first entry on the SITES1 file since most of his users were more likely to want to connect to an American site. Currently, the United States entry sits last because the file's arrangement is alphabetic. Other members have decided that they do not wish to have particular files in their copy because of limited disk space or because they have no interest in certain information and have, therefore, deleted those files.

A user of HYTELNET may also wish to create links to files that represent a unique local situation. For instance, it may be felt pertinent to add an extra help file for one's own online catalog system or TELNET escape sequence. As long as the new links lead to the correct information, then all is well.

ADAPTING HYPERREZ TO RUN ON
DIFFERENT PLATFORMS

HyperRez, originally a DOS-based program, has recently been adapted by Earl Fogel of the Computing Services Department at the University of Saskatchewan to run in a UNIX environment.[7] He wrote a shell that not only allows for the retention of the original hypertext links, but also automatically makes a connection to a remote site. This has allowed users without DOS machines to take full advantage of the information available in HYTELNET. Internet users are free to download both the DOS and UNIX versions of HYTELNET. There is also a version of HYTELNET that runs under Windows, called CATALIST,[8] designed by Richard Duggan of the University of Delaware.

Perhaps the best example of the UNIX version of HyperRez can be seen at the University of Western Australia. Deidre Stanton, at Murdoch University Library, Australia, along with some of her colleagues, is in the process of designing an Information Resources Access System for the Australian Academic Research Network (Figure 7).

Note the START.TXT file in Figure 7. Notice the traditional HELP and WHATIS files. Linking to the file IRASINDEX brings up an index of available bibliographies, guides, and directories, plus links to the actual files (Figure 8).

Let's return to the START.TXT file. From this menu, a user can actually run other programs connected to the UNIX machine. These programs include archie, the Gopher, NetLib, HYTELNET, and SWAIS. Archie allows a user to query the anonymous FTP archie server in Australia, to discover if certain files or programs are available for downloading. The Gopher[9] is a distributed document delivery service

```
+---------------------------------------------------+  Return to select
|Welcome to the Information Resources Access System|  q  to QUIT
+---------------------------------------------------+  arrows to move

                    Key-stroke commands    <HELP>

   What is the Information Resources Access System?    <WHATIS>

            Academic Discussion List Directory    <HYDIRECT>

            Anonymous ftp Database Information    <ARCHIE>

          Distributed Document Delivery Service    <GOPHER>

        Information Resources Access System Index    <IRASINDEX>

            Netlib Library Catalogue Access    <NETLIB>

                  Telnet Site Directory    <HYTELNET>

              Wide Area Information Servers    <SWAIS>
```

Figure 7. IRAS START.TXT

```
            +--------------------------------------------+
            | INFORMATION RESOURCES ACCESS SYSTEM INDEX  |
            +--------------------------------------------+

                    Key-stroke commands    <HELP>

    Bibliographies on Internet Use and Resources    <BIBLIO>

            Directories to Network Services    <DIRSERV>

Directories to Networked Information Resources    <DIRINFO>

                  Electronic Journals    <EJOURNALS>

            Guides to Network Services    <GDESERV>

    Guides to Networked Information Resources    <GDEINFO>

Reports and Surveys Related to Use of AARNet    <REPORTS>

    Software Related to Information Resources    <SOFTINFO>
```

Figure 8. IRASINDEX

that allows a user to access various types of data residing on multiple
hosts in a hypertext-like interface. The NetLib program provides a user
interface to library catalogs around the world using the **LIBS.COM**
software from Sonoma State University. The SWAIS is a collection of
programs that provide access to information distributed over wide area
networks.

It is obvious, then, that editing, adding, and deleting information in a utility based on HyperRez is a fairly straightforward procedure. In fact, a developer can create many different and useful utilities with the software.

WHAT LIBRARIANS CAN DO WITH HYPERTEXT

Each year libraries produce thousands of paper documents printed in various sizes and colors. A typical piece of paper might be a listing of library-owned information resources of interest to a social studies student. The library dutifully makes 200 copies on pink paper, whereas the list for philosophy students is printed on green paper. Shelf space is made available to house these papers in the hope that the students might be interested enough to pick them up. Other pieces of paper are produced for other purposes and scattered around the library system. How disastrous, though, if there are typographical errors that need correction. After going to the enormous trouble of compiling the information, buying the paper, waiting for the photocopier to warm up, and hand correcting the errors, one might feel that there is a better way.

Instead, would it not be more sensible to make the information available on a disk? Not just a disk containing a series of unrelated files, but, in fact, a hypertext index of all information regarding all aspects of the library's services. This information could be designed in such a way as to allow a reader of the utility to gain information on library hours, special collections, expert staff, library rules and policies, maps of the stack areas, and so on. The original and fully updated hypertext files could be sitting on a personal computer in the reference department. That personal computer itself could be made available for library users to browse the most up-to-date information relevant to their needs. The "new" students are computer literate, and many, indeed, can be seen wandering the halls of academe clutching their laptops. They are the last people who want to be given a handful of colored paper.

Librarians could also begin the process of producing customized hypertext information packages on demand. Not only would this be a valuable exercise in its own right, but it would also allow the librarians to gain a renewed credibility in the eyes of their patrons. They would be seen as disseminators of information rather than its wardens.

There is no reason why librarians should not take an active role in the design and implementation of a campuswide information system based on the principles of hypertext indexing. Apart from the usual opening-hours statement, librarians could also add interesting bibliographies, electronic journals, important conference announcements, and other useful Internet resource packages. Once the information has become outdated, it is just a matter of deleting the appropriate file.

OTHER HYPERTEXT FOUND ON THE INTERNET

When browsing around the Internet, one can find many hypertext utilities designed by both computer specialists and librarians. One such is HYCLASS, developed by Clifford Urr, Director of Information and Library Services, James Martin Associates. HYCLASS is designed to be run under HyperRez. Its subject matter aids librarians who need to access Library of Congress classifications assigned to computer- and software-related materials. A cataloger may instantly access the utility by depressing the hot-key and browse the files to find the most appropriate classification number. Once identified, the number is noted, the program returned to memory, and the number is then entered into the cataloging software. This process can save the cataloger a great deal of time, and it is more likely that correct information is found by this method than by wading through the paper indexes. Of course, this program could be expanded to include all Library of Congress classifications.

Librarians in acquisitions departments could also develop and make use of hypertext indexing. Take for instance the vendor file. This is usually a computer-produced paper index, sorted alphabetically by vendor name. This is useful if only a name is being searched, but what if someone wanted to find a particular vendor specializing in foreign language material or perhaps a vendor situated in a particular country? Clearly hypertext is the solution.

Reference was made earlier to the Internet utilities Gopher and SWAIS. These are both hypertext-like resources that allow a browser to discover useful information in a hierarchical structure. The Gopher opens with a main menu, rather like the opening screen of a HyperRez utility. The user selects a line number to start the process of deep jumps. One such jump would lead to a submenu containing the names of other accessible Gophers. Selecting a number would connect the user to that site almost immediately, even if it were a continent away. The menu process begins again with the new site. The Gopher allows links not only to remote sites but also to fully searchable databases, such as electronic versions of public domain books, newspapers, and information files concerning many topics. The current version will also send a retrieved file to the searcher's electronic mail address, wherever it happens to be.

SWAIS, the Simple Wide Area Information Server, also has hypertext qualities. After logging in, a user is presented with a menu of over 120 databases situated on sites worldwide. Any number of these databases may be selected by merely hitting the space bar. A keyword or phrase is entered, and the argument is run against the selected files. The result is returned in a menu structure, allowing the user to read each individual file. The SWAIS will also mail selected files to a user's electronic mail address. Billy Barron,[10] at the University of North Texas, has loaded the information contained in HYTELNET to a server at his site. A SWAIS searcher may select that file and issue a keyword argument. The server will return all the files containing that term. This example shows how one hypertext utility can interact with another.

These two programs can be run on many different types of computer platforms, and developers are free to add any type of information that they feel is useful to the community.

This paper has been stressing the uses to which HyperRez can be put. MaxThink has also produced a stablemate called Hyplus,[11] which is based on a similar philosophy of file linking but which contains some extra features. It is not memory-resident, running instead in a stand-alone mode. It can search for a term with a glossary utility and can also run another program simultaneously. It has the ability to dial a telephone number and allow a user to see a list of all previous jumps— a useful feature if an immediate jump to a particular file is required.

Whichever of the two programs a developer chooses to create utilities, one thing is for sure. He or she will gain a greater understanding of the subject matter being organized. This also holds true for the user. You are invited to test this statement by obtaining a copy of the software packages described above and by creating your own utilities. (More information on the software packages is given in the Appendix.)

APPENDIX

Hypertext Software and Utilities Available from
wuarchive.wustl.edu
(Directory PD1:<MSDOS.HYPERTEXT>)*

Filename	Type**	Length	Date	Description
ARJHLP23.ZIP	B	327172	920214	HyperText helpfile for ARJ v2.3. Can be TSR
CPPTOUR.ARC	B	72187	891208	Hypertext-based tutorial on using C++
DOSEA5.ZIP	B	128906	910831	Hypertext program explaining DOS 5.0.
EBK.ZIP	B	48545	911005	Topic-oriented hypertext viewing program
EBKSRC.ZIP	B	56013	911005	Borland C++ src for EBK.ZIP hypertext viewer
HS25.ARC	B	301370	890717	HyperShell hypertext browser, v2.5
HTEX06.ZIP	B	246184	920206	Hypertext authoring system, create/convert/edit
HYCLASS.ZIP	B	69120	910414	Hypertext LC class & computer-related material
HYDOS10.ZIP	B	86977	910615	Hypertext browser for all DOS commands, v1.0
HYENVOY1.ZIP	B	64779	910622	Hypertext browser for all ENVOY100 commands
HYPER.ARC	B	171621	880503	Construct your own hypertext network
HYPERH15.ZIP	B	63851	900428	Hypercard-like help util. Make your own stacks
HYPERREZ.ARC	B	113258	891021	Hypertext reader using plain ASCII files
HYPLUS.ZIP	B	155030	910628	Stand-alone Hypertext program from Maxthink
HYPRVX11.ZIP	B	75776	901211	Hypertext browser for VAX/VMS mail help, v1.1
HYTELN50.ZIP	B	348957	920123	Hypertext browser for finding TELNET addresses
MAGIC15A.ARC	B	208998	891126	BlackMagic hypertext reader/develop. sys. 1of3
MAGIC15B.ARC	B	217234	891126	BlackMagic hypertext reader/develop. sys. 2of3
MAGIC15C.ARC	B	328463	891126	BlackMagic hypertext reader/develop. sys. 3of3
NUHLP45.ZIP	B	90642	910628	Norton Utilities 4.5 Hypertext help browser
SENSES.ZIP	B	108544	910414	Demonstration of HYPLUS hypertext compiler
TP55TOUR.ARC	B	63504	891208	Hypertext-based tutorial on using OOP in TP5.5

*This list was created on Saturday, 28 March 1992 20:16:21 MST.
Some files may have been added or deleted since that date.
See file PD1:<MSDOS.FILEDOCS>AAAREAD.ME for additional information.
**Type B is Binary; Type A is ASCII.

NOTES

[1]Larson, Neil. (1989). HyperRez. Berkeley, CA: MaxThink. Available via FTP from wuarchive.wustl.edu in the mirrors/msdos/hypertext subdirectory as hyperrez.arc. Change file type to "binary" when fetching.

[2]Scott, Peter <scott@sklib.usask.ca>. (1992). HYTELNET. Saskatoon, SK: The author. Available via FTP from wuarchive.wustl.edu in the mirrors/msdos/hypertext subdirectory as hyteln50.zip. Change file type to "binary" when fetching.

[3]Scott, Peter <scott@sklib.usask.ca>. (1991). HYDOS. Saskatoon, SK: The author. Available via FTP from wuarchive.wustl.edu in the mirrors/msdos/hypertext subdirectory as hydos10.zip. Change file type to "binary" when fetching.

[4]Scott, Peter <scott@sklib.usask.ca>. (1990). HYPERVAX. Saskatoon, SK: The author. Available via FTP from wuarchive.wustl.edu in the mirrors/msdos/hypertext subdirectory as hyprvx.zip. Change file type to "binary" when fetching.

[5]Scott, Peter <scott@sklib.usask.ca.> (1991). HYENVOY. Saskatoon, SK: The author. Available via FTP from wuarchive.wustl.edu in the mirrors/msdos/hypertext subdirectory as hyenvoy1.zip. Change file type to "binary" when fetching.

[6]LIB—HYTELNET. (1990). To subscribe send an e-mail message to scott@sklib.usask.ca with the subject "Add me to LIB—HYTELNET."

[7]Fogel, Earl <fogel@skyfox.usask.ca.> (1992). Direct all enquiries fogel@skyfox.usask.ca.

[8]Duggan, Richard <duggan@brahms.udel.edu>. (1990). CATALIST. Newark, DE: University of Delaware. Available via FTP from ftp.unt.edu in the library subdirectory.

[9]Internet Gopher. (1992). Telnet to consultant.micro.umn.edu and log in with gopher. Emulate vt100. Use menus to find "libraries" entry.

[10]Barron, Billy <billy@vaxb.acs.unt.edu>. (1992). Telnet to quake.think.com and log in with wais. Find the entry for the "hytelnet" server, hit the space bar to mark, select keyword to search, and hit enter. The file(s) containing your keyword will be retrieved.

[11]Larson, Neil. (1989). Hyplus. Berkeley, CA: MaxThink. Available via FTP from wuarchive.wustl.edu in the mirrors/msdos/hypertext subdirectory as hyplus.zip. Change file type to "binary" when fetching.

KATHARINA KLEMPERER

Director of Library Automation
Dartmouth College
Hanover, New Hampshire

Delivering a Variety of Information in a Networked Environment

ABSTRACT

The volume and variety of electronic information resources, the increase in desktop computing power, and the pervasiveness of networks have combined to make access to information fundamentally different from that of a decade ago. This paper describes the nature of information resources that libraries are dealing with now and discusses the different needs of each with regard to access and delivery.

INTRODUCTION

Information science has undergone a fundamental change during the past 10 or 15 years. While libraries still provide the same service that they always have—access to information—the tools and skills are entirely different from those that were taught in library schools a decade ago. The volume and variety of electronic information resources, the increase in desktop computing power, and the pervasiveness of networks have combined to challenge the resources of information providers. This paper will describe the nature of information resources that libraries are dealing with now and will discuss the different needs of each with regard to access and delivery.

The different kinds of electronic information that we have available for delivery today can be divided into rough categories:

- text, including
    indexes
    structured full text
    unstructured full text
- numeric
- multimedia, including
    images
    full-motion video
    sound

Each of these has different needs in terms of access and delivery.

TEXT

Indexes

The kind of information that libraries have dealt with for years, and which they have handled with great success, is indexes to larger bodies of information. Among these we find card catalogs (and their online cousins), indexes to the journal literature, and catalogs of objects such as museum artifacts. The characteristics of this kind of textual information follow:

- It divides neatly into "records," all of which include roughly the same fields.
- It is highly structured, that is, each record is composed of distinct and identifiable fields such as authors and ID numbers.
- The records are of similar size.

A whole generation of systems grew up to support online catalogs, and because other types of indexes are so similar, it was easy to force them into systems that were designed to handle online catalog records, usually in MARC format. Each of these indexes has a reasonably small number of access points that can be indexed and reasonably short fields that can be displayed and comprehended easily.

Compare the following two examples of data structures from the Dartmouth College Library Online System. The first is from the online catalog, the second from the locally mounted MEDLINE database.

Author: Symposium on Immunology of Milk and the Neonate
           (1990 : Miami, Fla.)
Title: Immunology of milk and the neonate / edited by Jiri
           Mestecky, Claudia Blair, and Pearay L. Ogra.
Imprint: New York : Plenum Press, c1991.
Series: Advances in experimental medicine and biology ; v. 310.
Location: Dana RJ/216/S945/1990

Author(s): Wilson NW, Self TW, Hamburger RN
Title: Severe cow's milk induced colitis in an exclusively breast-
           fed neonate. Case report and clinical review of cow's milk
           allergy.
Source: Clinical pediatrics 1990 Feb;29(2):77-80.
NLM ID: 90150935
Location: Health Sciences Serial

Structured Full Text

There is a conceptual difference between index-type databases and
full-text databases. Indexes *represent* a complete document, whether it
be a book, a phonograph record, or a museum object. A full-text file
is the document; once you have retrieved it you need look no further.
Among full-text formats, we find ourselves on a continuum. At one
end are highly structured data files that are in fact full text but that
can be forced into the traditional online catalog database structure
without too much effort. It may not consist of bibliographic data, but
once new field names have been defined, search and retrieval can proceed
basically as if one were retrieving catalog records. An example of highly
structured full text is a dictionary entry. The following example is from
the *American Heritage Electronic Dictionary,* as mounted at Dartmouth
College Library:

          Word: kin*dle (1)
Part of Speech: verb
Inflected Form: -dled, -dling, -dles.
Part of Speech: transitive verb
         Sense: 1. a. To build or fuel (a fire).
                   1. b. To set fire to; ignite.
                   2. To cause to glow; light up, as in: The sunset kindled
                      the skies.
                   3. a. To inflame; make ardent.
                   3. b. To arouse; inspire, as in: "No spark had yet
                      kindled in him an intellectual passion"(George
                      Eliot).

Part of Speech:	intransitive verb
Sense:	1. To catch fire; burst into flame.
	2. To become bright; glow.
	3. a. To become inflamed.
	3. b. To be stirred up; rise.
Etymology:	Middle English kindelen < Old Norse kynda.
Derivative:	kin'dler
Part of Speech:	noun

These data, although in fact full text, display the characteristics of index data proposed above: they divide into records, they are highly structured, and the records are of similar size. Consequently, it was a fairly easy task to load the data into the same database manager that was used for the index-type databases. Notice however the repeating groups of fields (Part of Speech and Sense). This feature of the data is not usually found in index-type databases.

When the entire full text is indexed, plenty of new ways to access information present themselves. For example, in the *American Heritage Electronic Dictionary:*

- Find all the words of Norwegian derivation in the English language (sample results: floe, iceberg, fiord, ski, slalom, telemark, lemming, troll).
- Find all the verbs that have to do with "fire" (sample results: anneal, barbecue, beacon, blaze, burn, crackle, discharge, douse, ignite).
- Find all the six-letter words that end in "ism" (sample results: ageism, cubism, Nazism, nudism, sadism, [Uncle] Tomism).

Unstructured Full Text

At the other end of the text continuum are complete texts of literature. These texts are minimally structured. Most have sentences, paragraphs, and chapters, but the information is structured not as a *collection of records* but as an *ordered string of words.*

This changes the methods of access and display significantly. In record-oriented data, one searches for a known feature (usually a keyword located in a specific field) in the entire database, and the goal is to locate all the records containing this feature. Boolean searching means that two or more features will be found in the same record. Thus, a search for the author word *Hemingway* and the title word *sun* will retrieve a number of catalog records (mostly Hemingway's *The Sun Also Rises;* see Figure 1). Nobody really cares which catalog records happen to precede or follow these retrieved records; the database records are basically unrelated to each other except perhaps alphabetically. Display of retrieved records is straightforward: one provides a short, medium, or long display of individual records, giving various depths of detail to allow users to scan the results and then look more closely at one or more retrieved records.

Full-text files have a completely different set of needs. Since full texts consist of a series of ordered words rather than unrelated records, it can be argued that a literary text is really nothing more than a long string of characters. Where "records" can be identified, they are of varying length and tend to consist of multiply occurring "fields," also of varying length. Fields may also be interleaved and must be displayed in their original order (e.g., chapter heading, subheading, multiple paragraphs containing multiple sentences; see Figure 2).

What we are searching for here is not so much *records* (e.g., paragraphs), but *matchpoints*. If I am searching for the word "rabbit"

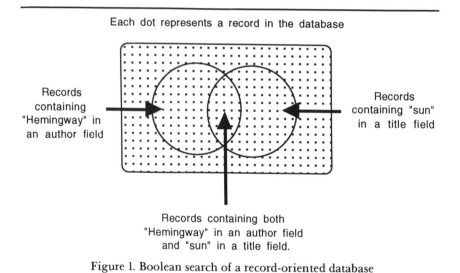

Figure 1. Boolean search of a record-oriented database

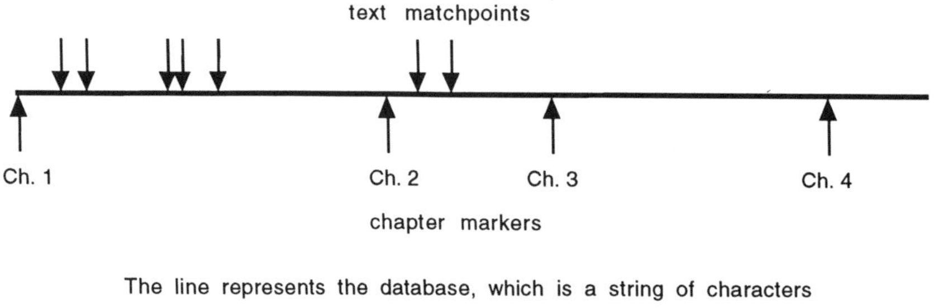

Figure 2. "Fields" in an unstructured full-text database

in the text of *Alice in Wonderland,* I don't want to find all the paragraphs or lines that contain the word, I want to locate the occurrences of the word itself and scan the text preceding and following the matchpoints I have found. Rather than Boolean combinations (find every "record" containing *rabbit* and *Alice*) full texts are better served by proximity operators, which locate occurrences within a certain distance of each other (find every occurrence of *rabbit* within five words of *Alice;* find every occurrence of *Alice* preceding *rabbit* by no more than 100 characters). Displays likewise have different requirements; rather than seeing a list of individual chapters or paragraphs, in which the target words might appear only after many lines, the user is better served by a display of matchpoints in context. The user needs to be able to see all the matchpoints in context at a glance, jump from one matchpoint to the next, and scroll forward and backward through the text from any given matchpoint. A further display requirement is to provide the ability to go to the beginning of the "segment" (e.g., paragraph, chapter, poem) for each matchpoint. An example will illustrate the initial display of matchpoints:

sorted by matchpoint:

18	suddenly a White	Rabbit with pink eyes ran close by her.
22	of the way to hear the	Rabbit say to itself, 'Oh dear! Oh dear!
25	natural); but when the	Rabbit actually TOOK A WATCH OUT
28	had never before seen a	rabbit with either a waistcoat-pocket, or
95	and the White	Rabbit was still in sight, hurrying down
99	to corner, but the	Rabbit was no longer to be seen:
07	CHAPTER 1 Down the	Rabbit-Hole Alice was beginning to get
30	it pop down a large	rabbit-hole under the hedge. In another
35	to get out again. The	rabbit-hole went straight on like a tunnel

sorted by appearance in the document:

07	CHAPTER 1 Down the	Rabbit-Hole Alice was beginning to get
18	suddenly a White	Rabbit with pink eyes ran close by her.
22	of the way to hear the	Rabbit say to itself, 'Oh dear! Oh dear!
25	natural); but when the	Rabbit actually TOOK A WATCH OUT
28	had never before seen a	rabbit with either a waistcoat-pocket, or
30	it pop down a large	rabbit-hole under the hedge. In another
35	to get out again. The	rabbit-hole went straight on like a tunnel
95	and the White	Rabbit was still in sight, hurrying down
99	to corner, but the	Rabbit was no longer to be seen: she

The surprise here is that this kind of display has long been with us, known as a KWIC display (KeyWord In Context). Its usefulness has not been lost.

The display above gives line numbers for each match; if the text were not broken into lines, the matches could just as easily be numbered sequentially. At this point, the user wants to zero in on one match and perhaps display a certain number of words around it. For example, displaying 100 words before and after the match at line 25 would result in the following:

> sleepy and stupid), whether the pleasure of making a daisy-chain would be worth the trouble of getting up and picking the daisies, when suddenly a White Rabbit with pink eyes ran close by her.
>
> There was nothing so **VERY** remarkable in that; nor did Alice think it so **VERY** much out of the way to hear the Rabbit say to itself, 'Oh dear! Oh dear! I shall be late!' (when she thought it over afterwards, it occurred to her that she ought to have wondered at this, but at the time it all seemed quite natural); but when the **Rabbit** actually TOOK A WATCH OUT OF ITS WAISTCOAT-POCKET, and looked at it, and then hurried on, Alice started to her feet, for it flashed across her mind that she had never before seen a rabbit with either a waistcoat-pocket, or a watch to take out of it, and burning with curiosity, she ran across the field after it, and fortunately was just in time to see it pop down a large rabbit-hole under the hedge.
>
> In another moment down went Alice after it, never once considering how in the world she was to get out again.

At this point, the user might want to keep scrolling forward or might want to go back to the beginning of the chapter in which this match was found. The whole procedure is more one of navigating around a text rather than looking at records in a file.

Between the strictly record-oriented indexes and the completely unstructured full texts, there is a wide variety of full texts that can be treated either as record oriented or as full-text files, for example, the Bible, collections of poems, plays, encyclopedias.

NUMERIC DATA

Beyond text files, there are completely different data formats that are now available electronically, each requiring different methods of access and display.

A completely different kind of data that has recently received a lot of attention, thanks to the U.S. government's decision to distribute its census data on CD-ROM, and consequently in great quantity, is *numeric* data. Numeric data of course require an entirely different sort of database management system and user interface. The ideal here is not simply to provide access to tables as if they were pages out of printed volume, but to provide access to the raw data that can then be manipulated statistically. Rather than searching for occurrences of terms in records or full text, one would like to select a subset of the universe of data and then perform statistical tabulations on it and produce visually pleasing displays. For example, using the U.S. census as an example, select the universe to be all households living in towns with a population less than 5,000 in the state of Vermont. Then perform statistics on household annual income: mean, median, standard deviation, frequency by $10,000 increments. Produce a bar graph to illustrate these results. Now perform the same operations using the analogous universe in the states of New York, California, and Mississippi.

A living example of such statistical manipulations is Dartmouth's SPSS server, which in this simple and somewhat trivial case is showing frequencies of occurrence of signs of the Zodiac for birthdays of individuals in a specific population (ICPSR 1991 General Social Survey). The chart is produced in real time, from variables selected by the user (Figure 3).

MULTIMEDIA

Of course the newest area of exploration is that of aural and visual media and the combinations of all media into what is known as multimedia. The emphasis in audiovisual media has been mostly on the *delivery* of the "documents"; no small problem in itself, but access to the contents is still largely text based.

For example, in a database of musical sound recordings, one would obviously need to access recordings by name, e.g., *Beethoven's Fifth Symphony* conducted by von Karajan with the Berlin Philharmonic Orchestra. Such indexing is nothing new; the main problem is delivering the sounds over a network and playing them on a workstation with reasonable fidelity. One would like to be able to retrieve songs by indexing the music itself; a user should be able to sing a melody or play it on a keyboard, or enter a harmonic progression and then retrieve the citations for the pieces that match it, and then hear the matching music. This is not an unknown concept; "thematic indexes" that organize musical themes by their melodic intervals have existed in paper for a long time. Indexing of images is even more complicated, since the actual shapes must somehow be encoded into structures that can be referenced.

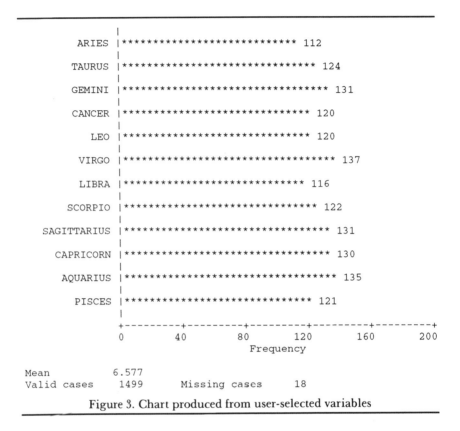

Figure 3. Chart produced from user-selected variables

At this point, the main effort in the multimedia area has been in the use of hypermedia as a presentation mechanism. Here still, the emphasis is on the presentation and delivery of media, with access following a kind of stream-of-consciousness model. Any actual indexing that is done is still textual.

CONCLUSION

The important point to remember, with the variety of information that can now be delivered to the desktops of users anywhere in the world, is that each has different needs regarding access and delivery. New database engines are needed to provide access to these data resources, and new delivery mechanisms will display them. The challenge is to develop the instruments that will accomplish this.

ARLENE MOORE SIEVERS

Head, Information Acquisition Department
University Library
Case Western Reserve University
Cleveland, Ohio

Free-Net in Cleveland and
Case Western Reserve University Library:
Linking Community and University

ABSTRACT

Free-Net Cleveland is a completely free, open-access community computer system operated and coordinated by Case Western Reserve University in Cleveland, Ohio. Through Free-Net, users can access a wide range of electronic services and features including free electronic mail and the Internet as well as valuable university information sources such as the university's online catalog, government documents, and links to faculty members in academic areas. Free-Net also functions as a communication medium for the university, providing opportunities for enhanced student/faculty interaction, and it functions as an educational resource for schoolchildren through its Academy One component. Free-Net relies heavily on volunteers from the community to operate it and keep it current. Free-Net Cleveland is part of the National Public Telecomputing Network (NPTN), which is being created to provide networked services and links between Free-Nets throughout North America and the world.

INTRODUCTION

Free-Net is something in which perspective determines what one knows about it, how one uses it, and most definitely how one perceives its impact. This becomes clear when seeking out diverse perspectives on something that people in Cleveland, and particularly at Case Western Reserve University, use in different ways, misunderstand, and yet take for granted, like any other utility. Cleveland holds the distinction of being the place where Free-Net began and is its first community site.

The idea of a free community computing network was conceived of and developed by Dr. T. M. Grundner at Case Western Reserve University in Cleveland. Dr. Grundner has subsequently helped numerous communities establish their own Free-Nets. He also gave freely of his time and knowledge in providing the essential background for this paper. His insights into the philosophy behind the system, how it has developed, just how one sets up a Free-Net, and his perspective into the future via the National Public Telecomputing Network (NPTN), which he is launching, were especially valuable.

Assistance was also provided by one of the few paid employees who actually runs Free-Net at Case Western Reserve University, and who knows a great deal about its inner workings, Martha Artzberger, of Information Network Services. She provided information on campus use of Free-Net, in academic departments by students and faculty, in university administration, and its important relationship to the Case Western Reserve University campuswide computer network, CWRUNET.

A third major source was George Barnum, University Library's government documents librarian, who is an experienced sysop (systems operator) and who has worked on the government documents part of Free-Net for some years.

Written documentation on Free-Net is virtually nonexistent. For this reason, it was necessary to rely on information gained through interviewing Dr. Grundner and others. Written documentation consists of a description of Free-Net prepared for the National Research and Education Network (NREN) hearings in Congress and fact sheets. One of the pitfalls of living in the age of the shift from print to digitized information is the absence of clear archiving responsibilities and the lack of a paper trail. One learns this firsthand preparing a paper about an electronic information source.

WHAT IS FREE-NET?

Free-Net is a completely free, open-access community computer system operated and coordinated by Case Western Reserve University. The Free-Net computer allows anyone to call in 24 hours a day and access a wide range of electronic services and features. These range from free electronic mail to information in various areas of the "electronic city." It is largely dependent on volunteers for the development of "areas," for inputting of information, answering questions, and creating what Free-Net will be in any community. It draws on a wide range of subject expertise in many areas as diverse as veterinary science, space science, a legal service, recipe exchange, and restaurant menus and reviews. It provides access for the community to the Internet through the teleport component and to numerous remote information sources through the library area. It provides numerous forums for users to communicate, ask questions, and air views (Grundner, 1990, p. 51).

Having been in operation since 1986, it has experienced numerous growing pains. Probably the greatest complaint anyone has about the network currently relates to the inadequate number of telephone lines, which sometimes creates difficulty connecting for those accessing via modems. For most university users, this problem is virtually nonexistent because the entire campus is connected to it fiber optically through the university's campuswide network, CWRUNET.

Perhaps the most important concept behind Free-Net is that of opening up computing to the widest possible user group. Personal access to online computer services for those not part of a university, a large corporation, or the government has been limited to those with the resources to afford the luxury of a Prodigy or CompuServe service (T. M. Grundner, personal communication, January 27, 1992). Free-Net allows access to a multitude of valuable services requiring only a terminal and modem access. New user registration is even accomplished online. There is no bureaucracy, forms to fill, or qualifications to meet.

Dr. Grundner sees the development of Free-Net and the Free-Net movement as similar in nature to the free public library concept that took hold in the United States in the middle to late 19th century (T. M. Grundner, personal communication, January 27, 1992). A certain amount of idealism is behind the concept of this populist computing network. In a time when access to information appears to be heading more and more to a privatized system, with perhaps the creation of new classes of "information wealthy" and "information poor," this concept is a breath of fresh air to those who still hold fast to the ideals behind the free public library and believe a democratic society is based on the principle of equality of access to information.

When asked what his biggest surprise has been in the years since Free-Net was developed and has been running, Dr. Grundner replied, "the use of Free-Net by working-class people 'from the neighborhoods' and their children" (T. M. Grundner, personal communication, January 27, 1992). His interpretation of this phenomenon is that there have been great numbers of computers bought by families in the hopes of advancing their children's education. Many of them remain relatively underused by the families who purchased them. Free-Net, which is heavily promoted in the schools in the Cleveland area, provides something interesting and useful to do with a family's personal computer at no charge (T. M. Grundner, personal communication, January 27, 1992). In the process, computer novices gain confidence and knowledge using an online computer database and an electronic mail system. The menus, commands, and functions are designed to be as simple and transparent as possible, and the organizational structure, developed around the "electronic city" concept, is an effective and readily understandable principle.

The community element and the idea of volunteerism are extremely important to the Free-Net concept. According to Dr. Grundner, there has been no lack of committed volunteers who create the Free-Net components. Indeed, the idea came directly from Dr. Grundner's positive experience with expert volunteers in another project. Free-Net started from a project Dr. Grundner created when working with the Medical School of Case Western Reserve University. This was a microcomputer-based health information system dependent on volunteer effort and the expertise of the doctors, many of whom were primarily researchers affiliated with university hospitals. Dr. Grundner was surprised by their willingness to contribute to the system, to input explanatory information in the system, and their interest in establishing one-to-one contact with the people who were asking the questions. The idea of forming a community-based computer network, based primarily on the efforts of volunteers but established at a university, came from this experience (T. M. Grundner, personal communication, January 27, 1992).

CWRUNET, FREE-NET, AND THE UNIVERSITY

Members of the university community are most in contact with Free-Net because it serves as the university electronic mail system. Many are only aware of Free-Net as a system rapidly outgrowing its original capacity. Since the vast number of community users connect via dial-up modem, and since the system is extremely busy during peak business hours, it has, at times, been very difficult to get a connection. When university buildings were fiber optically wired for CWRUNET, of which Free-Net is a component, this problem ended for most. University users complain when Free-Net is down for maintenance on Friday mornings and on the occasional instance when it is not operational, but the truth is that the electronic mail component has caught on and flourished on campus where previous efforts in the library and university failed. This is due to the simplicity of the Free-Net electronic mail component and the recent almost complete campus access to CWRUNET connections.

In many ways, for users in the university and University Library, Free-Net is something of an afterthought. Perhaps explaining that Free-Net is just one information node of CWRUNET, the campuswide system network, and that it provides the conduit for electronic mail gives an indication why. Case Western Reserve holds the distinction of being the first campus completely fiber optically wired for its system. The system can handle not only extremely large amounts of data very quickly but audio, video, and imaging transmissions as well. Cable TV, among numerous other services such as networked CD-ROMs, shared software, and data files, are offered to students in their dormitory rooms via CWRUNET. An exciting electronic imaging and multimedia project, which Case Western Reserve University is exploring with IBM, is intended to offer enhanced materials in music and medical science networked on CWRUNET. Free-Net is nonetheless an important community and extra-university node of the system, so to speak, and conversely CWRUNET supplies the Internet connection for Free-Net users.

FREE-NET, STUDENTS, AND FACULTY

These same academic components that connect community users to university experts function for class members and instructors as a structured, expansive electronic mail system, a question-and-answer forum, and a problem-solving medium. Many university academic departments have Free-Net sections for each class, where not only students on campus, who have access to CWRUNET, but those living elsewhere in the community, out of town, or home for vacation can communicate as well. Expansive course descriptions are given online and are of great use to students planning their class schedules. It is interesting that humanities areas such as English and art history, not only engineering and science departments, use Free-Net options to enhance student/faculty communication possibilities. Martha Artzberger confirmed that the Free-Net communication mode is acknowledged by instructors to be helpful in encouraging shy students or those with imperfect conversational English to participate in class discussions on a more comfortable basis and at leisure (M. Artzberger, personal communication, January 28, 1992).

This paper began with the idea that perspective is significant when considering Free-Net. Those who work with it in the academic area see it as an Internet connection, an electronic mail medium, and a way to provide enhanced access for learning between instructors and students. It is a convenient campus-access mode for students who live off campus and want to be part of the learning that goes on between students getting together, going over assignments, and exchanging views outside of class.

THE UNIVERSITY, FREE-NET, AND THE PUBLIC

The role of the university and the University Library in Free-Net is important, and it truly is a two-way street. Obviously, the community has benefited from the university research that created Free-Net and from the administration's commitment that continues to support its operation and enhancement. Actually, Cleveland Free-Net, and all Free-Nets, operate on a minimum of paid labor. The equivalent of only two and one-half full-time employees are needed for a Free-Net the size of Cleveland's. Smaller communities operate with only one (T. M. Grundner, personal communication, January 27, 1992).

The other major university contribution is the expertise of faculty. There is a Case Western Reserve University component of Free-Net in the University Circle segment of the electronic city menu that has an academic section where departmental information, student rosters, office hours, and course information are posted. Many of the departments have a general question-and-answer forum not limited to students.

Some academic sections are active, others rarely used, but the interaction between Free-Net users and faculty in some areas, like the sciences, is steady and obviously rewarding. These university components give the public easy access to experts in specialized fields and at the research university level. Case Western Reserve University, with internationally recognized programs in chemistry, physics, engineering, and medicine, is able to offer some of the expertise of a first-rate faculty to the public at large.

The public aspect of Free-Net brings its own challenges to the university. With the current debate about freedom of speech and political correctness on campuses and the heavy use of Free-Net by all age groups in the community as well as by university undergraduates, the free-spirited adult exchanges on some of the Free-Net chat groups became something of a problem. As a community system, Free-Net is like any public space and is subject to a degree of misuse. The solution has been the establishment of some obscenity standards for most of Free-Net and the establishment of "Adult only 18 or older" areas for those who wish to exercise complete freedom of expression in Free-Net communications (T. M. Grundner, personal communication, January 27, 1992).

It is interesting that Case Western Reserve University, which no longer has an education degree program nor a library school, sad to say, does a great deal for schools and the K-12 age group through Free-Net. Dr. Grundner, who has a doctorate in education, is especially involved in this rapidly expanding segment of Free-Net called Academy One.

FREE-NET, CHILDREN, AND SCHOOLS

One of the best uses of Free-Net has been in its K-12 applications in Cleveland and a number of communities worldwide. To participate, schools must establish Internet access through a sponsoring university and must supply their own terminals and modems. All other elements of participation involved are free. What participating classes and schools get from Free-Net is unlimited access to the full range of Free-Net possibilities including personal electronic mail, access to distant library resources, and curriculum enrichment through specially designed programs and activities that link schools across the country and the world (National Public Telecomputing Network, 1991a, p. 1).

The Academy One component sponsors a number of projects that link schools together and provide interesting learning experiences. For example, there are simulated space launch projects that school children participate in through Free-Net. These exercises run simultaneously on all Free-Net systems and work as organized projects to launch a space shuttle. School sites are given different roles in each mission, some being landing sites, tracking stations, alternate landing sites, and weather stations. Some schools become other shuttles, perform docking maneuvers, and conduct joint experiments such as monitoring solar disturbances. Coordination and communication between the shuttle's mission control and schools are conducted through conferences on NPTN Free-Net systems. Electronic mail is sent back and forth, hourly reports are posted, and progress is reported. Schools involved in past shuttle missions included ones throughout the United States, Finland, Czechoslovakia, and Russia (T. M. Grundner, personal communication, January 27, 1992).

Another Academy One Free-Net program is a "virtual worlds" project that allows students to apply science, mathematics, reading, and telecomputing skills to solve problems they encounter while conducting expeditions to other worlds. Each expedition is one school day long and consists of problems to solve, with each school posting mission reports on Free-Net about what they encounter. Other schools are given problems to solve relating to these adventures, such as identifying creatures they meet. These experiences and exercises appear to be popular and fun for the children participating and do provide practice for computer skills as well as an early introduction to networking (National Public Telecomputing Network, 1991a, p. 3).

The Academy One component of Free-Net has a lot of projects in preparation and is limited only by the number of telephone lines available to it. Ten more will be added if a grant to put the ERIC database online as a Free-Net resource is successful (T. M. Grundner, personal communication, January 27, 1992).

FREE-NET AND LIBRARIES

Major libraries, such as the Cleveland Public Library, Case Western Reserve University Library, the Cleveland Area Metropolitan Library

System (CAMLS), and the Special Libraries Association (SLA) have been actively involved in Free-Net from the very beginning. The additional library resources Free-Net provides, such as numerous distant online catalogs, are popular resources. However, it may be that these efforts have only scratched the surface of what even more expansive library/Free-Net involvement could accomplish. Dr. Grundner sees a great deal of unrealized potential in this area, where there would appear to be an affinity of missions (T. M. Grundner, personal communication, January 27, 1992).

At University Library, instituting online reference service, making the online catalog Euclid available, allowing CARL UnCover to be accessed on a trial basis, and putting together two innovative government documents projects have been major contributions to Free-Net. Certainly, however, these are just a few of the things that could be done and for which the potential exists. Perhaps self-interest rules because the electronic mail component has been universally embraced by the library.

Many of the innovative efforts of the University Library have been in the direction of CWRUNET, our campuswide information system, doing such things as putting CD-ROMs on a networked jukebox and making data files accessible. Much of the University Library's attention has been diverted by preparations to migrate to a new automated library system as one of the first-to-be-activated OhioLink sites. University Library is also in the midst of planning, designing, and building a new "library of the future," which will be heavily committed to the new information technologies.

The Cleveland Public Library has been very involved with Free-Net from the start making their card catalog available online to all users and allowing registered borrowers, and borrowers in allied systems, to locate materials, have them checked out, and sent to agencies for pickup. This is an ideal use of Free-Net because the Cleveland Public Library, while a very rich resource, is far removed from many people in the metropolitan Cleveland area who might wish to use it.

In the Medina Ohio Free-Net, the public library also plays a very central role, as it also does in the Peoria Free-Net. This is the ideal model and should be a very common one in future Free-Nets in smaller cities. Where the public library plays a leading, active role in the community, it will also play an active role in Free-Net. Public libraries, working with universities, are the ideal combinations to initiate Free-Netting in their communities.

CAMLS is a very active local consortium of 16 academic libraries, 15 public libraries, 12 medical libraries, 12 corporate libraries, and 3 school systems representing about 344 total sites and approximately 10.5 million volumes. CAMLS has taken the lead in providing a reference bulletin board manned by librarians from participating libraries, promising a two-day turnaround time in answering questions. Scanning through recent questions and responses reveals that questions tend to be answered the same day. There are the usual interesting reference questions, queries about libraries' borrowing policies, and other questions that point to library services Free-Net users would like to see added. Chief among these appear to be an online encyclopedia and online magazine sources that could be downloaded. Some of these materials are on the university's CWRUNET, but are generally limited to university student use because of site licensing restrictions. A few sources are on Free-Net in full text, and they are heavily used.

Chief among these in the "library" area of the electronic city is "The Freedom Shrine." This is a section of full-text freedom documents, such as the Declaration of Independence, U.S. Constitution, and the Magna Carta. Famous speeches such as Lincoln's Gettysburg Address and Martin Luther King's "I Have a Dream . . ." speech are in full text, as are patriotic songs and poems. There are many other documents accessible, and more are being added. All are searchable by keyword and are immensely popular with schools and reference librarians. Other online full-text sources include a few books, primarily limited to those not covered by copyright. These include religious texts such as the Book of Mormon and the Koran. An explanation of the Gutenberg Project and how to participate in the project is also online in this section.

Numerous online catalogs are available directly on Free-Net, including a Data Research Associates version of the Library of Congress catalog with title and author search capabilities. Other online catalogs include almost all the major academic collections in the area, including that of Ohio State University. These are of real assistance to students home from college trying to do classwork and papers as well as to unaffiliated users locating resources on their own. A few major area resources are not online, and these gaps inevitably limit usability. University of California's MELVYL, Boston University's online catalog, and a host of others are reachable through the "library" or the "teleport" area of the electronic city menu, which provides the Internet connection. Resources of much more limited use on Free-Net are those such as Dartmouth's Dante Project, a Renaissance literature database.

Librarians also use Free-Net as a way to communicate with each other locally. SLA has a large, active, far-flung Cleveland chapter and uses a Free-Net section for member communication, newsletters, meeting listings, and a popular jobline. CAMLS, the area consortium, also uses the medium in this way, as does the Ohio Government Documents Roundtable (GODORT). The Northeast Ohio Major Academic Research Libraries (NEOMARL) group, which has a number of sections, also uses Free-Net to communicate. On the campus of Case Western Reserve

University, cooperation among libraries is increasing due to joint participation in the OhioLink project, and Free-Net has served as a valuable communication mode in this effort.

When reading through many of the Free-Net listings of the card files and directories of local service agencies, those with public library backgrounds may be reminded of the information public libraries have always endeavored to establish and keep current. These were often called "community resource files." It was always difficult to determine just which community sources of information might help patrons, and many of the agencies and people one would list were difficult to reach or kept strict business hours. Even successful telephone contact was often awkward to achieve. Many public libraries were always aware that the answers to many questions were not in the public library but were scattered in the community. Looking at Free-Net from a public library perspective, one cannot help but see that important among its many benefits is the fact it acts as a gateway to many more resources.

FREE-NET AND GOVERNMENT DOCUMENTS

Case Western Reserve University Library has a number of connections with Free-Net as an information provider. A specific area that has great potential for use to the public and the community, and in which two different approaches have been tried to present information, is government documents. A six-month pilot project undertaken by Case Western Reserve University Library and carried out by George Barnum, government documents librarian, illustrates the strengths, possibilities, and some shortcomings of Free-Net in practical applications. The CWRU Government Documents Department was chosen by the Government Printing Office (GPO) and the General Accounting Office (GAO) to determine the extent of possible use of the online Department of Commerce Economic Bulletin Board (EBB) as a free service. The EBB is generally available for a fee only. The six months' fee waiver was offered to 100 depository libraries. Case Western Reserve University Library was one of only a very few libraries to make the information accessible to users in a digitized form, and the only one to attempt to present it online to the public at large (G. D. Barnum, personal communication, January 23, 1992).

In the test he designed, Mr. Barnum, who is a sysop, or systems operator, in charge of the government documents component on Free-Net, posted a monthly list of all tables of data that were available from the EBB. These included such things as monthly retail sales, employment and earnings, and currency exchange rates from the Federal Reserve. Each month there would be a listing of around 200 available files.

Free-Netters could browse the list of available tables and listings and request a file directly or send an electronic mail message to Mr. Barnum in Free-Net citing the ones they wanted to see and access. On receipt of such a message, Mr. Barnum would access the Department of Commerce EBB via modem and download the requested table or chart to disk. A small amount of editing was required before uploading the information on Free-Net. It would then be available generally, not just to whomever had requested it.

It seemed to be a good idea, and it was if considered in terms of popularity with users and prompt distribution of important government information. However, it became a tremendously labor-intensive activity, and there were technical complications such as the 2400-baud rate of transmission used by the Department of Commerce for downloading, which made the process very slow and time-consuming. This kind of thing was compounded by certain technical limitations of Free-Net, which sometimes necessitated extensive editing of files. Free-Net only accepted ASCII files, which made uploading of tabular information slow (G. D. Barnum, personal communication, January 23, 1992).

There were, however, steady requests for tables and statistics, some from the university community and many others from businesses, local governments, and other segments of the public. The Cleveland area is made up of numerous small municipalities, and these were frequent requesters and users of the data. There were requests from much farther afield as well, since Free-Net is accessible through Internet. Once users were aware of the electronic availability of the information, there were usually repeat requests.

Mr. Barnum soon learned that in dealing with a diverse population of Free-Net users there were abusers of the system and troublemakers, even ones smitten with Department of Commerce information. This is a relatively minor problem that affects nearly all Free-Net sysops to some extent and occasionally other Free-Net users as well. The system lets those who are online at any time know who else is using the system at that time. Occasionally there are rude messages, but this really is an infrequent problem for most using the system. There are policies in place now to deal with this sort of disturbance, which really can be likened to misuse of the airwaves.

Along with the individually requested tables and files, there were a number that were automatically put onto Free-Net. These included such popular things as the Gross National Product (GNP), the Consumer Price Index (CPI), employment statistics, economic indicators, and the Federal Reserve credit rates. Of course, some of these statistics are announced publicly immediately on release but usually not in their complete form, and then only the most general statistics or those that show significant newsworthy change. The advantage of the online EBB to Free-Net was that it made all the tables available immediately on release, which was usually about two months before they would be received in printed form in one of the usual publication sources.

Since any time lag on time-sensitive statistics makes them incrementally less valuable in hard-copy publication, the online immediate access was significant for those who used them for planning purposes. Case Western Reserve University's Weatherhead School of Management, business people in the community, and mayors of suburban communities are examples of information users to whom this criterion applied.

The test was run from June to December 1990, and was not continued due to, simply, the inability of the Government Documents Department to man such a service on a volunteer basis and accomplish what was required in the amount of time that was needed. Some of the technical problems encountered could perhaps have been fairly easily solved had the project continued. Lack of time and staffing was the main deterrent.

The reality is that Free-Net is operated mainly by volunteers. This means that incorporating its services into those of a university library must involve stretching limited time and personnel resources. It is a factor that cannot be ignored. Dr. Grundner sees a more practical role for public libraries in supporting Free-Net through active involvement. As already described, the Cleveland Public Library and CAMLS are actively participating in Free-Net. In other communities, such as Peoria, the public library has taken a central role as a driving force in Free-Net. Making terminal access available to the public is a key service in this effort.

The end of the test involving the Government Documents Department at Case Western Reserve University, the Department of Commerce online Economic Bulletin Board, and Free-Net did not mean a cessation of Free-Net activity for the Government Documents Department. Their leadership and participation has taken a new turn and now is committed to a new, perhaps more viable, Free-Net government documents option.

Free-Net is now providing a means of uniting electronically the Ohio Government Documents Roundtable (GODORT) members. These include representatives from the 38 Ohio libraries with government documents collections. They include the State Library and major university libraries as well as small public libraries with very limited collections. GODORT is creating a Free-Net section to aid their own cooperative efforts, as well as to make information available to the public more readily. New Free-Net government documents offerings include an online directory of state government documents collections, the

GODORT newsletter and the GPO depository newsletter available electronically, and a section for requests, offers, and exchanges of documents between members.

The State Library also uses Free-Net to publicize a list of available state documents and their distribution status. It also maintains a current list of Ohio government officials. A section called "Get government information" still makes available popular Department of Commerce Electronic Bulletin Board information such as the CPI, employment data, and economic indicators. As with all Free-Net areas, there is a question-and-answer section open to all, which is monitored and answered by GODORT members. Free-Net Cleveland reaches to such areas as Oberlin, a GODORT site, and connects with other Ohio Free-Nets such as the one in Youngstown, Ohio. Other Ohio GODORT members connect via the Internet. In establishing the GODORT Free-Net option, much attention is being paid to setting up clear areas of responsibility for maintaining and updating the information. This is one of the most important determinants of a successful Free-Net section. Now Free-Net has even better capabilities to measure use, and these capabilities will be used to expand or limit the options GODORT makes available (G. D. Barnum, personal communication, January 23, 1992).

Through the example of the experience of the Case Western Reserve University Library Government Documents Department in Free-Net, one can gain an understanding of the ways Free-Net continues to change and evolve as needs and capabilities of its operators and users do. New areas of Free-Net activity are proposed and set up continually. Others lose interest or willing volunteers to operate them.

From a user's standpoint, inactive Free-Net areas are a disappointment. This view is also supported by the university coordinator for Free-Net who noted that one of the biggest problems in coordinating Free-Net is in monitoring areas that have gone dormant, contacting the sysops responsible or finding new ones, and getting the areas active and current again or deciding whether they should be dropped. Some sections, such as culinary arts, veterinary medicine, computer groups, the legal section, and the area run by Cleveland's Lewis NASA Research Center need no such prodding. They are busy and active all the time, have lots of enthusiastic contributors and users, and obviously have good and competent sysops.

FREE-NET, GOVERNMENT, THE LAW, AND POLITICS

One area of intense daily activity on Free-Net is the legal one in the government area of the electronic city. Many of the elements of this section are a result of the emphasis in Free-Net on community participation in government. It is within the framework of a project called the NPTN Teledemocracy Project. This includes such things as the Hermes Project, which puts U.S. Supreme Court decisions, dissenting opinions, and arguments online, as well as other U.S. Federal Court decisions. It is augmented by an interpretation section to these decisions and rulings. There is also a question-and-answer legal forum, which is quite active with participation among the legal community of Cleveland, business people with legal questions relating to agencies such as the Occupational Safety and Health Administration (OSHA), and students and faculty of Case Western Reserve University Law School asking and answering questions.

Government and politics is an area of substantial Free-Net use with an even greater potential for growth in the future. In some Free-Nets, sadly not in Cleveland, discourse between government officials and the citizenry is an important feature. Only one or two small communities in the Cleveland area appear to be using Free-Net to provide a one-to-one link between officials and those whom they represent. In the few such community links that do exist, the system does perform the function of getting messages directly to those in charge and of getting responses. The usual local complaints concerning such matters as barking dogs, problems with garbage pickup, and needed street repairs are common messages. There is an incentive to officialdom to reply since they must know that a larger audience than just the person who complains will see if the query goes unanswered.

Even taking into consideration those who do not participate, the government center of Free-Net is one of its most vital elements. OSHA and the Environmental Protection Agency (EPA) information is dispersed, interpreted, and commented on in Free-Net. An up-to-date directory of governmental hotlines, name listings, addresses, and telephone numbers for elected officials from the president on down is maintained. The county engineer's office maintains an area issuing news bulletins and answering questions.

The NPTN Teledemocracy Project consists not only of information online, but during times of important political campaigns provides all major candidates with "electronic campaign office space," at least on the Cleveland Free-Net system. This is intended to allow users to access information directly from candidates, not only that interpreted by the media (National Public Telecomputing Network, 1991c, p. 2).

THE FREE-NET MOVEMENT

Dr. Grundner's pioneering efforts are these days directed toward establishing Free-Nets in other communities and cities and in linking these through the NPTN, which he created. He sees the NPTN as the community computing equivalent to National Public Radio or the Public Broadcasting Service (T. M. Grundner, personal communication, January 27, 1992).

Linked Free-Nets, which would still be entirely community created and driven since this is an integral concept of Free-Net, could rely on some network feeds to fill out their programming, so to speak. Dr. Grundner calls this cybercasting. Popular examples currently on Free-Net are the daily *USA Today News* in an electronic edition and national weather service forecasts as well as Academy One features. "Go weather" probably has the most logins next to personal electronic mail on Cleveland Free-Net. Other such networked offerings would be NASA space shuttle launch and mission transmissions, which is offered on Cleveland Free-Net through the NASA Air and Space SIG. Electronic journals are another possibility as networked utilities of NPTN.

The main role of NPTN currently is in helping communities establish their own Free-Nets, both in the United States and abroad. NPTN makes available the technical expertise and software necessary to operate community systems (National Public Telecomputing Network, 1991b, pp. 1-2).

Establishing comprehensive electronic mail linkups between Free-Nets is another objective of NPTN, one that has tremendous capacity for use by the widest range of people, for example, connecting families with children in college. NPTN plans to establish a national news organization to serve the telecomputing public as well as to establish NPTN international connections with overseas information resources. Other large cities that would be important NPTN resources are slated to establish Free-Nets. One of the current sites organizing is Los Angeles in coordination with UCLA and its library school (T. M. Grundner, personal communication, January 27, 1992).

A significant international aspect of Free-Net, other than the Internet connection, is the establishment of direct links to a number of foreign libraries. Dr. Grundner is keenly interested in establishing more overseas Free-Nets and in linking them with those in the United States. During the Gulf War, electronic mail access through Free-Net was established to enable friends and relatives of troops stationed in the Middle East to communicate quickly. The most interesting and visible international connection of Free-Net remains that of the schoolhouse area of the electronic city, which includes the Academy One space launches.

ESTABLISHING A FREE-NET

The steps involved in organizing and establishing a community Free-Net are fairly straightforward. Important questions related to this issue are how much it costs, who needs to be involved, and what kind of support NPTN can provide. Dr. Grundner estimates the initial cost as approximately $10,000, this being the amount one needs to buy the requisite computer equipment. An energetic, leadership-minded organizing committee composed of representative members of the community is essential. Help and advice are available from the start from NPTN, who provide the software, some organizing information, and certain network feeds (T. M. Grundner, personal communication, January 27, 1992).

Of course, an Internet connection, usually through the local college or university, is essential, as is institutional cooperation in the project. All Free-Nets operate primarily through volunteers, so it must be determined if enough dedicated people are available in the community, with computers, modems, and the willingness to give of their time to the project. A Free-Net in a medium-sized community might require only one full-time person to run it. Of course, equipment such as computers and modems is needed in any public areas to be made available as public Free-Net sites. Often this equipment exists and is available in the libraries, schools, and community centers. Free-Net is an obvious project for communities to put forward for grant aid. In large cities, the firm commitment of a university would probably be required. In Cleveland, two and one-half full-time employees from Case Western Reserve University run Free-Net out of Information Services, which also administers the university computing center and University Libraries. Free-Net is an ongoing commitment of the university.

SUMMING UP FREE-NET

This description of Free-Net in Cleveland, from the primary perspective of an academic librarian, is intended to provide an insight into what community computing is all about, how it relates to the university and to libraries of all kinds, and what its potential is. In a time when it is important that universities demonstrate their relevance to the states and communities in which they exist, as well as to the taxpayers who provide funding directly or indirectly, initiating a Free-Net or becoming an integral part of one that develops is a fairly inexpensive way to establish this relevance. Currently, universities are the vital link for community Free-Nets because of the necessity of Internet access.

When the National Research and Education Network (NREN) was being debated in Congress, Free-Net documents were presented as an example of a potential community use of the network. Future Free-Nets will need to draw on public library resources, but universities may be bypassed if connections are possible without them. The scenario of libraries being somehow omitted as important links in providing information as the information technology revolution forges ahead is a common one. The public may not relate an information technology revolution as having to do with public or other kinds of libraries unless the connection is made apparent. Librarians are often startled by this misperception since almost all are intensely involved in the shift to making information available and accessible in digitized form. Reaching out and being part of collective efforts are essential to staying at the center of providing access to information in the future. Free-Net is an avenue for providing this access.

REFERENCES

Grundner, T. M. (1990). Free-Netting: The development of free, public access community computer systems. In C. A. Parkhurst (Ed.), *Library perspectives on NREN: The national research and education network* (pp. 51-52). Chicago: Library and Information Technology Association.

National Public Telecomputing Network. (1991a). *Academy One: A national online educational community. Project summary.* (Available from Dr. T. M. Grundner, President, NPTN, Case Western Reserve University, 303 Wickenden Building, Cleveland, OH 44106).

National Public Telecomputing Network. (1991b). *Community computing and the National Public Telecomputing Network.* (Available from Dr. T. M. Grundner, President, NPTN, Case Western Reserve University, 303 Wickenden Building, Cleveland, OH 44106).

National Public Telecomputing Network. (1991c). *NPTN Teledemocracy Project. Project summary.* (Available from Dr. T. M. Grundner, President, NPTN, Case Western Reserve University, 303 Wickenden Building, Cleveland, OH 44106).

M.E.L. JACOB

M.E.L. Jacob Associates
Columbus, Ohio

New Technology, New Tools, New Librarians: Shaping the Future

ABSTRACT

Speakers' comments from the Annual Clinic on Library Applications of Data Processing are summarized. The focus of the clinic was designing information, and topics discussed include design principles, knowledge management, applications of technology to information workstations, graphical interfaces, public library use of the Internet, electronic information in school libraries, computer-mediated instruction, computer-based staff training, design techniques, hypertext, information delivery in a networked environment, and the Cleveland Free-Net.

INTRODUCTION

Most of the authors for the clinic have focused on current state-of-the-art technology. This is the technology in use in most libraries and likely to be applied in the near future. While the business of predicting the future is fraught with minefields and notable failures, it is likely that the limits of technology will continue to be pushed forward, and more capability and capacity will be available at ever lower unit cost. Librarians are both the early adapters of new technology and the followers. The authors represented in this volume are among the leaders, pioneers, and early adapters.

DESIGNING INFORMATION

Information Technologies

Among the current technologies that affect information services are workstations, multimedia support, optical and CD-ROM storage media, and networking. Tools in the form of software and some hardware are increasingly available, although as Katharina Klemperer noted, different media require the use of different tools and not all have reached the same level of refinement and application. Among these software tools are various hypermedia packages. A number have been described by Peter Scott. Other tools librarians can and should use in learning about and adapting technology and tools are the technology itself, colleagues, continuing education activities, the literature, and of course the Internet. Themes that have been repeated are information creation, maintenance, use, and evaluation.

Design Principles

Edward Tufte reminds us that we live in a multidimensional environment, but our displays are limited to two dimensions. However, we can use technology and graphic design to achieve apparent multidimensional presentations. He presented a variety of examples to illustrate this showing both good and bad ways of displaying information. His examples, however, required the verbal context he provided for understanding. The pictures alone were insufficient to illustrate his points.

Tufte, like Richard Saul Wurman (1989) and Ronnie Peters, believes that good design and organization can enhance intelligibility of information. He also agreed with Richard Greenfield that most graphical user interfaces are examples of poor design. Some supposed advances he noted are in fact regressions. He also urged using comparisons in display to enhance analysis and comprehension.

High-resolution displays are essential. Some of these begin to approach the print medium in resolution, but the displays available to most users are limited and a poor substitute for the printed page.

Graphical techniques are especially useful when there is an overwhelming amount of information to be conveyed. These techniques can focus attention on the primary points while still including some aspects of the whole. Professional designers can enhance information displays and should be used. Design by committee is fraught with failure. There is no substitute for creativity and for the coherence a single good designer can provide.

Knowledge Management

Carolyn Gray and Richard Lucier covered related aspects of knowledge management. Gray described the Gesher Project, a joint effort of Digital Equipment Corporation and the Brandeis University Library to study scholarly communication and information use and to develop a personal information system for scholars. An ethnographer on the Brandeis Library staff enabled them to apply ethnographic techniques to their study, providing a better understanding of the context and a richer view of critical factors. Gray cautioned that what appears to be inefficient in isolation, such as lunches and coffee klatches, may be highly effective channels for communicating information and teaching. She also cautioned that ethnographic techniques are time-consuming but reveal information that might otherwise be missed.

Gray defined knowledge activity as consisting of seven aspects: diagnosis and problem finding, planning and decision making, monitoring and control, organizing and scheduling, authoring and presentation, communication, and lastly system development. The information chain involves production, distribution, acquisition, and use. These two views must be linked. Librarians must build bridges between scholars and themselves and the information resources. The world is in a constant state of change. Scholars are changing and so is scholarly work and research. Librarians must change too.

Richard Lucier provided an overview of the knowledge management model developed at the Welch Library of Johns Hopkins University. He proposed a new role for librarians as the creators and maintainers of scholarly and research databases and illustrated his view with examples of the support provided by the library to the Human Genome Mapping project.

Librarians must be active or lose the initiative to others. Budget problems are not an excuse. The present constraints are part of an overall systemic change and not just the effect of escalating serial and material prices. Structural changes are necessary. Librarians must reallocate existing resources and seek new resources outside traditional bounds. Changing people is difficult if not impossible.

Too many librarians focus on replacement strategies rather than innovation or transformation. Knowledge management requires transforming people, functions, and organizations. Revolution, not evolution, is needed. Lucier has found it better to separate functions and set up new units with new people to develop knowledge management activities. Once such groups become viable, they act as change agents for the more traditional units such as the library. However, librarians must find ways to maintain critical traditional services while making such transitions.

Identifying the critical institutional needs is one way of establishing priorities and identifying potential new resources. The major barriers are legal, technical, and financial. Knowledge management will come. Librarians must decide what role they want to play.

Information Workstations

William Mischo of the University of Illinois and Virginia Tiefel of Ohio State University (OSU) described applications and innovative uses of technology at their respective institutions. Mischo discussed the library information workstation project based on an IBM workstation providing access to local databases, campus resources, the library catalog, and external resources including the Internet. Tiefel presented the OSU Gateway software that helps students to formulate a search query and execute a search using an encyclopedia, dictionary, CD-ROM indexes, and the library catalog. The Macintosh-based Gateway encourages use of both print and electronic resources. Both are focused on providing seamless, one-stop shopping for the user.

Mischo noted that current information retrieval systems deliver both too much and too little. They either overwhelm the user with many documents or fail to retrieve anything. Many users are uncertain which information resources to use or how to formulate their questions.

Mischo noted that keeping all workstation software updated is a problem. At present, sneakernet is used; i.e., a staff member individually loads new software into each workstation. Eventually he hopes to use the network to distribute such software. Since Illinois has a number of branch libraries, each can offer local databases and customize the software interface, particularly help screens, default search values, and vocabulary. Future changes will incorporate searching multiple databases, multimedia databases and functions, and more image data storage and transmission.

Tiefel said that OSU has a continuous evaluation process for The Gateway. At present, use is limited to units within the main library, but network access for dormitory and remote use is planned. With such a large user education program, the tutoring nature is particularly helpful in providing new students with an easy-to-use access to electronic resources that requires no prior knowledge of the system or of the resources used.

Graphical Interfaces

Richard Greenfield, consultant, provided an illustrated tour of several graphical user interfaces with examples of what not to do as well as examples that were well done. He urged avoiding most icons, pointing out that they were not intuitive and were often confusing. He also noted that naive users do not care where information comes from. Like Joe Friday, they just "want the facts, ma'am."

Public Libraries and the Internet

Jean Polly, Liverpool Public Library, continued her paean on the Internet. While it is not easy to use, it has a wealth of resources that public libraries can use to better serve their patrons. As more resources become available only in electronic form, access to the Internet and its resources becomes increasingly important.

While most university staff have access via stable, permanent connections, these are too expensive for most public libraries. Instead they can use dynamic, inexpensive connections to the Internet. While more difficult to use, they are cheap.

Her list of needs are better interfaces, cheaper interfaces, more and better training, and more vision regarding Internet use and resources. Her message to librarians: GET INVOLVED.

Electronic Information in School Libraries

David Loertscher, Hi Willow, discussed the role of the school librarian and the use of technology in schools. He noted that a number of the publications, print and diskette, published by Libraries Unlimited are created by school librarians.

Technology is being used routinely in more schools, and the school media center is often a major resource in such use. Schools use personal computers for most administrative tasks such as letters to parents, scheduling, inventories, and accounts. A large number are also using computers in the curriculum. He suggested that the best way to teach students information and computer literacy is to teach them to create databases in support of projects related to the curriculum.

Computer-Mediated Instruction

Ruth Small, Syracuse University, provided insights into the principles for designing computer-mediated instructional programs. Critical factors are the learner, the information, the task, and the instruction. She recommended use of the ARCS Model: Attention, Relevance, Confidence, and Satisfaction. Her own examples were clear, consistent, well ordered, logical, and used repetition.

Computer-Based Staff Training

Joe Rader, University of Tennessee, Knoxville (UTK), described the project at UTK to create a computer-based training program for staff. He noted that industry spends some $40 million annually on staff training. There is no estimate available for what libraries spend or how much time they devote to staff training.

Lessons learned include (a) staff participation is critical, (b) experts can make the job easier and the finished products better, (c) technology can make the task manageable, (d) libraries can adapt tools to their needs as well as the products created by other libraries, and (e) staff and supervisors need to feel they have control of the process. He recommended considering development of packages for both staff and users or with other libraries to reduce costs. He also asked whether libraries should consider more standardization of practices and procedures to enable easy transference of training software.

Design Techniques

Ronnie Peters, graphic designer, reiterated some of Dr. Tufte's observations and provided copious examples of design techniques. Among the most interesting of these, however, were his illustrations from Korean artists showing different approaches to perspectives and horizons. His illustrations underscored that different cultural perspectives must also be considered in designing information systems and graphical interfaces. Context matters.

Peters noted that there is a well-established body of design principles for print media, and some of these apply equally well to computer displays. Others must be modified to accommodate the more limited resolution, size, shape, and color of computer displays. Designers may use representations of the object itself or symbols standing for the object. Flags are often used to represent countries. Icons are a formalized symbol. He noted that icons in a system should have similar shapes and formats. The eye first perceives the shape and then what it contains.

Type fonts should be used with care. Some fonts are not well suited to screens. Peters ended by asserting and demonstrating that good design clarifies and enhances communication, echoing Dr. Tufte.

Hypertext

Peter Scott spoke as an advocate of hypertext programs. He provided an overview of available software, focusing mostly on tools created with HyperRez. He said such packages are easy to use, create, maintain, and adapt for local needs. Paper is a waste, and electronic exchange can replace it. Scott provides access to information on library and information services and resources available on the Internet.

Information Delivery in a Networked Environment

Katharina Klemperer provided an overview of Dartmouth services then focused mainly on three information trends: an increasing volume and variety of information, workstations, and networking. She identified five types of information sources: indexes, structured full text, full text, numeric, and multimedia. Most information systems handle indexes—periodical indexes, online abstracting and indexing databases, and library catalogs—well. They can also handle many structured full-text files satisfactorily such as dictionaries, almanacs, and the Bible. They do not handle unstructured full text such as a large monograph adequately.

Different search engines, display formats, and systems are needed for unstructured files. Most multimedia files rely on words and codes for providing access. Work is underway on other access means.

Klemperer echoed Polly on the need for better navigating tools for locating information resources in networked environments. She provided examples of some of the categorized displays Dartmouth is experimenting with.

Cleveland Free-Net

Sievers provided an overview of Cleveland Free-Net: its history, use, and relationships with Case Western Reserve University. The community access system is supported by the university, and staff interact with the community through it. Both gain. Most support comes from volunteers. It opens access to computing and information resources to all citizens. Schools and libraries use the resources heavily. Other communities have established their own Free-Nets.

CONCLUSION

These writers provide multiple answers to what the new roles for librarians could be. Gray and Lucier suggest that knowledge managers may be the future: creating bridges to resources, building databases, and assisting in providing scholarly information systems. Mischo, Tiefel, Klemperer, Sievers, Scott, and Polly see providing enhanced access to information and support and guidance to users as major roles. All of them advocate an active role and involvement in the use of new technology and resources. Electronic resources are proliferating, and users need assistance in locating and accessing the information needed for problem solving, decision making, and even entertainment. The role librarians play depends on the willingness of the individual librarian to become involved, participate, learn, and contribute. These leaders have provided examples of how they have done it and where they expect to move in the future. The rest of us need to follow their examples and begin making changes in ourselves and in our environments so we can remain effective contributors to society and scholarship. The turtle only moves forward when he sticks his neck out.

REFERENCE

Wurman, R. S. (1989). *Information anxiety*. New York: Doubleday.

CONTRIBUTORS

WINNIE CHAN is the Automated Records Maintenance Coordinator and Assistant Professor of Library Administration at the University of Illinois at Urbana-Champaign (UIUC) Library. She holds a B.S. in Chemistry from Chinese University of Hong Kong and an M.S. in Library Science from Louisiana State University. She was previously a serial cataloger/serials coordinator at the UIUC Library. Her current responsibilities include coordinating the online catalog production and batch maintenance activities, involvement in development and design of interface software for the online catalog, and troubleshooting of microcomputer software/hardware problems.

TIMOTHY W. COLE received both his B.S. in Aeronautical and Aerospace Engineering (1978) and his M.S. in Library and Information Science (1989) from the University of Illinois at Urbana-Champaign (UIUC). Since 1989, he has worked as Assistant Librarian at UIUC, with a joint appointment to the Engineering Library and the Beckman Institute Library. He has been heavily involved with the upgrading of microcomputer hardware and software throughout the UIUC library system that has taken place over the past three years. In particular, he has been one of the principal programmers working on the UIUC's microcomputer end-user interfaces to bibliographic databases. Prior to earning his library science degree, Mr. Cole worked as an aerospace engineer at Martin-Marietta Aerospace and at the Jet Propulsion Laboratory.

PRUDENCE W. DALRYMPLE is Director of the Office on Accreditation with the American Library Association (ALA). Formerly a faculty member of the Graduate School of Library and Information Science at the University of Illinois at Urbana-Champaign, she received her Ph.D. in Library and Information Studies from the University of Wisconsin-Madison. Dr. Dalrymple has published several articles in her fields of interest, which include information retrieval, particularly studies of end-user access to electronic information systems, and health sciences librarianship. Her experience prior to ALA includes more than

212

10 years as a reference librarian, search analyst, and manager in health sciences libraries.

CAROLYN M. GRAY is Associate Director at Brandeis University Libraries. She received a Ph.D. from the Florence Heller School of Social Policy, Brandeis University, an M.L.S. from the School of Library Science, University of Oklahoma, and a B.A. in English from the University of Missouri at St. Louis. Her responsibilities at Brandeis include library systems, public services, and library development. Dr. Gray has consulted with a number of different organizations in the area of library technology. Her fields of interest include information policy and scholarly communication. Sue Woodson-Marks, Ph.D., an anthropologist on the library staff, helped with the preparation of the paper.

M. E. L. JACOB is a writer, consultant, and publisher of *Entrak*. She teaches workshops in strategic planning and library networking. Ms. Jacob is active in a number of library and information science associations and societies and is a frequent speaker at conferences. She has worked at OCLC and in university, public, and special libraries.

KATHARINA KLEMPERER is Director of Library Automation at Dartmouth College. She holds a B.A. from Swarthmore College and an M.A. in Music from San Francisco State University, as well as an M.L.S. from the University of California at Berkeley. Prior to her appointment at Dartmouth, she was a member of the MELVYL system development team at the Division of Library Automation of the University of California.

DAVID V. LOERTSCHER is President, Hi Willow Research and Publishing. He has degrees from the University of Utah, the University of Washington, and a Ph.D. in Library Science from Indiana University. He has been a library media specialist in elementary and secondary schools in Nevada and Idaho and taught library media education at Purdue, the University of Arkansas, and the University of Oklahoma.

RICHARD E. LUCIER is University Librarian and Assistant Vice Chancellor for Academic Information Management at the University of California, San Francisco. He holds a B.M. in Music and Philosophy from the Catholic University of America and an M.L.S. in Library Science from Rutgers University; he has completed extensive work in health policy and administration at the University of North Carolina at Chapel Hill. Previously, Mr. Lucier was the cofounder and director of the Laboratory for Applied Research in Academic Information at the Johns Hopkins University. Known for his development of the Knowledge Management Model, he has special interests in scientific and scholarly communication, and the development and management of scientific databases. Among his publications is a forthcoming book of knowledge management to be published by the Johns Hopkins University Press in 1993.

WILLIAM H. MISCHO is Engineering Librarian, Beckman Institute Librarian, and Professor of Library Administration at the University of Illinois at Urbana-Champaign. His research interests include enhanced access to bibliographic resources, interface design and development, and microcomputer applications in libraries.

RONNIE PETERS is Art Director at Dynamic Diagrams. He was educated as a graphic designer at the University of Canterbury, New Zealand, and has a master's degree from Rhode Island School of Design. He has worked as a designer at numerous positions in New Zealand and the United States including the Waikato Museum of Art and History, IRIS (Brown University's Institute for Research in Information and Scholarship), Studio Works (New York), and Graphic Design Continuum (Ohio). He won an award at the World Design Expo, Design Eye Competition in Japan. At Dynamic Diagrams, a design studio dedicated to the creation of information graphics in both print and electronic media, his work includes design and production of all aspects of both print and electronic publications. He also teaches part time at Rhode Island School of Design. He coauthored a paper, "Design of Hypermedia Publications: Issues and Solutions," presented as part of the conference, EP91.

JEAN ARMOUR POLLY is the Manager of Network Development and User Training at NYSERNet, Inc., the New York State Education and Research Network. She was formerly the Assistant Director for Public Services at the Liverpool Public Library in central New York. She has a B.A. in Medieval Studies and an M.S.L.S., both from Syracuse University. Author of two books and numerous articles in the library literature, she is currently a columnist for *Library Journal* on topics of technology and computer books. Her interests involve use of the Internet by the public in library settings as well as human/machine interface design.

JOE C. RADER is Associate Professor and Head of University Archives, University of Tennessee, Knoxville, Libraries. Prior to this appointment in July 1990, he served as Head of Circulation Services. Codirector for 15 months, in 1989-90, of a largely externally funded project to develop computer-based training for library staff, he has published several articles and made presentations based on the project and its results. Pre-librarianship careers, a summer's internship at the Lawrence Livermore Laboratory in California, and the experience of the Modern Archives Institute have contributed to the diversity represented in his interests. He is a long-time active member of many local and regional information professional societies and national organizations, including the American Library Association, the American Association of University Professors, and the Society of American Archivists.

PETER SCOTT is Manager, Small Systems, at the University of Saskatchewan Libraries, Canada. He was formerly Order Unit Manager, Technical Services, at the same institution. He received his B.A. in Philosophy and Literature at the Middlesex Polytechnic, England, in 1973. He is a frequent speaker at library and networking conferences and is the author of many hypertext utilities including HYTELNET, HYPERVAX, HYENVOY, and HYDOS.

ARLENE MOORE SIEVERS is Head of the Information Acquisition Department at Case Western Reserve University Library. She received her M.L.S. from Indiana University and worked for a number of years in public libraries in Indiana. Her work in serials and library automation began as an account executive with Swets Subscription Service in the Netherlands. She is active in the United Kingdom Serials Group and is the North American Correspondent for their Journal *Serials.*

RUTH V. SMALL is Assistant Professor and Coordinator of the School Media Program in the School of Information Studies at Syracuse University. She received her Ph.D. in Instructional Design, Development and Evaluation at Syracuse University. Her areas of interest focus on how people access, process, and present multimedia information. She has designed and evaluated educational and training courses and materials for business and industry, schools, colleges and universities, and social services agencies and has published book chapters and articles, including "Learning Situations and Instructional Models" (with Charles M. Reigeluth) in *Educational Technology: Foundations* (edited by Robert M. Gagné), "The Contributions of Technology to Instruction and Learning" in the 1990 edition of *School Library Media Annual,* and "Information Based Education: An Investigation of the Nature and Role of Information Attributes in Education" (with Michael B. Eisenberg) in *Information Processing and Management.*

LINDA C. SMITH is Associate Professor in the Graduate School of Library and Information Science at the University of Illinois at Urbana-Champaign. She joined the faculty in 1977 and teaches in the areas of reference, science reference, and online information systems. Her research interests include information retrieval, artificial intelligence, and science information. She is active in a number of professional associations including the American Society for Information Science, the American Association for the Advancement of Science, and the Association for Library and Information Science Education.

VIRGINIA TIEFEL has been Director of Library User Education at the Ohio State University Library since 1978. She is a graduate of the University of Michigan School of Information and Library Studies and has published numerous articles on library user education. She is a recipient of the 1986 Miriam Dudley Bibliographic Instruction Award and was chosen Outstanding Ohio Academic Librarian in 1984. She is Project Director of Ohio State's Gateway to Information Project.

LESLIE TROUTMAN is Music-User Services Coordinator and Assistant Professor at the University of Illinois at Urbana-Champaign. A graduate of Bowling Green State University, the University of North Carolina at Chapel Hill, and the University of Illinois at Urbana-Champaign, her research interests include music materials in the online environment and the discography of early music. Currently, she is collaborating with Donald W. Krummel on a book about musical titles.

INDEX

Prepared by Laurel Preece